P9-BZQ-378

WITHDRAWN

Schaumburg Township District Library

130 South Roselle Road
Schaumburg, Illinois 60193

WORD
PLAYS

An Anthology of New American Drama

Performing Arts Journal Publications
New York

SCHAUMBURG TOWNSHIP DISTRICT LIBRARY
130 SOUTH ROSELLE ROAD
SCHAUMBURG, ILLINOIS 60193

8/99
DON

812.08
WORD

3 1257 01300 5243

WORDPLAYS
©1980 Copyright by Performing Arts Journal Publications
FEFU AND HER FRIENDS
©1978, 1980 Copyright by Maria Irene Fornes
DOMINO COURTS
©1977, 1980 Copyright by William Hauptman
THE VIENNA NOTES
©1979, 1980 Copyright by Richard Nelson
BOY ON THE STRAIGHT-BACK CHAIR
©1969, 1980 Copyright by Ronald Tavel
NAROPA
©1979, 1980 Copyright by Jean-Claude van Itallie
STARLUSTER
©1980 Copyright by John Wellman

First Edition
All rights reserved
No part of this publication may be reproduced or transmitted in any form or by any means, electronic or mechanical, including photocopy, recording, or any information storage or retrieval system now known or to be invented, without permission in writing from the publishers, except by a reviewer who wishes to quote brief passages in connection with a review written for inclusion in a magazine, newspaper, or broadcast.

Library of Congress Cataloging in Publication Data
Wordplays
Library of Congress Catalog Card No.: 80-83855
ISBN: 0-933826-10-9
ISBN: 0-933826-11-7 (pbk)

All rights reserved under the International and Pan-American Copyright Conventions. For information, write to Performing Arts Journal Publications, P.O. Box 858, Peter Stuyvesant Station, New York, N.Y. 10009.

For production rights, refer to individual plays. Professionals and amateurs are warned that the plays appearing herein are fully protected under the Copyright Laws of the United States and all other countries of the Copyright Union. All rights including professional, amateur, motion picture, recitation, lecturing, public readings, radio and television broadcasting, and the rights of translation into foreign languages, are strictly reserved.

Design: Gautam Dasgupta
Printed in the United States of America

Publication of this book has been made possible in part by grant from the National Endowment for the Arts, Washington, D.C., a federal agency, and public funds received from the New York State Council on the Arts.

PAJ Playscripts/General Editors:
Bonnie Marranca and Gautam Dasgupta

Contents

Fefu and Her Friends

Maria Irene Fornes

©1978, 1980 Copyright by Maria Irene Fornes.
CAUTION: No performances or readings of this work may be given without the ex-
press authorization of the author's agent. For production rights contact: Bertha
Case, 345 West 58th Stret, New York, N.Y. 10019.

Fefu and Her Friends was first performed on May 5, 1977, by the New York Theatre Strategy at the Relativity Media Lab, New York. It was directed by Maria Irene Fornes. The cast included:

FEFU . . . . *Rebecca Schull*
CINDY . . . . *Gwendolyn Brown*
CHRISTINA . . . . *Carolyn Hearn*
JULIA . . . . *Margaret Harrington*
EMMA . . . . *Gordana Rashovich*
PAULA . . . . *Connie LoCurto Cicone*
SUE . . . . *Janet Biehl*
CECILIA . . . . *Joan Voukides*

The play was subsequently produced by the American Place Theatre, New York, on January 8, 1978.

Set: L.L. Powers
Costumes: Lana Fritz
Lighting: Candice Dunn

Cast of Characters:

FEFU
CINDY
CHRISTINA
JULIA
EMMA
PAULA
SUE
CECILIA

New England, Spring 1935

Part I. Noon. The living room. The entire audience watches from the auditorium.

Part II. Afternoon. The lawn, the study, the bedroom, the kitchen. The audience is divided into four groups. Each group is guided to the spaces. These scenes are performed simultaneously. When the scenes are completed the audience moves to the next space and the scenes are performed again. This is repeated four times until each group has seen all four scenes.

Part III. Evening. The living room. The entire audience watches from the auditorium.

Part I

The living room of a country house in New England. The style is simple and although ample it resembles a farm house. To the left, French doors leading to a terrace, the lawn and a pond. To the rear right, two steps up is a landing that leads to the stairs to the upper floor. On the left of the landing there is an archway which is the entrance to other rooms in the main floor. A couch faces the audience. There is a coffee table, two small chairs on each side of the table. Upstage right there is a piano. Against the right wall there is a bar with a siphon. A double barrel shotgun leans near the French doors. On the table there is a dish with chocolates. On the sofa there is a silk shawl. FEFU *stands on the landing.* CINDY *lies on the couch.* CHRISTINA *sits on the chair to the right.*

FEFU: My husband married me to have a constant reminder of how loathsome women are.
CINDY: What?
FEFU: Yup.
CINDY: That's just awful.
FEFU: No it isn't.
CINDY: It isn't awful?
FEFU: No.
CINDY: I don't think anyone would marry for that reason.
FEFU: He did.
CINDY: Did he say so?
FEFU: He tells me constantly.
CINDY: Oh, dear.
FEFU: I don't mind. I laugh when he tells me.
CINDY: You laugh?
FEFU: I do.

CINDY: How can you?

FEFU: It's funny. — And it's true. That's why I laugh.

CINDY: What is true?

FEFU: That women are loathsome.

CINDY: . . . Fefu!

FEFU: That shocks you.

CINDY: It does. I don't feel loathsome.

FEFU: I don't mean that you are loathsome.

CINDY: You don't mean that I'm loathsome.

FEFU: No . . . It's something to think about. It's a thought.

CINDY: It's a hideous thought.

FEFU: I take it all back.

CINDY: Isn't she incredible?

FEFU: Cindy, I'm not talking about anyone in particular. I'm talking about . . .

CINDY: No one in particular, just women.

FEFU: Yes.

CINDY: In that case I am relieved. I thought you were referring to us.

(*They are amused.* FEFU *speaks affectionately.*)

FEFU: You are being stupid.

CINDY: Stupid and loathsome. (*To* CHRISTINA.) Have you ever heard anything more . . .

CHRISTINA: (*Interrupting.*) I am speechless.

(*Short pause.*)

FEFU: Why are you speechless?

CHRISTINA: I think you're outrageous.

FEFU: Don't be offended. I don't take enough care to be tactful. I know I don't. But don't be offended. Cindy is not offended. She pretends to be, but she isn't really. She understands what I mean.

CINDY: I do not.

FEFU: Yes, you do. — I like exciting ideas. They give me energy.

CHRISTINA: And how is women being loathsome an exciting idea?

FEFU: (*With mischief.*) It revolts me.

CHRISTINA: You find revulsion exciting?

FEFU: Don't you?

CHRISTINA: No.

FEFU: I do. It's something to grapple with. — What do you do with revulsion?

CHRISTINA: I avoid anything that's revolting to me.

FEFU: Hmm. (*To* CINDY.) You too?

CINDY: Yes.

FEFU: Hmm. — Have you ever turned a stone over in damp soil?

CHRISTINA: Ahm.

FEFU: And when you turn it there are worms crawling on it?

CHRISTINA: Ahm.

FEFU: And it's damp and full of fungus?

CHRISTINA: Ahm.

FEFU: Were you revolted?

CHRISTINA: Yes.

FEFU: Were you fascinated?

CHRISTINA: I was.

FEFU: There you have it. You too are fascinated with revulsion.

CHRISTINA: Hmm.

FEFU: You see, that which is exposed to the exterior . . . is smooth and dry and clean. That which is not . . . underneath, is slimy and filled with fungus and crawling with worms. It is another life that is parallel to the one we manifest. It's there. The way worms are underneath the stone. If you don't recognize it . . . (*Whispering.*) it eats you. — That is my opinion. — Well, who is ready for lunch?

CINDY: I'll have some fried worms with lots of pepper.

FEFU: (*To* CHRISTINA.) You?

CHRISTINA: I'll have mine in a sandwich with mayonnaise.

FEFU: And to drink?

CHRISTINA: Just some dirty dishwater in a tall glass with ice.

(FEFU *looks at* CINDY.)

CINDY: That sounds fine.

FEFU: All right. I'll go dig them up. (FEFU *starts toward the steps. She looks through the doors. She speaks to* CHRISTINA.) You haven't met Phillip. Have you?

CHRISTINA: No.

FEFU: (*Looking outside.*) Look. That's him.

(CHRISTINA *walks to the door.*)

CHRISTINA: Which one?

(FEFU *reaches for the gun, aims and shoots.* CHRISTINA *hides behind the couch. She and* CINDY *scream.*)

FEFU: That one! (FEFU *smiles proudly. She blows on the mouth of the barrel. She puts down the gun and looks out again.*) There he goes. He's up.

CINDY: Christ, Fefu.

FEFU: It's a game we play. I shoot and he falls. Whenever he hears the blast he falls. No matter where he is, he falls. One time he fell in a puddle of mud and his clothes were a mess. (*She looks out.*) It's not too bad. He's just dusting off some stuff. (*She waves to Phillip and starts to go upstairs.*) He's all right. Look.

(CHRISTINA *looks out.* CINDY *takes a deep breath.*)

CINDY: A drink?

CHRISTINA: Yes.

(CINDY *goes to the bar.*)

CINDY: What would you like?

CHRISTINA: Bourbon and soda . . . (CINDY *puts ice in a glass, opens a bottle of bourbon and pours it. She reaches for the soda.*) lots of soda. Just soda. (CINDY *takes another glass and starts to squirt soda.*) Wait. (CINDY *stops squirting.*) I'll have an ice cube with a few drops of bourbon.

CINDY: One or two ice cubes?

CHRISTINA: One. Something to suck on. (CINDY *puts one ice cube in another glass, and pours in a few drops of bourbon.*)

CINDY: She's unique. There's no one like her.

CHRISTINA: Thank God. (CINDY *gives the drink to* CHRISTINA *who is still behind the couch.*) Thanks.

CINDY: But she is lovely you know. She really is.

CHRISTINA: She's crazy.

CINDY: A little. She has a strange marriage.

CHRISTINA: Strange? It's revolting. — What is he like?

CINDY: He's crazy too. They drive each other crazy. They are not crazy really. They drive each other crazy.

CHRISTINA: Go on.

CINDY: I finished.

CHRISTINA: Why do they stay together?

CINDY: They love each other.

CHRISTINA: Love?

CINDY: It's love.

CHRISTINA: Who are the other two men?

CINDY: Fefu's younger brother, John. He's visiting from school. And the gardener. His name is Tom. — The gun is not loaded.

CHRISTINA: How do you know?

CINDY: It's not. Why should it be loaded?

CHRISTINA: Hmm?

CINDY: Why do you think it's loaded?

CHRISTINA: It seemed to be loaded a moment ago.

CINDY: That was just a blank.

CHRISTINA: It sounded like a cannon shot.

CINDY: That was just gun powder. There's no bullet in a blank.

CHRISTINA: The blast alone could kill you. One can die of fright, you know.

CINDY: True.

CHRISTINA: My heart is still beating.

CINDY: That's just fright.

CHRISTINA: Of course it's just fright. It's fright.

CINDY: I mean, you were just scared. You didn't get hurt.

CHRISTINA: Just scared. I guess I was lucky I didn't get shot.

CINDY: Fefu won't shoot you. She only shoots Phillip.

CHRISTINA: That's nice of her.

CINDY: You're being a scaredy cat.

CHRISTINA: All right, put the gun away. I don't like looking at it. (CHRISTINA *sits on the chair to the right.*)

CINDY: I don't like touching guns.

CHRISTINA: Why not?

CINDY: I never did.

CHRISTINA: It's not loaded.

CINDY: You never know.

CHRISTINA: You're not making sense.

CINDY: I'm not?

CHRISTINA: No. Either you think it's loaded, or you think it's not loaded.

CINDY: I don't see why I can't believe it's not loaded and yet think it might be loaded.

CHRISTINA: Well, you could, but you couldn't be absolutely certain that it's not loaded and think that it might be loaded.

CINDY: I suppose not. I suppose I could only be absolutely certain if I looked. But I wouldn't look because it might go off while I'm looking.

(*They laugh.*)

CHRISTINA: Oh, I would say that you think there's a good chance it's loaded.

CINDY: No, I wouldn't say that.

CHRISTINA: Shall we look?

CINDY: . . . No . . .

CHRISTINA: Well, put the gun away.

CINDY: You do it.

CHRISTINA: You do it.

CINDY: You do it.

(CHRISTINA *walks to the gun and draws the curtain in front of it. She then gestures like a magician after accomplishing a magic feat.* FEFU *enters and surprises* CHRISTINA *in the middle of her theatrical gesture.* CHRISTINA *stops her action.*)

FEFU: Oh, don't stop.

CHRISTINA: No. I was . . . just . . . I . . . I'm not a dancer.

FEFU: It looked nice. (CHRISTINA *draws the curtain back.* FEFU *speaks to* CINDY.) I just fixed the toilet in your bathroom.

CINDY: You did?

FEFU: I did. The water stopper didn't work. It drained. I adjusted it. I'm waiting for the tank to fill up. Make sure it all works.

CHRISTINA: You do your own plumbing?

FEFU: I just had to bend the metal that supports the rubber stopper so it falls right over the hole. What happened was it fell to the side so the water wouldn't stop running into the bowl. (FEFU *sits near* CINDY.) He scared me this time you know. He looked like he was really hurt.

CINDY: I thought the guns were not loaded.

FEFU: I'm never sure.

CHRISTINA: Hmm!

CINDY: Fefu, what do you mean?

FEFU: He told me one day he'll put real bullets in the guns. — He likes to make me nervous. (*There is a moment's silence.*) I have upset you. . . . I don't mean to upset you. That's the way we are with each other. We always go to extremes but it's not anything to be upset about.

CHRISTINA: You scare me.

FEFU: That's all right. I scare myself too, sometimes. But there's nothing wrong with being scared. . . . It makes you stronger. — It does me. — He won't put real bullets in the guns. — It suits our relationship . . . the game, I mean. If I didn't shoot him with blanks, I might shoot him for real. Do you see the sense of it?

CHRISTINA: I think you're crazy.

FEFU: I'm not. I'm sane.

CHRISTINA: You're very stupid.

FEFU: I'm not. I'm very bright.

CHRISTINA: (*Not hostile.*) You depress me.

FEFU: Don't be depressed. Laugh at me if you don't agree with me. Say I'm ridiculous. I know I'm ridiculous. Come on, laugh. I hate to think I'm depressing to you.

CHRISTINA: All right. I'll laugh.

FEFU: I'll make you a drink.

CHRISTINA: No, I'm just sucking on the ice.

FEFU: Oh, don't you feel well?

CHRISTINA: No, there was a little bourbon on it.

FEFU: Would you like some more?

CHRISTINA: Yes, I think so. Just a couple of drops.

(FEFU *goes to the bar and pours a little bourbon on the ice cube.*)

FEFU: Like that?

CHRISTINA: Yes, thank you.

(FEFU *gives her the drink and looks at her for a moment.*)

FEFU: That's the cutest thing I've ever seen. (CHRISTINA *puts the cube to her lips.*) It's cold. (CHRISTINA *nods.*) You need a stick in the ice, like a popsicle stick. You hold the stick and your fingers won't get cold. I have some sticks. I'll do some for you.

CHRISTINA: Don't. . . . This is not the way I usually drink my bourbon.

FEFU: It won't be hard to do. You might want some later. — I'm strange, Christina. But I am fortunate in that I don't mind being strange. It's hard on others sometimes. But not that hard. Is it, Cindy. Those who love me, love me precisely because I am the way I am. (*To* CINDY.) Isn't that so? (CINDY *nods and shakes her head.*)

CINDY: I would love you even if you weren't the way you are.

FEFU: You wouldn't know it was me if I weren't the way I am.

CINDY: I would still know it was you underneath.

FEFU: (*To* CHRISTINA) You see? — There are some good things about me. — I'm never angry for example.

CHRISTINA: But you make everyone else angry.

(FEFU *thinks a moment.*)

FEFU: No.

CHRISTINA: You've made me furious.

FEFU: I know. And I might make you angry again. Still I would like it if you liked me. — You think it unlikely.

CHRISTINA: I don't know.

FEFU: . . . We'll see. (FEFU *goes to the doors. She stands there for a moment before she speaks.*) I still like men better than women. — I envy them. I like being like a man. Thinking like a man. Feeling like a man. — They are well together. Women are not. (CHRISTINA *puts her glass to her mouth.*) I'm driving you to alcohol. (FEFU *looks outside. She speaks reflectively.*) Look at them. They are checking the new grass mower . . . Out in the fresh air and the sun, while we sit here in the dark . . . Men have natural strength. Women have to find their strength, and when they do find it, it comes forth with bitterness and it's erratic . . . Women are restless with each other. They are like live wires . . . either chattering to keep themselves from making contact, or else, if they don't chatter, they avert their eyes . . . like Orpheus . . . as if a god once said "and if they shall recognize each other, the world will be blown apart." They are always eager for the men to arrive. Whey they do, they can put themselves at rest, tranquilized and in a mild stupor. With the men they feel safe. The danger is gone. That's the closest they can be to feeling wholesome. Men are muscle that cover the raw nerve. They are the insulators. The danger is gone, but the price is the mind and the spirit . . . High price. — Why? — What is feared? — Hmm. Well . . . — Do you know? Perhaps the heavens would fall. — Have I offended you again?

CHRISTINA: No. I too have wished for that trust men have for each other. The faith the world puts in them and they in turn put in the world. I know I don't have it.

FEFU: Hmm. Well, I have to see how my toilet is doing. (FEFU *goes to the landing and exits. She puts her head out.*) Plumbing is more important than you think.

(CHRISTINA *falls of her chair in a mock faint.* CINDY *smiles.*)

CINDY: What do you think?

CHRISTINA: Think? I hurt. I'm all shreds inside.

CINDY: Anything I can do?

CHRISTINA: Sing.

(CINDY *sings the first verse of "Winter Wonderland." She does a dance step taking the silk shawl as she moves toward* CHRISTINA.)

CHRISTINA: Ohh.
CINDY: You don't like that song?
CHRISTINA: I do. I do.

(CINDY *sits on the chair. They sing the second verse of "Winter Wonderland"* *as they move their legs and fingers in the style of the time. There is the sound* *of a horn.* FEFU *enters.*)

FEFU: It's Julia. (*They stop singing. To* CHRISTINA.) Are you all right?
CHRISTINA: Yes.

(FEFU *exits through the foyer.* CHRISTINA *sits up.*)

CHRISTINA: Darn it. She always catches me.
FEFU: (*Off-stage.*) Julia . . . let me help you.
JULIA: I can manage. I'm much stronger now.
FEFU: There you go.
JULIA: You have my bag.
FEFU: Yes.
CINDY: I can't get used to it.
CHRISTINA: She's better. Isn't she?
CINDY: Not really.

(JULIA *and* FEFU *enter.* JULIA *is in a wheelchair.*)

JULIA: Hello Cindy.
CINDY: Hello darling. How are you?
JULIA: I'm very well now. I'm driving now. You must see my car. It's very
    clever the way they worked it all out. You might want to drive it. It's not
    hard at all. (*Turning to* CHRISTINA.) Christina . . .
CHRISTINA: Hello Julia.
JULIA: I'm glad to see you.
FEFU: I'll take this to your room. You're down here, if you want to wash up.
    (FEFU *exits through the upstage exit.* JULIA *follows her.*)
CHRISTINA: Was she actually hit by the bullet?
CINDY: No . . . I was with her.
CHRISTINA: I know.
CINDY: I thought the bullet hit her, but it didn't . . . How do you know if a
    person is hit by a bullet?
CHRISTINA: Cindy . . . there's a wound and . . . there's a bullet.
CINDY: Well, the hunter aimed . . . at the deer. He shot.
CHRISTINA: He?
CINDY: Yes.
CHRISTINA: (*Pointing in the direction of* FEFU.) It wasn't . . . ?
CINDY: Fefu? . . . No. She wasn't even there. She used to hunt but she doesn't
    anymore. She loves animals.
CHRISTINA: Go on.
CINDY: He shot. Julia and the deer fell. The deer was dead . . . dying. Julia

was unconscious. She had convulsions . . . like the deer. He died and she didn't. I screamed for help and the hunter came and examined Julia. He said, "She is not hurt." Julia's forehead was bleeding. He said, "It is a surface wound. I didn't hurt her." I know it wasn't he who hurt her. It was someone else. He went for help and Julia started talking. She was delirious. — Apparently there was a spinal nerve injury but the doctors are puzzled because it doesn't seem her spine was hurt when she fell. She hit her head and she suffered a concussion but that would not affect the spinal nerve. So there seems to be no reason for the paralysis. She blanks out and that is caused by the blow on the head. It's a scar in the brain. It's called the petit mal.

(FEFU *enters. She remains by the door.*)

CHRISTINA: What was it she said?

CINDY: Hmm? . . .

CHRISTINA: When she was delirious.

CINDY: When she was delirious? That she was persecuted. — That they tortured her. . . . That they had tried her and that the shot was her execution. That she recanted because she wanted to live. . . . That if she talked about it . . . to anyone . . . she would be tortured further and killed. And I have not mentioned this before because . . . I fear for her.

CHRISTINA: It doesn't make any sense, Cindy.

CINDY: It makes sense to me. (FEFU *goes to* CINDY.) You heard? (FEFU *nods. She holds* CINDY.)

FEFU: Who hurt her?

CINDY: I don't know.

FEFU: (*To* CHRISTINA.) Did you know her?

CHRISTINA: I met her once years ago.

FEFU: You remember her then as she was. . . . She was afraid of nothing. . . . Have you ever met anyone like that? . . . She knew so much. She was so young and yet she knew so much. . . . How did she learn all that? . . . (*To* CINDY.) Did you ever wonder? (*She ruffles* CINDY's *hair.*) Well, I still haven't checked my toilet. Can you believe that. I still haven't checked it. (FEFU *goes upstairs.*)

CHRISTINA: How long ago was the accident?

CINDY: A year . . . a little over a year.

CHRISTINA: Is she in pain?

CINDY: I don't think so.

CHRISTINA: We are made of putty. Aren't we?

(*There is the sound of a car, car doors opening and closing. A window opening.*)

FEFU: (*Off-stage.*) Emma! What is that you're wearing? You look marvelous.

EMMA: (*Off-stage.*) I got it in Turkey.

FEFU: Hi Paula, Sue.

PAULA: Hi.

SUE: Hi.

(CINDY *goes out to greet them.* JULIA *enters. She wheels herself to the downstage area.*)

FEFU: I'll be right down. (*Short pause.*) Hey, my toilet works.

EMMA: That's marvelous Stephany. Mine does too.

FEFU: Don't be funny.

EMMA: Come down. (FEFU *enters.*)

FEFU: They're here. (*She goes to the foyer as* EMMA, SUE *and* PAULA *enter.* EMMA *and* FEFU *embrace.*) How are you, my child?

EMMA: Good ... good ... good ... (*Still embracing* FEFU, EMMA *sees* JULIA.) Julia! (*She runs to* JULIA *and sits on her lap.*)

FEFU: Emma!

JULIA: It's all right.

EMMA: Take me for a ride. (JULIA *wheels the chair.* EMMA *waves as they ride.*) Hi, Cindy, Paula, Sue, Fefu.

JULIA: Do you know Christina?

EMMA: How do you do.

CHRISTINA: How do you do.

EMMA: (*Pointing.*) Sue ... Paula ...

SUE: Hello.

PAULA: Hello.

CHRISTINA: Hello.

PAULA: (*To* FEFU.) I liked your talk at Flossie Crit.

FEFU: Oh god, don't remind me. I thought I was awful. Come, I'll show you your rooms. (*She starts to go up.*)

PAULA: I thought you weren't. I found it very stimulating.

EMMA: When was that? ... What was it on?

FEFU: Aviation.

PAULA: It wasn't on aviation. It was on Voltairine de Cleyre.

JULIA: I wish I had known.

FEFU: It wasn't important.

JULIA: I would have gone, Fefu.

FEFU: Really, it wasn't worth the trouble.

EMMA: Now you'll have to tell Julia and me all about Voltairine de Cleyre.

FEFU: You know all about Voltairine de Cleyre.

EMMA: I don't.

FEFU: I'll tell you at lunch.

EMMA: Oh, I had lunch.

JULIA: You can sit and listen while we eat.

EMMA: I will. When do we start our meeting?

FEFU: After lunch. We'll have something to eat and then we'll have our meeting. Who's ready for lunch?

(*The following lines are said almost simultaneously.*)

CINDY: I am.

JULIA: I'm not really hungry.

CHRISTINA: I could eat now.

PAULA: I'm ready.

SUE: I'd rather wait.

EMMA: I'll have coffee.

FEFU: . . . Well . . . We'll take a vote later.

CINDY: What are we doing exactly?

FEFU: About lunch?

CINDY: That too, but I meant the agenda. (CINDY *looks at* SUE.)

SUE: Well, I thought we should first discuss what each one of us is going to talk about, so we don't duplicate what someone else is saying, and then we have a review of it, a sort of rehearsal, so we know in what order we should speak and how long it's going to take.

EMMA: We should do a rehearsal in costume. What color should each wear? It matters. Do you know what you're wearing?

PAULA: I haven't thought about it. What color should I wear?

EMMA: Red.

PAULA: Red!

EMMA: Cherry red or white.

SUE: And I?

EMMA: Dark green.

CINDY: The treasurer should wear green.

EMMA: It suits her too. Who else wants to know? (FEFU *raises her hand.*) For you, all the gold in Persia.

FEFU: There is no gold in Persia.

EMMA: In Peru.

FEFU: O.K.

EMMA: I brought my costume. I'll put it on later.

FEFU: You're not in costume?

EMMA: No. This is just a dress. My costume is . . . dramatic. I won't tell you any more about it. You'll see it.

SUE: I had no idea we were going to do theatre.

EMMA: Life is theatre. Theatre is life. If we're showing what life is, can be, we must do theatre.

SUE: Will I have to act?

EMMA: It's not acting. It's being. It's springing forth with the powers of the spirit. It's breathing.

JULIA: I'll do a dance.

EMMA: I'll stage a dance for you.

JULIA: Sitting?

EMMA: On a settee.

JULIA: I'm game.

EMMA: It'll be stunning. (*She throws herself on the couch, kisses whoever is there and takes a deep breath.*) I'm happy. (*Walks toward the lawn.*) Glorious day. Isn't it a beautiful day?... — (*Going out.*) Phillip! What are you doing? — Hello. — Hello, John. — What?
FEFU: We'll never see her again. — Come.

(FEFU, PAULA *and* SUE *go upstairs.* JULIA *goes to the gun, takes it and smells the mouth of the barrel. She looks at* CINDY.)

CINDY: It's a blank.

(JULIA *takes the remaining slug out of the gun. She lets it fall on the floor.*)

JULIA: She's hurting herself.

(JULIA *looks blank and is motionless.* CINDY *picks up the slug. She notices* JULIA's *condition.*)

CINDY: Julia ... (*To* CHRISTINA.) She's absent. (*She takes the gun from* JULIA.)
CHRISTINA: What do we do?
CINDY: Nothing, she'll be all right in a moment.

(JULIA *comes to.*)

JULIA: It's blank ...
CINDY: It is.
JULIA: She's hurting herself. (JULIA *lets out a strange whimper. She goes to the coffee table, takes a piece of chocolate, puts it in her mouth and goes toward her room. She stops.*) I must lie down a while.
CINDY: Call me if you need anything.
JULIA: I will. (*She exits.* CINDY *tries to put the slug in the rifle.*)
CINDY: Do you know how to do this?
CHRISTINA: Of course not.

(CINDY *succeeds in putting the slug in the gun.* CECILIA *enters.*)

CECILIA: I am Cecilia Johnson. Do I have the right place?
CINDY: Yes.

(*Lights fade all around* CECILIA. *Then they fade on her.*)

Part II

IN THE LAWN

There is a bench. A game of croquet is set on the grass. FEFU *and* EMMA *eat apples and play croquet.*

EMMA: Do you think about genitals all the time?

FEFU: Genitals? No, I don't think about genitals all the time.

EMMA: I do, and it drives me crazy. Each person I see in the street, anywhere at all . . . I keep thinking of their genitals; what they look like, what position they are in. I think it's odd that everyone has them. Don't you?

FEFU: No. I think it'd be odder if they didn't have them.

(EMMA *laughs.*)

EMMA: I mean, people act as if they don't have genitals.

FEFU: How do people with genitals act?

EMMA: I mean, how can business men and women stand in a room and discuss business without even one reference to their genitals. I mean everybody has them. They just pretend they don't.

FEFU: I see. You mean (*She wiggles her pelvis.*) they should do this all the time.

(EMMA *laughs.*)

EMMA: No, I don't mean that. Think of it. Don't you think I'm right?

FEFU: Yes, I think you're right. (EMMA *sits on the bench.*) Oh, Emma, Emma, Emma, Emma.

EMMA: That's m'name. — Well, you see, it's generally believed that you go to heaven if you are good. If you are bad you go to hell. That is correct. However, in heaven they don't judge goodness the way we think. They don't. They have a divine registry of sexual performance. In that registry they mark down every little sexual activity in your life. If your faith is not entirely in it, if you just perform as an obligation and you don't feel the most profound devotion, if your spirit, your heart and your flesh is not religiously delivered to it, you are condemned. They put you down in the black list and you don't go to heaven. Heaven is populated with divine lovers. And in hell live the duds.

FEFU: That's probably true.

(EMMA *hits the ball.*)

EMMA: I knew you'd see it that way.

FEFU: Oh, I do. I do. You see, on earth we are judged by public acts, and sex is a private act. The partner cannot be said to be the public, since both partners are engaged. So naturally, it stands to reason that it must be angels who judge our sexual life.

EMMA: Naturally.

(*Pause.*)

FEFU: You always bring joy to me.

EMMA: Thank you.

FEFU: I thank you. (FEFU *becomes distressed. She sits.*) I am in constant pain. I don't want to give in to it. If I do I am afraid I will never recover. . . . It's not physical, and it's not sorrow. It's very strange Emma. I can't describe it, and it's very frightening. . . . It is as if normally there is a lubricant . . . not in the body . . . a spiritual lubricant . . . it's hard to describe . . . and without it, life is a nightmare, and everything is distorted. — A black cat started coming to my kitchen. He's awfully mangled and big. He is missing an eye and his skin is diseased. At first I was repelled by him, but then, I thought, this is a monster that has been sent to me and I must feed him. And I fed him. One day he came and shat all over my kitchen. Foul diarrhea. He still comes and I still feed him. — I am afraid of him. (EMMA *kisses* FEFU.) How about a little lemonade?

EMMA: Yes.

(FEFU *exits.* EMMA *recites the following sonnet improvising either movement or song.*)

EMMA: Not from the stars do I my judgement pluck.
              And yet methinks I have astronomy;
              But not to tell of good or evil luck,
              Of plagues, of dearths, or seasons' quality;
              Nor can I fortune to brief minutes tell,
              Pointing to each his thunder, rain, and wind,
              Or say with princes if it shall go well
              By oft predict that I in heaven find.

> But from thine eyes my knowledge I derive,
> And, constant stars, in them I read such art
> As truth and beauty shall together thrive
> If from thyself to store thou wouldst convert:
> Or else of thee this I prognosticate,
> They end is truth's and beauty's doom and date.

(FEFU *enters with a pitcher and two glasses.* PAULA *and* CECILIA *follow. When the scene is done a fourth time* CINDY *and* CHRISTINA *will also join them. From there they will go to places for the third part in the living room while the audience returns to their seats, except for* PAULA *who will go to the piano in the living room and sing Schubert's "Who is Sylvia?")*

IN THE STUDY

There are books on the walls, a desk, Victorian chairs, a rug on the floor. CHRISTINA *sits behind the desk. She reads a French text book. Her lips move but her voice is almost inaudible.* CINDY *sits to the left of the desk with her feet up on a chair. She looks at a magazine. A few moments pass.*

CHRISTINA: (*Practicing.*) Etes-vous externe ou demi-pensionnaire? La cuisine de votre cantine est-elle bonne, passable ou mauvaise? (*She continues reading almost inaudibly. A moment passes.*)

CINDY: (*Reading.*) A lady leopard in Africa divorced her husband because he was a cheetah.

CHRISTINA: Oh, dear. (*They laugh. They go back to their reading. A moment passes.*) Est-ce que votre professeur interroge souvant les eleves? (*They go back to their reading A moment passes.*)

CINDY: I suppose ... when a person is swept off their feet ... the feet remain and the person goes off ... with the broom.

CHRISTINA: No ... when a person is swept off their feet ... there is no broom.

CINDY: What does the sweeping?

CHRISTINA: An emotion ... a feeling.

CINDY: Then emotions have bristles?

CHRISTINA: Yes.

CINDY: Now I understand. (*Pause.*) Do the feet remain?

CHRISTINA: No, the feet fly also ... but separate from the body. At the end of the leap, just before the landing, they join the ankles and one is complete again.

CINDY: Oh, that sounds nice.

CHRISTINA: It is. Being swept off your feet is nice. Anything else?

CINDY: Not for now. (*They go back to their reading.*)

CHRISTINA: (*Questioning* CINDY.) Aimez-vous mieux le francais ou l'anglais?

CINDY: ... Le francais.

CHRISTINA: Votre pere, et-il militaire, avocat, ou pharmacien?

CINDY: Moi?

CHRISTINA: Non, votre pere.
CINDY: Oui.
CHRISTINA: Vous etes une mauvaise eleve.
CINDY: Oui.
CHRISTINA: Bon. (*They go back to their reading.*)
CINDY: A lady leopard in Africa divorced her husband because he was a
  cheetah. Huh huh huh huh. (CHRISTINA *smiles at* CINDY.) Are you having
  a good time?
CHRISTINA: Yes, I'm very glad I came.
CINDY: Do you like everybody?
CHRISTINA: Yes.
CINDY: Do you like Fefu?
CHRISTINA: I do. . . . She confuses me a little. —I try to be honest . . . and I
  wonder if she is . . . I don't mean that she doesn't tell the truth. I know
  she does. I mean a kind of integrity. I know she has integrity too. . . . But
  I don't know if she's careful with life . . . something bigger than the self
  . . . I suppose I don't mean with life but more with convention. I think
  she is an adventurer in a way. Her mind is adventurous. I don't know if
  there is dishonesty in that. But in adventure there is taking chances and
  risks, and then one has to, somehow, have less regard or respect for things
  as they are. That is, regard for a kind of convention, I suppose. I am
  probably ultimately a conformist, I think. And I suppose I do hold back
  for fear of being disrespectful or destroying something—and I admire
  those who are not. But I also feel they are dangerous to me. I don't think
  they are dangerous to the world, they are more useful than I am, more
  important, but I feel some of my life is endangered by their way of thinking. Do you understand?
CINDY: Yes, I do.
CHRISTINA: I guess I am proud and I don't like thinking that I am thought-
  ful of things that have no value. —I like her.
CINDY: Hmm.

(*They go back to their reading. There is a knock on the door.* SUE *looks in.*)

SUE: Julia is not here?
CINDY: No.
SUE: She must be in her bedroom.
CINDY: Yes, I think she's resting. (SUE *starts to go.*) Come back and join us.
SUE: I will.
CINDY: I had a terrible dream last night.
CHRISTINA: What was it?
CINDY: I was at a dance. And there was a young doctor I had seen in connec-
  tion with my health. We all danced in a circle and he identified himself
  and said that he had spoken to Mike about me, but that it was all right,
  that he had put it so that it was all right. I was puzzled as to why Mike
  would mind and why he had spoken to him. Then, suddenly everybody

sat down on the floor and pretended they were having singing lessons and one person was practicing Italian. The singing professor was being tested by two secret policemen. They were having him correct the voice of some-one they had brought. He apparently didn't know how to do it. Then, one of the policemen put his hands on his vocal cords and kicked him out the door. Then he grabbed me and felt my throat from behind with his thumbs while he rubbed my nipples with his pinkies. Then, he pushed me out the door. Then, the young doctor started cursing me. His mouth moved like the mouth of a horse. I was on an upper level with a railing and I said to him, "Stop and listen to me." I said it so strongly that he stopped. Everybody turned to me in admiration because I had made him stop. Then, I said to him, "Restrain yourself." I wanted to say respect me. I wasn't sure whether the words coming out of my mouth were what I wanted to say. I turned to ask my sister. The young man was bending over and trembling in mad rage. Another man told me to run before the young man tried to kill me. Meg and I ran downstairs. She asked me if I wanted to go to her place. We grabbed a taxi, but before the taxi got enough speed he came out and ran to the taxi and was on the verge of opening the door when I woke up.

(*The door opens.* FEFU *looks in. Her entrance may interrupt* CINDY's *speech at any point according to how long it takes her to reach the kitchen.*)

FEFU: Who's for a game of croquet?
CHRISTINA: In a little while.
FEFU: See you outside. (*She exits.*)
CHRISTINA: That was quite a dream.
CINDY: What do you think it means?
CHRISTINA: I think it means you should go to a different doctor.
CINDY: He's not my doctor. I never saw him before.
CHRISTINA: Well good. I'm sure he's not a good doctor.

(*At the end of the fourth repeat, when* FEFU *invites them for croquet,* CINDY *says, "Let's play croquet," and they follow* FEFU.)

IN THE BEDROOM

A plain unpainted room. Perhaps a room that was used for storage and was set up as a sleeping place for JULIA. *There is a mattress on the floor. To the right of the mattress there is a small table, to the left is* JULIA's *wheelchair. There is a sink on the wall. There are dry leaves on the floor although the time is not fall. The sheets are linen.* JULIA *lies in bed covered to her shoulders. She wears a white hospital gown.* JULIA *hallucinates. However, her behavior should not be the usual behavior attributed to a mad person. It should be rather still and luminous. There will be aspects of her hallucination that frighten her, but hallucinating itself does not.*

JULIA: They clubbed me. They broke my head. They broke my will. They broke my hands. They tore my eyes out. They took my voice away. They didn't do anything to my heart because I didn't bring my heart with me. They clubbed me again, but my head did not fall off in pieces. That was because they were so good and they felt sorry for me. The judges. You didn't know the judges? — I was good and quiet. I never dropped my smile. I smiled to everyone. If I stopped smiling I would get clubbed because they love me. They say they love me. I go along with that because if I don't . . .

(*With her fingers she indicates her throat being cut and makes the sound that usually accompanies that gesture.*)

JULIA: I told them the stinking parts of the body are the important ones: the genitals, the anus, the mouth, the armpit. All important parts except the armpits. And who knows, maybe the armpits are important too. That's what I said. He said that all those parts must be kept clean and put away. He said that women's entrails are heavier than anything on earth and to see a woman running creates a disparate and incongruous image in the mind. It's anti-aesthetic. Therefore women should not run. Instead they should strike positions that take into account the weight of their entrails. Only if they do, can they be aesthetic. He said, for example, Goya's Maja. He said Ruben's women are not aesthetic. Flesh. He said that a woman's bottom should be in a cushion, otherwise it's revolting. He said that there are exceptions. Ballet dancers are exceptions. They can run and lift their legs because they have no entrails. Isadora Duncan had entrails, that's why she should not have danced. But she danced and for this reason became crazy. She wasn't crazy.

(*She moves her hand as if guarding from a blow.*)

JULIA: She was. He said that I had to be punished because I was getting too smart. I'm not smart. I never was. Neither is Fefu smart. They are after her too. Well, she's still walking!

(*She guards from a blow. Her eyes closed.*)

JULIA: Wait! I'll say my prayer. I'm saying it.

(*She mumbles. She opens her eyes with caution.*)

JULIA: You don't think I'm going to argue with them do you. I repented. I told them exactly what they wanted to hear. They killed me. I was dead. But I repented and they said, "Live but crippled. And if you tell. . ."

(*She repeats the throat cutting gesture.*)

JULIA: Why do you have to kill Fefu, for she's only a joker? "Not kill, cure. Cure her." Will it hurt?

(*She whimpers.*)

JULIA: Oh, dear, dear, my dear, they want your light. Your light my dear. Your precious light. Oh dear, my dear.

(*Her head moves as if slapped.*)

JULIA: Not cry. I'll say my prayer. I'll say it. Right now. Look.

(*She sits up.*)

JULIA: The human being is of the masculine gender. The human being is a boy as a child and grown up he is a man. Everything on earth is for the human being, which is man. To nourish him. — There are evil things on earth for man also. For him to fight with, and conquer and turn its evil into good. So that it too can nourish him. — There are Evil Plants, Evil Animals, Evil Minerals, and Women are Evil. — Woman is not a human being. She is: 1-A mystery. 2-Another species. 3-As yet undefined. 4-Unpredictable; therefore wicked and gentle and evil and good which is evil. — If a man commits an evil act, he must be pitied. The evil comes from outside him, through him and into the act. Woman generates the evil herself. — God gave man no other mate but woman. The oxen is good but it is not a mate for man. The sheep is good but it is not a mate for man. The mate for man is woman and that is the cross man must bear. — Man is not spiritually sexual, he therefore can enjoy sexuality. His sexuality is physical which means his spirit is pure. Women's spirit is sexual. That is why after coitus they dwell in nefarious feelings. Because that is their natural habitat. That is why it is difficult for them to return to the human world. Their sexual feelings remain with them till they die. And they take those feelings with them to the afterlife where they corrupt the heavens, and they are sent to hell where through suffering they may shed those feelings and return to earth as man.

(*Her head moves as if slapped.*)

JULIA: Don't hit me. Didn't I just say my prayer?

(*A smaller slap.*)

JULIA: I believe it.

(*She lies back.*)

JULIA: They say when I believe the prayer I will forget the judges. And when I forget the judges I will believe the prayer. They say both happen at once. And all women have done it. Why can't I?

(SUE *enters with a bowl of soup on a tray.*)

SUE: Julia, are you asleep?

(*Short pause.*)

JULIA: No.

SUE: I brought your soup.
JULIA: Put it down. I'm getting up in a moment.

(SUE *puts the soup down.*)

SUE: Do you want me to help you?
JULIA: No, I can manage. Thank you, Sue.

(SUE *goes to the door.*)

SUE: You're all right?
JULIA: Yes.
SUE: I'll see you later.
JULIA: Thank you, Sue.

(SUE *exits.* JULIA *closes her eyes. As soon as each audience group leaves, the tray is removed, if possible through a back door.*)

IN THE KITCHEN

A fully equipped kitchen. There is a table and chairs and a high cutting table. On a counter next to the stove there is a tray with three soup bowls, three spoons and a ladle. On the cutting table there are two empty glasses. Soup is heating on a burner. A kettle with water sits on an unlit burner. In the refrigerator there is an ice tray with wooden sticks in each cube and two pitchers; one with water, one with lemonade. In one of the cabinets there are three complete sets of dishes and other utensils used in the scene. PAULA *sits at the table. She is writing on a pad.* SUE *leans on the cutting table. She is waiting for the soup to heat.*

PAULA: I have it all figured out.
SUE: What?
PAULA: A love affair lasts seven years and three months.
SUE: It does?
PAULA: (*Reading.*) 3 months of love. 1 year saying: It's all right. This is just a passing disturbance. 1 year trying to understand what's wrong. 2 years knowing the end has come. 1 year finding the way to end it. After the separation, 2 years trying to understand what happened. 7 years, 3 months. (*No longer reading.*) At any point the sequence might be interrupted by another love affair that has the same sequence. That is, it's not really interrupted, the new love affair relegates the first one to a second plane and both continue their sequence at the same time.

(SUE *looks over* PAULA's *shoulder.*)

SUE: You really added it up.
PAULA: Sure.
SUE: What do you want to drink?
PAULA: Water. (SUE *takes the water pitcher from the refrigerator and fills*

the two glasses.) The old love affair may fade, so you are not aware the process goes on. A year later it may surface and you might find yourself figuring out what's wrong with the new one while trying to end the old one.

SUE: So how do you solve the problem?

PAULA: Celibacy?

SUE: (*Going to the refrigerator with the pitcher.*) Celibacy doesn't solve any-thing.

PAULA: That's true.

SUE: (*Taking out the ice tray with the sticks.*) What's this? (PAULA *shakes her head.*) Dessert? (PAULA *shrugs her shoulders.* SUE *takes an ice cube and places it against her forehead.*) For a headache. (*She takes another cube and moves her arms in a judo style.*) Eskimo wrestling. (*She places one stick begind her ear.*) Brain cooler. That's when you're thinking too much. You could use one. (*She tries to put the ice cube behind* PAULA'*s ear. They wrestle and laugh. She puts the stick in her own mouth. She takes it out to speak.*) This is when you want to keep chaste. No one will kiss you. (*She puts it back in to demonstrate. Then takes it out.*) That's good for celibacy. If you walk around with one of these in your mouth for seven years you can keep all your sequences straight. Finish one before you start the other. (*She puts the ice cube in the tray and looks at it.*) A frozen caterpillar. (*She puts the tray away.*)

PAULA: You're leaving that ice cube in there?

SUE: I'm clean. (*She pours soup in three bowls, brings the tray to the table and places a bowl and spoon in front of* PAULA.) So what else do you have on love? (SUE *places another bowl and spoon on the table and sits.*)

PAULA: Well, the break up takes place in parts. The brain, the heart, the body, mutual things, shared things. The mind leaves but the heart is still there. The heart has left but the body wants to stay. The body leaves but the things are still at the apartment. You must come back. You move everything out of the apartment. You must come back. You move every-thing out of the apartment but the mind stays behind. Memory lingers in the place. Seven years later, perhaps seven years later, it doesn't matter any more. Perhaps it takes longer. Perhaps it never ends.

SUE: It depends.

PAULA: Yup. It depends.

SUE: Something's bothering you.

PAULA: No.

SUE: (*Taking the tray.*) I'm going to take this to Julia.

PAULA: Go ahead.

(*As* SUE *exits,* CECILIA *enters.*)

CECILIA: May I come in?

PAULA: Yes . . . Would you like something to eat?

CECILIA: No, I ate lunch.

PAULA: I didn't eat lunch. I wasn't very hungry.

CECILIA: I know.

PAULA: Would you like some coffee?

CECILIA: I'll have tea.

PAULA: I'll make some.

CECILIA: No, you sit. I'll make it. (CECILIA *looks for tea.* PAULA *also looks, finds it and gives it to* CECILIA.)

PAULA: Here it is.

CECILIA: (*She lights the burner.*) I've been meaning to call you. (PAULA *walks to the table.*)

PAULA: It doesn't matter. I know you're busy.

CECILIA: Still I would have called you but I really didn't find the time.

PAULA: Don't worry.

CECILIA: I wanted to see you again. I want to see you often.

PAULA: There's no hurry. Now we know we can see each other.

CECILIA: Yes, I'm glad we can.

PAULA: I have thought a great deal about my life since I saw you. I have questioned my life. I can't help doing that. It's been many years and I wondered how you see me now.

CECILIA: You're the same.

PAULA: I felt small in your presence . . . I haven't done all that I could have. All I wanted to do. Our lives have gone in such different directions I cannot help but review what those years have been for me. I gave up, almost gave up. I have missed you in my life. . . . I became lazy. I lost the drive. You abandoned me and I kept going. But after a while I didn't know how to. I didn't know how to go on. I knew why when I was with you. To give you pleasure. So we could laugh together. So we could rejoice together. To bring beauty to the world. . . . Now we look at each other like strangers. We are guarded. I speak and you don't understand my words. Time has changed you more than it has changed me. You have forgotten. I remember every day.

(FEFU *enters. Taking two glasses.*)

FEFU: Emma and I are having a hell of a game of croquet. (*Taking the lemonade pitcher from the refrigerator.*) You want to join us? . . . No. You're having a serious conversation.

PAULA: Very serious. (PAULA *smiles at* CECILIA *in a conciliatory manner.*) Too serious.

FEFU: (*As she exits.*) Come.

PAULA: I'm sorry. Let's go play croquet. — I'm not reproaching you.

CECILIA: (*Reaching for* PAULA's *hand.*) I know. I've missed you too.

(*They exit. As soon as the audience leaves the props are reset.*)

Part III

The living room. It is dusk. There are flowers in the bar. EMMA *enters, checks the lights in the room on her hand, looks around the room and goes upstairs. The rest enter through the rear.* CECILIA, SUE *and* JULIA *are last.* CECILIA *enters speaking.*

CECILIA: Well, we each have our own system of receiving information, placing it, responding to it. That system can function with such a bias that it could take any situation and translate it into one formula. That is, I think, the main reason for stupidity or even madness, not being able to tell the difference between things.

SUE: Like?

CECILIA: Like . . . this person is screaming at me. He's a bully. I don't like being screamed at. Another person screams, or the same person in a different situation is screaming and they have a good reason. You know you have done something that justly provokes them to scream. They are two different things. Often that distinction is not made.

SUE: I see.

CECILIA: We cannot survive in a vacuum. We must be part of a community, perhaps 10, 100, 1000. It depends on how strong you are. But even the strongest will need a dozen, three, even one who sees, thinks and feels as they do. The greater the need for that kind of reassurance, the greater the number that we need to identify with. Some need to identify with the whole nation. Then, the greater the number, the more limited the number of responses and thoughts. A common denominator must be reached. Thoughts, emotions that fit all, have to be limited to a small number. That is, I feel, the concern of the educator — to teach how to be sensitive to the differences, in ourselves as well as outside ourselves, not to supervise the memorization of facts. (EMMA's *head appears in the door-*

way to the stairs.) Otherwise the unusual in us will perish. As we grow we feel we are strange and fear any thought that is not shared with everyone.

JULIA: As I feel I am perishing. My hallucinations are madness, of course, but I wish I could be with others who hallucinate also. I would still know I am mad but I would not feel so isolated. — Hallucinations are real, you know. They are not like dreams. They are as real as all of you here. I have actually asked to be hospitalized so I could be with other nuts. But the doctors don't want to. They can't diagnose me. That makes me even more isolated. (*There is a moment's silence.*) You see, right now, it's an awful moment because you don't know what to say or do. If I were with other people who hallucinate they would say, "Oh yeah. Sure. It's awful. Those dummies, they don't see anything." (*The others begin to relax.*) It's not so bad, really. I can laugh at it . . . Emma is ready. We should start. (*The others are hesitant. She speaks to* FEFU.) Come on.

FEFU: Sure. (FEFU *begins to move the table. Others help move the table and enough furniture to clear a space in the center. They form a semi-circle facing upstage.*) All right. I start. Right?

CINDY: Right.

(EMMA *sits on the steps. Only her head and legs are visible.*)

FEFU: I talk about the stifling conditions of primary school education etc.... etc.... The project . . . I know what I'm going to say but I don't want to bore you with it. We all know it by heart. Blah blah blah blah. And so on and so on. And so on and so on. Then I introduce Emma . . . And now Miss Emma Blake. (*They applaud.* EMMA *shakes her head.*) What.

EMMA: Paula goes next.

FEFU: Does it matter?

EMMA: Of course it matters. Dra-ma-tur-gia. It has to build. I'm in costume.

FEFU: Oh. And now, ladies and gentlemen, Miss Paula Cori will speak on Art as a Tool for Learning. And I tell them the work you have done at the Institute, community centers, essays, etc. Miss Paula Cori.

(*They applaud.* PAULA *goes to center.*)

PAULA: Ladies and gentlemen, I, like my fellow educator and colleague, Stephany Beckmann . . .

FEFU: I am not an educator.

PAULA: What are you?

FEFU: . . . a do gooder . . . a girl scout.

PAULA: Well, like my fellow girl scout Stephany Beckmann say blah blah blah blah blah blah blah blah and I offer the jewels of my wisdom and experience, which I will write down and memorize, otherwise I would just stand there and stammer and go blank. And even after I memorize it I'm sure I will just stand there and stammer and go blank.

EMMA: I'll work with you on it.

PAULA: However, after our other colleague Miss Emma Blake works with me on it . . . (*In imitation of* EMMA *she brings her hands together and opens*

her arms as she moves her head back and speaks.) My impulses will burst
forth through a symphony of eloquence.
EMMA: Breathe . . . in . . . (PAULA *inhales slowly.*) And bow. (PAULA *bows.*
They applaud. She comes up from the bow.)
PAULA: Oh, I liked that. (*The walk to her seat has the same quality as the*
previous movements. She sits.)
EMMA: Good . . .

(*They applaud.*)

FEFU: And now, ladies and gentlemen, the one and only, the incompara-
ble, our precious, dear Emma Blake.

(EMMA *walks in rather casually. She wears a robe which hangs from her arms*
to the floor. She demonstrates the possibilities of the robe.)

EMMA: From the prologue to "The Science of Educational Dramatics" by
Emma Sheridan Fry.*

> Environment knocks at the gateway of the senses. A rain of summons
> beats upon us day and night. . . . We do not answer. Everything
> around us shouts against our deafness, struggles with our unwill-
> ingness, batters our walls, flashes into our blindness, strives to sieve
> through us at every pore, begging, fighting, insisting. It shouts,
> "Where are you? Where are you?" But we are deaf. The signals do not
> reach us.
>
> Society restricts us, school straight jackets us, civilization submerges us,
> privation wrings us, luxury feather-beds us. The Divine Urge is checked.
> The Winged Horse balks on the road, and we, discouraged, defeated,
> dismount and burrow into ourselves. The gates are closed and Divine
> Urge is imprisoned at Center. Thus we are taken by indifference that is
> death.
>
> Environment finding the gates closed tries to break in. Turned away, it
> comes another way. Keep back, it stretches its hands to us. Always
> scheming to reach us. Never was a suitor more insistent than Environ-
> ment, seeking admission, claiming recognition, signaling to be seen,
> shouting to be heard. And through the ages we sit inside ourselves
> deaf, dumb and blind, and will not stir. . . .
>
> . . . Maybe you are not deaf. . . . Perhaps signals reach you. Maybe
> you stir. . . . The gates give. . . . Eternal Urge pushes through the
> stupor of our senses, making paths to meet the challenging suitor, win-
> dows through which to see him, ears through which to hear him. Envi-
> ronment shouting, "Where are you?" and Center battering at the inner

---

*Emma Sheridan Fry taught acting to children at The Educational Alliance in New York from
1903 to 1909. In 1917, her book *Educational Dramatics* was published by Lloyd Adams' Noble.
The text of Emma's speech is taken from the prologue.

side of the wall crying, "Here I am," and dragging down bars, wrenching gates, prying at port-holes. Listening at cracks, reaching everywhere, and demanding that sense gates be flung open. The gates are open! Eternal Urge stands at the threshold signaling with venturous flag. An imperious instinct lets us know that "all" is ours, land that whatever anyone has ever known, or may ever have known, we will call and claim. A sense of life universal surges through our life individual. We attack the feast of this table with an insatiable appetite that cries for all.

What are we? A creation of God's consciousness coming now slowly and painfully into recognition of ourselves.

What is Personality? A small part of us. The whole of us is behind that hungry rush at the gates of Senses.

What is Civilization? A circumscribed order in which the whole has not entered.

What is Environment? Our mate, our true mate that clamors for our reunion.

We will meet him. We will seize all, learn all, know all here, that we may fare further on the great quest! The task of Now is only a step toward the task of the Whole! Let us then seek the laws governing real life forces, that coming into their own, they may create, develop and reconstruct. Let us awaken life dormant! Let us, boldly, seizing the star of our intent, left it as the lantern of our necessity, and let it shine over the darkness of our compliance. Come! The light shines. Come! It brightens our way. Come! Don't let its glorious light pass you by! Come! The day has come!

(EMMA *throws herself on the couch.* PAULA *embraces her.*) Oh, it's so beautiful.
JULIA: It is, Emma. It is.

(*They applaud.*)

CINDY: Encore! Encore!

(EMMA *stands.* PAULA *sits on the couch.*)

EMMA: Environment knocks at the gateway ... (*She laughs and joins the others in the semi-circle.*) What's next.
FEFU: I introduce Cecilia. (*She goes to center.*) I don't think I should introduce Cecilia. She should just come out after Emma. Now things don't need introduction. (*Imitating* EMMA) They are happening.
EMMA: Right!

(CECILIA *goes to center.*)

CECILIA: Well, as we say in the business, that's a very hard act to follow.

EMMA: Not very hard. It's a hard act to follow.

CECILIA: Right. I should say my name first.

FEFU: Yes.

CECILIA: I should breathe too. (*She takes a breath. One starts singing "Cecilia." All except* PAULA *join in.* CECILIA *sits next to* PAULA. *She leans against* PAULA *and puts her hand on* PAULA's *leg. At the end of the song* CECILIA *realizes where she is and stands.*) I should go before Emma. I don't think anyone should speak after Emma.

CINDY: Right. It should be Fefu, Paula, Cecilia, then Emma, and then Sue explaining the finances and asking for pledges. And the money should roll in. It's very good. (*They applaud.*) Sue . . .

(SUE *goes to center.*)

SUE: Yes, blahblahblahblah, pledges and money. (*She indicates she is finished. They applaud.*)

FEFU: Who's ready for coffee?

CINDY: And dishes.

CHRISTINA: I'll help.

EMMA: Me too.

(*They put the furniture back.* EMMA *and* SUE *start to go to the kitchen.* SUE *tries to go ahead of* EMMA. EMMA *speeds ahead of her.*)

FEFU: Don't all come. Sit. Sit. You have done enough, relax.

(*All except* CINDY *and* JULIA *exit.*)

JULIA: I should go do the dishes. I haven't done anything.

CINDY: You can do them tomorrow.

JULIA: True. — So how have you been?

CINDY: Hmm.

JULIA: Let me see. I can tell by looking at your face. Not so bad.

CINDY: Not so bad.

(*There is the sound of laughter from the kitchen.* CHRISTINA *runs in.*)

CHRISTINA: They're having a water fight over who's going to do the dishes. (*She hides behind the left curtain.*)

CINDY: Emma?

CHRISTINA: And Paula, and Sue, all of them. Fefu was getting into it when I left. Cecilia got out the back door.

(CHRISTINA *walks back to the kitchen with some caution. She runs back and lies on the couch covering her head with a cushion.* EMMA *enters with a pan of water in her hand. She is wet.* CINDY *and* JULIA *point to the lawn.* EMMA *runs to the lawn. There is the sound of knocking from upstairs.*)

PAULA: Open up.

FEFU: There's no one here.

PAULA: Open up you coward.

FEFU: I can't. I'm busy.
PAULA: What are you doing?
FEFU: I have a man here. Ah ah ah ah ah.
PAULA: O.K. I'll wait. Take your time.
FEFU: It's going to take quite a while.
PAULA: It's all right. I'll wait.
FEFU: Do me a favor?
PAULA: Sure. Open up and I'll do you a favor.

(*There is the sound of a pot falling, a door slamming.*)

FEFU: Fill it up for me.
PAULA: O.K.
FEFU: Thank you.
PAULA: Here's water. Open up.
FEFU: Leave it there. I'll come out in a minute.
PAULA: O.K. Here it is. I'm leaving now.

(*Loud steps.* PAULA *comes down with a filled pan. She hides by the entrance to the steps. She waits a moment, realizes* FEFU *is not coming down. She comes down from the landing. She walks to the rear exit, screams and runs to the lawn.* EMMA *follows her. Water splashes.*)

EMMA: You missed!
PAULA: Truce!
EMMA: Who's the winner?
PAULA: You are. You do the dishes.
EMMA: I'm the winner. You do the dishes.

(SUE *comes down the steps and looks out the window.*)

SUE: Psst. (PAULA *and* EMMA *scream.*) Gotcha!
EMMA: Please don't.
PAULA: Truce. Truce.
SUE: O.K. Back to the kitchen. Empty that pan. . . . Right there! Back to the kitchen. (PAULA *and* EMMA *come in with empty pans.* SUE *steps down from the landing.* PAULA *tries to run.*) Halt! (PAULA *stops.*) To the kitchen. (*They go to the kitchen. A moment later they scream.*)
FEFU: (*Off-stage.*) O.K. Line up. (*To* SUE.) Put that down. (*There is a moment's silence.*)
JULIA: It's over.
CINDY: We're safe.
JULIA: (*To* CHRISTINA.) You can come up now. (CHRISTINA *stays down.*) You rather wait a while. (CHRISTINA *nods.*)
CHRISTINA: (*Playful.*) I feel danger lurking.
CINDY: She's been hiding all day.

(FEFU *enters and sits.*)

FEFU: I won. I got them working in there.

JULIA: I thought the fight was over who'd do the dishes.

FEFU: Yes. — I have to change. I'm soaked. (*Starting to go.*)

CHRISTINA: They forgot what the fight was about.

FEFU: We did?

JULIA: That's usually the way it is.

FEFU: (*To* CHRISTINA) Are you ready for an ice cube?

(FEFU *exits upstairs.* EMMA *tip-toes in. She signals* CINDY *and* JULIA *to be silent. She reaches the couch, pours water on* CHRISTINA *and runs back to the kitchen.* CHRISTINA *runs upstairs. There is silence.*)

CINDY: So. — And how have you been?

JULIA: All right. I've been taking care of myself.

CINDY: You look well.

JULIA: I do not . . . Have you seen Mike?

CINDY: No, not since Christmas.

JULIA: I'm sorry.

CINDY: I'm O.K. — And how's your love life?

JULIA: Far away. . . . I have no need for it.

CINDY: I'm sorry.

JULIA: Don't be. I'm very morbid these days. I think of death all the time.

PAULA: (*Standing in the doorway.*) Anyone for coffee? (*They raise their hands.*) Anyone take milk? (*They raise their hands.*)

JULIA: Should we go in?

PAULA: I'll bring it out. (PAULA *exits.*)

JULIA: I feel we are constantly threatened by death, every second, every instant, it's there. And every moment something rescues us. Something rescues us from death every moment of our lives. For every moment we live we have to thank something. We have to be grateful to something that fights for us and saves us. I have felt lifeless and in the face of death. Death is not anything. It's being lifeless and I have felt lifeless sometimes for a brief moment, but I have been rescued by these . . . guardians. I am not sure who these guardians are. I only know they exist because I have felt their absence. I think we have come to know them as life, and we have become familiar with certain forms they take. Our sight is a form they take. That is why we take pleasure in seeing things, and we find some things beautiful. The sun is a guardian. Those things we take pleasure in are usually guardians. We enjoy looking at the sunlight when it comes through the window. Don't we? We as people, are guardians to each other when we give love. And then of course we have white cells and antibodies protecting us. Those moments when I feel lifeless have occurred, and I am afraid one day the guardians won't come in time and I will be defenseless. I will die . . . for no apparent reason.

(*Pause.* PAULA *stands in the doorway with a bottle of milk.*)

PAULA: Anyone take rotten milk? (*She smiles, No one laughs.*) I'm kidding. This one is no good but there's more in there . . . (*Remaining in good spirits.*) Forget it. It's not a good joke.

JULIA: It's good.

PAULA: In there it seemed funny but here it isn't. It's a kitchen joke.(PAULA *shrugs her shoulders.*) . . . Bye . . . (*She exits.*)

JULIA: (*After her.*) It is funny, Paula. (*To* CINDY.) It was funny.

CINDY: It's all right, Paula doesn't mind.

JULIA: I'm sure she minds. I'll go see . . . (JULIA *starts to go.* PAULA *appears in the doorway.*)

PAULA: Hey, who was the lady I saw you with? — That was no lady. That was my rotten wife. That one wasn't good either, was it? (*Exiting.*) Emma. . . . That one was no good either.

(SUE *comes in with a tray with sugar, milk and two cups of coffee. She stops at the doorway to look at* PAULA *and* EMMA *who are behind the wall.*)

SUE: (*Whispering.*) What are you doing? — What? — O.K., O.K. (*She comes in and puts the tray down. She whispers.*) They're plotting something.

(PAULA *comes out.*)

PAULA: Ladies and gentlemen. Ladies, since our material is too shocking and avant-garde, we have decided to uplift our subject matter so it's more palatable to the sensitive public. (PAULA *takes a pose.* EMMA *comes out. She lifts an imaginary camera to her face.*)

EMMA: Say cheese.

PAULA: Cheese (PAULA *smiles. They both turn front.*)

PAULA and EMMA: Ha ha! (*The others smile.*)

PAULA: Ah, success, success. Make it clean and you'll succeed. — Coffee's in the kitchen.

SUE: I brought theirs out.

PAULA: Oh, shall we have it here?

JULIA: No. We can all go in the kitchen. (*They each take their coffee and go toward the kitchen.*)

PAULA: Either here or there. (*She sits by the rear door.*) I'm exhausted.

(CECILIA *enters from the lawn. She looks at* PAULA *for a moment before* PAULA *notices her.*)

CECILIA: Is the war over?

PAULA: Yes.

CECILIA: It's nice out. (PAULA *nods in agreement.*) Where's everybody?

PAULA: In the kitchen, having coffee.

(CECILIA *walks toward the kitchen. She speaks when she reaches the archway.*)

CECILIA: We must talk. (PAULA *is ready to talk.*) Not now. I'll call you. (CECILIA *starts to go.*)

PAULA: When?

CECILIA: I don't know. I have to . . .

PAULA: I don't want you, you know.

CECILIA: I know.

PAULA: No, you don't. I'm not lusting after you.

CECILIA: I know that. (*She starts to go*.) I'll call you.

PAULA: When?

CECILIA: As soon as I can.

PAULA: At what time?

CECILIA: . . . I don't know.

PAULA: I won't be home then.

CECILIA: When will you be home?

PAULA: I'll check my book and let you know.

CECILIA: Do that. — I'll be leaving after coffee. I'll say good-bye now.

PAULA: Good-bye. (CECILIA *exits*. PAULA *starts toward the steps*. FEFU *appears on the landing*.)

FEFU: You're still wet.

PAULA: I'm going to change now.

FEFU: Do you need anything?

PAULA: No, I have something I can change to. Thank you.

(PAULA *goes upstairs*. FEFU *takes a step down and stops. There is a slight change of atmosphere. She is downcast. She turns to see the flowers on the bar and goes to them. She smells one and turns to look behind her.* JULIA *enters. She is walking. She goes to the coffee table, gets the sugar bowl, lifts it in* FEFU'*s direction, takes the cover off, puts it back on and walks to the kitchen. As soon as* JULIA *exits,* SUE'*s voice is heard speaking the following lines. Immediately after,* JULIA *re-enters wheeled by* SUE. CINDY, CHRISTINA, EMMA, *and* CECILIA *are with them. On the arms of the wheelchair rests a tray with a coffee pot and cups. As they reach the sofa and chairs they sit and take cups.*)

SUE: I was terribly exhausted and run down. I lived on coffee so I could stay up all night and do my work. And they used to give us these medical check-ups all the time. But all they did was ask how we felt and we'd say "Fine," and they'd check us out. In the meantime I looked like a ghost. I was all bones. Remember Susan Austin? She was very naive and when they asked her how she felt, she said she was nervous and she wasn't sleeping well. So she had to see a psychiatrist from then on.

EMMA: Well, she was crazy.

SUE: No, she wasn't. — Oh god, those were awful days. . . . Remember Julie Brooks?

EMMA: Sure.

SUE: She was a beautiful girl.

EMMA: Ah yes, she was gorgeous.

(PAULA *comes down as soon as possible and stands on the landing*.)

SUE: At the end of the first semester they called her in because she had been out with 28 men and they thought that was awful. And the worst thing was that after that, she thought there was something wrong with her.

CINDY: She was a nymphomaniac, that's all.

(*They are amused.*)

SUE: She was not. She was just very beautiful so all the boys wanted to go out with her. And if a boy asked her to go have a cup of coffee she'd sign out and write in the name of the boy. None of us did of course. All she did was go for coffee or go to a movie. She was really very innocent.

EMMA: And Gloria Schuman? She wrote a psychology paper the faculty decided she didn't write and they called her in to try to make her admit she hadn't written it. She insisted she wrote it and they sent her to a psychiatrist also.

JULIA: Everybody ended going to the psychiatrist.

(FEFU *exits through the foyer.*)

EMMA: After a few visits the psychiatrist said: Don't you think you know me well enough now that you can tell me the truth about the paper? He almost drove her crazy. They just couldn't believe she was so smart.

SUE: Those were difficult times.

PAULA: We were young. That's why it was difficult. On my first year I thought you were all very happy.

EMMA: Oh god.

PAULA: I had been so deprived in my childhood that I believed the rich were all happy. During the summer you spent your vacations in Europe or the Orient. I went to work and I resented that. But then I realized that many lives are ruined by poverty and many lives are ruined by wealth. I was always able to manage. And I think I enjoyed myself as much when I went to Revere Beach on my day off as you did when you visited the Taj Mahal. Then when I stopped feeling envy, I started noticing the waste. I began feeling contempt for those who, having everything a person can ask for, make such a mess of it. I resented them because they were not better than the poor. If you have all you need you should be generous. If you can afford to go to school your mind should be better. If you didn't have to fight for your place on earth you should be nobler. But I saw them cheating and grabbing like the kids in the slums, or wasting away with self-indulgence. And I saw them be plain stupid. If there is a reason why some are rich while others starve it must be so they put everything they have at the service of others. They should take the responsibility of everything that happens in the world. They are the only ones who can influence things. The poor don't have the power to change things. I think we should teach the poor and let the rich take care of themselves. I'm sorry, I know that's what we're doing. That's what Emma has been doing. I'm sorry . . . I guess I feel it's not enough. (PAULA *sobs.*) I'll wash my face. I'll be right back. (*She starts to go.*) I think highly of all of you.

(*She goes through the rear doorway.* SUE *starts to go after her.* CECILIA *follows* SUE. PAULA *turns.* SUE *walks back.* CECILIA *kisses* PAULA *on the lips. They exit.* FEFU *enters from the lawn.*)

FEFU: Have you been out? The sky is full of stars.

(SUE, CHRISTINA, *and* CINDY *exit.*)

JULIA: What's the matter?

(FEFU *smiles and shakes her head.* JULIA *starts to go toward the door.*)

FEFU: Stay a moment, will you?
JULIA: Of course.
FEFU: Did you have enough coffee?
JULIA: Yes.
FEFU: Did you find the sugar?
JULIA: Yes. There was sugar in the kitchen. What's the matter?
FEFU: Can you walk? (JULIA *is hurt. She opens her arms implying she hides nothing.*) I am sorry, my dear.
JULIA: What is the matter?
FEFU: I don't know, Julia. Every breath is painful for me. I don't know. (FEFU *turns* JULIA*'s head to look into her eyes.*) I think you know.

(JULIA *looks away.*)

JULIA: No, I don't know. I haven't seen very much of you lately. I have thought of you a great deal. I always think of you. Cindy tells me how you are. I always ask her. How is Phillip? Things are not well with Phillip?
FEFU: No.
JULIA: What's wrong?
FEFU: A lot is wrong.
JULIA: He loves you.
FEFU: He can't stand me.
FEFU: He loves you.
FEFU: He's left me. His body is here but the rest is gone. I exhaust him. I torment him and I torment myself. I need him, Julia.
JULIA: I know you do.
FEFU: I need his touch. I need his kiss. I need the person he is. I can't give him up. (*She looks into* JULIA*'s eyes.*) I look into your eyes and I know what you see. (JULIA *closes her eyes.*) It's death. (JULIA *shakes her head.*) Fight!
JULIA: I can't.
FEFU: I saw you walking.
JULIA: No. I can't walk.
FEFU: You came for sugar, Julia. You came for sugar. Walk!
JULIA: You know I can't walk.
FEFU: Why not? — Try! — Get up! — Stand up!
JULIA: What is wrong with you?

FEFU: You have given up!

JULIA: I get tired! I get exhausted! I am exhausted!

FEFU: What is it you see? (JULIA *doesn't answer.*) What is it you see! Where is it you go that tires you so?

JULIA: I can't spend time with others! I get tired!

FEFU: What is it you see!

JULIA: You want to see it too?

FEFU: No, I don't. You're nuts, and willingly so.

JULIA: You know I'm not.

FEFU: And you're contagious. I'm going mad too.

JULIA: I try to keep away from you.

FEFU: Why?

JULIA: I might be harmful to you.

FEFU: Why?

JULIA: I am contagious. I can't be what I used to be.

FEFU: You have no courage.

JULIA: You're being cruel.

FEFU: I try to swallow my feelings but I can't. They choke me. I want to rest, Julia. How does a person rest. I want to put my mind at rest. I am frightened. (JULIA *looks at* FEFU.) Don't look at me. (*She covers* JULIA's *eyes with her hand.*) I lose my courage when you look at me.

JULIA: May no harm come to your head.

FEFU: Fight!

JULIA: May no harm come to your will.

FEFU: Fight, Julia!

JULIA: I have no life left.

FEFU: Fight, Julia!

JULIA: May no harm come to your hands.

FEFU: I need you to fight.

JULIA: May no harm come to your eyes.

FEFU: Fight with me!

JULIA: May no harm come to your voice.

FEFU: Fight with me!

JULIA: May no harm come to your heart.

(CHRISTINA *enters.* FEFU *sees* CHRISTINA, *releases* JULIA. *To* CHRISTINA.)

FEFU: Now I have done it. Haven't I. You think I'm a monster. (*To* JULIA.) Forgive me if you can. (JULIA *nods.*)

JULIA: I forgive you.

(FEFU *gets the gun.*)

CHRISTINA: What in the world are you doing with that gun?

FEFU: I'm going to clean it.

CHRISTINA: I think you better not.

FEFU: I think you're silly.

(CECILIA *appears on the landing. She is ready to go.*)

CHRISTINA: I don't care if you shoot yourself. I just don't like the mess you're making.

(FEFU *starts to go to the lawn and turns.*)

FEFU: I enjoy betting it won't be a real bullet. You want to bet?

CHRISTINA: No. (FEFU *exits.* CHRISTINA *goes to* JULIA.) Are you all right?

JULIA: Yes.

CHRISTINA: Can I get you anything?

JULIA: Water. (CECILIA *goes to the bar for water.*) Put some sugar in it. Could I have a damp cloth for my forehead? (CHRISTINA *goes toward the kitchen.*) I didn't tell her anything. Did I? I didn't.

CECILIA: About what?

JULIA: She knew. (*There is the sound of a shot.* CHRISTINA *and* CECILIA *run out.* JULIA *puts her hand to her forehead. Her hand goes down slowly. There is blood on her forehead. Her head falls back.* FEFU *enters holding a dead rabbit in her arms. She stands behind* JULIA.)

FEFU: I killed it . . . I just shot . . . and killed it . . . Julia.

(SUE *and* CINDY *enter from the foyer,* EMMA *from the backstage entrance,* PAULA *from upstairs,* CHRISTINA *and* CECILIA *from the lawn. They surround* JULIA. *The lights fade.*)

Domino Courts

William Hauptman

©1977, 1980 Copyright by William Hauptman.
CAUTION: No performances or readings of this work may be given without the express authorization of the author's agent. For production rights contact: Ellen Neuwald, Inc., 905 West End Avenue, New York, N.Y. 10025.

Domino Courts was originally performed by the Second Company of the Williamstown Theatre Festival in August, 1975; produced by Nikos Psacharpoulos; under the direction of Barnet Kellman; with the following cast:

FLOYD . . . . *Jay Sanders*
RONNIE . . . . *Linda Varvel*
ROY . . . . *Josh Clark*
FLO . . . . *Diane Patterson*

Domino Courts was first produced professionally by Wynn Handman and Julia Miles at the American Place Theatre in New York in December, 1975; under the direction of Barnet Kellman; with the following cast:

FLOYD . . . . *Guy Boyd*
RONNIE . . . . *Mary-Elaine Monti*
ROY . . . . *Conard Fowkes*
FLO . . . . *Regina Baff*

This production was based on the original set and lighting designs by Rich Eisbrouch; costume designs by Carol Oditz; production stage manager, Andrea Naier.

Domino Courts was subsequently produced by Wynn Handman and Julia Miles at the American Place Theatre in November, 1976; under the direction of Barnet Kellman; with the following cast:

FLOYD . . . . *Guy Boyd*
RONNIE . . . . *Jane Galloway*
ROY . . . . *Conard Fowkes*
FLO . . . . *Regina Baff*

Set design by Henry Millman; lighting design by Eddie Greenberg; costumes by Carol Oditz; production stage manager, Richard S. Viola.

PLACE: a tourist court in Southern Oklahoma
TIME: an afternoon in August, 1939

Pre-show music is heard. The Mill Brothers singing "Paper Doll." As the song plays, the houselights dim; as it ends the houselights go dark and the stage goes black.

Noon. FLOYD *sitting on the bed, wearing a suit, holding his hat in his hand. His jacket is on the coat-rack. Another identical hat sits on the chair in the center of the room. When the stage brightens,* FLOYD *speaks:*

FLOYD: The Hot Grease Boys, that's what they used to call us. We thought we were hot grease. You should have seen us in those days, walking in a bank and sticking our guns in their faces and saying hand over your money. Hot Grease. That was before Roy and I split up. When I close my eyes, I can still see us driving down the highway, the centerline disappearing under the hood. I can see us driving at night, headlights shining in our faces and those silver posts going by along the sides of the road. Then they found out who we were. You started seeing our pictures everywhere — in the papers, in the post office. Oklahoma was getting too hot for us; so I retired and Roy drove North. (*Crossing to chair where hat sits.*) Wait up, Roy, I shouted, you forgot your hat. But the car was already moving and he couldn't hear me and I watched him vanish in a cloud of dust. That was four years ago. Now Roy's coming back, and I can see the look on his face when I show him I've still got his good hat. (FLOYD's *wife,* RONNIE, *enters. She wears a bathrobe over a bathing suit. She sits at the vanity, ignoring* FLOYD, *and starts brushing her hair, looking in the mirror.* FLOYD *doesn't look at her.*) I remember the day we busted that bank in Mound City. I remember us on the road. I remember that last hot day, the car moving and me shouting and the car gone. Dust on my good shoes. Hot — hot — oh, we thought we were so hot . . . (*Pause.*)

RONNIE: Talking to yourself again, Floyd?

FLOYD: I get worked up. They'll be here soon.

RONNIE: I don't know why they couldn't come to our house in town.

FLOYD: It's private out here in the country. Nobody knows our faces out here, we can do what we want.

RONNIE: Nobody knows us in town either.

FLOYD: (*Crossing suddenly to window.*) There's a car coming.

RONNIE: It's not them.

FLOYD: It's not slowing down . . . it's gone past. How'd you know?

RONNIE: I always know what's going to happen. Sit down, Floyd, they're not coming yet. (FLOYD *sits in chair by window and continues to stare out.*) You should go for a swim.

FLOYD: Not me. I'm not going to be standing around without any clothes on when Roy comes. Nosir. (*Pause.*)

RONNIE: I think you're jealous of Roy. He's still working. You'd like to be famous again.

FLOYD: No. No, he's not that famous now. You never see his name in the papers anymore, not now that we've split up. But when we were together, nobody could stop us. (*Crossing back to the hat on the chair.*) I hope you brought your gun along, Roy. We could still show them. What a character you were, you old pisspot. I always said if we were a deck of cards, you'd be the joker. I'm talking about Roy. That's his hat. (*He puts it on, leaving his own hat on the chair.*) How do I look?

RONNIE: It looks like your hat.

FLOYD: But this is Roy's hat . . . (*He advances toward her menacingly.*)

RONNIE: Let's play dominos.

(FLOYD *stops instantly; turns and starts unfolding the card table. When he starts talking again, he talks like a hoodlum.*)

FLOYD: She likes to play dominos. Do you? I've always thought it was a waste of time myself. Cards — that's my game. And bingo. I do like the way the dominos look. There's several versions of dominos. One's called forty-two and another's called moon, and that's how I got to know you, Roy. Yeah. (*He works silently for a moment.* RONNIE *ignores him. He moves the chair with his hat left in front of the bed and positions the card table* C. S.) Good old Roy. We both had the same dream when we were boys, didn't we? That's how close we were. We dreamed about the Man in the Moon. I always thought I looked like him. When I was a boy I used to lie awake at nights and watch him floating there, outside the window, thinking we both had the same ghostly grin. So does Fred Astaire. Those are the only other people I've ever wanted to be. Good old Roy. We burned up the roads in those days, didn't we? (*Normal voice, crossing to window.*) There's another car coming —

RONNIE: It's not them. Sit down, Floyd. (*He sits, instantly.* RONNIE *drags her chair from the vanity to the table, sits* U. C. *and starts setting up a row of dominos.* FLOYD *joins her, bringing the chair he was sitting in and placing it* S.L. *He drags it very slowly so it scrapes the floor.*)

FLOYD: That scare you? That loud noise?

RONNIE: No.

FLOYD: (*Sitting; sadly.*) I used to scare you when we were first married. That's the trouble, I don't now.

RONNIE: This is making you nervous, isn't it?

FLOYD: What?

RONNIE: Seeing Roy again.

FLOYD: Why should I be nervous? You're the one who should be nervous. You're going to be meeting his new wife, comparing yourself to her. (*Pause.*) I just hope he brought his gun along. That scare you?

RONNIE: It's your move. (*He tips over a row of dominos. She starts setting up another one.*)

FLOYD: Why should I be nervous?

RONNIE: It's been four years. People change.

FLOYD: Not Roy. Some people would, but not him. (*Standing, getting excited.*) That's what was so important about the day we stuck up the Mound City Bank. Roy was disguised as Clark Gable. We always did our jobs disguised as movie stars. He'd drawn a little moustache on his face with a pencil; he said he only wished his ears stuck out more. I was disguised as Fred Astaire. I had on my patent leather shoes and my trousers with the black satin stripe. When he asked me who I was, and I told him, he said that was all wrong: Clarke Gable and Fred Astaire never made a movie together yet, and anyway, who ever heard of a dancing stick up team? Then he looked at me, and he rubbed off that pencilled moustache. Let it go, Floyd, he said. Hell — let's be ourselves. So he shook my hand and I stopped grinning and we busted that bank as the Oklahoma Hot Grease Boys, and it went for over four thousand dollars. (*Almost like a boy.*) There's another car coming, can I go look?

RONNIE: You could never go back on the road again, Floyd. Not now.

FLOYD: You talk about me as if there was something wrong with me. I'm not old.

RONNIE: I didn't say you were old.

FLOYD: (*Agitated.*) There's nothing wrong with me, Ronnie. Why...you talk about me as if I was an alcoholic! (*Laughs loudly.*) Maybe I do want to join up with Roy again. Maybe he feels the same way. Maybe I brought something along that would make your blood run cold.

RONNIE: (*Bored.*) Did you bring your gun?

FLOYD: That's for me to know and you to find out. (ROY *appears behind them in the door.* RONNIE *sees him over* FLOYD's *shoulder, gasps and points.* ROY *is dark-haired, handsome, sleek, and looks apprehensive. He wears a suit almost identical to* FLOYD's *and carries two yellow suitcases like a porter.*) Roy ... (ROY *says nothing. He just grins.*) You old pisspot. (ROY *starts back outside.*) Roy — it's me — Floyd! Don't you know me? This is my wife, Ronnie. (FLOYD *starts toward him.* ROY *abruptly motions no. He cases the cabin first, disappearing into the kitchen.* FLOYD *gets his jacket from the coat-rack and puts it on,* RONNIE *straightens her robe.* ROY *reappears, every move alert, and manhandles the suitcases* D. S. R. *, taking a long time, looking around the room. When he speaks, it is almost in a whisper.*)

ROY: Everything looks so small now. So small and flat . . .

FLOYD: You don't look any different, Roy!

ROY: The buildings are so much larger up North. That must be it. But the driving down here, things get smaller and smaller. The road changes. Goes from a turnpike to a blacktop to that narrow little dirt road outside. When you finally get here, Oklahoma's no bigger than a tablecloth. . . . Your house looks like a doll house, Floyd. Look at that chair! (*He points and laughs.* FLOYD *laughs, then catches* ROY's *eye and stops abruptly.*) Like to introduce my wife, Flo. Flo! (*He crosses and shouts out the door. Nobody appears.*)

FLOYD: (*Starting towards them.*) Those suitcases look heavy —

ROY: (*Crossing quickly back to suitcases.*) There's nothing in them. Nothing but Flo's things and some hotel towels. I can't stop stealing them . . . (*Pause.*)

RONNIE: Can we see her? (FLO's *face appears at the door. She is drab and timid.*)

FLOYD: (*Booming.*) Well, come on in, honey, and let us have a look at you! (FLO *disappears again.*)

RONNIE: Floyd, not so loud. (FLO *reappears.*) I'm Ronnie.

(*She holds out her arms.* FLO *steps hesitantly into the cabin, first removing her hat and wiping her feet. She hands* RONNIE *flowers. Then they suddenly embrace.* FLOYD *backslaps* ROY, *and* RONNIE *takes the flowers into the kitchen.*)

FLOYD: This is something! Boy, it's good to see you, Roy!

ROY: Same here.

FLOYD: Hey! You remember the invisible rope? (*They leap apart* D. S., *stand facing each other.*) We stand on either side of the road. A car comes along and — (*They pull an imaginary rope taut between them.* FLO *gasps.*) Can you see it?

FLO: It looks real.

FLOYD: He slams on his brakes, and when he gets out we make him give us all the money he's got. Go on — try to cross it.

FLO: (*She puts her hands over her eyes and runs through it.*) Oooh.

FLOYD: Go on, Ronnie. Can't you almost feel it?

RONNIE: (*Crossing slowly to rope, smiling.*) Yes.

FLOYD: (*Scornfully.*) You can't feel it, there's nothing there. (*He embraces* ROY. RONNIE *clears dominos from card table and sets tablecloth and four plates while* FLO *wanders.*) Boy, this is gonna be great. We'll stay up all night talking about the days of the Hot Grease Boys, the Mound City Bank, the old invisible rope trick, and our dream about the moon.

ROY: ...Dream about the moon?

FLOYD: Sure, you know. Our dream.

ROY: We had a lot of trouble finding this place. (*Looking around, easing somewhat.*) I think you gave us the wrong directions, Floyd. Maybe not. I didn't dream the town would look so small now. We almost didn't find it at all.... Just four houses. That's not much of a town.

FLOYD: You're not in town, Roy. This is a tourist court.

ROY: No wonder we had so much trouble finding it. Why'd you do that?

RONNIE: Who knows? Floyd wanted to rent a cabin for some reason.

FLOYD: So we could do what we wanted. (*Booming.*) So we could make as much noise as we wanted.

ROY: (*Crossing to* RONNIE *at table.*) Floyd wrote me lots about you. I don't know how he got such a good-looking woman.

FLOYD: (*Bringing the remaining chair* D. S. *and trying to get between them.*) You haven't changed, Roy. Not a particle.

ROY: Neither have you, Horseface.

FLOYD: So tell us about things, about things up North.

ROY: For one thing, I'm thinking about joining a mob.

FLO: (*Picking up a shrivelled balloon off end table* D. R. *and putting it in her purse.*) Somebody had a party ... (*The others ignore her.*)

FLOYD: A mob?

RONNIE: He means a gangster mob, Floyd, like in the movies.

FLOYD: I know that; sounds good.

RONNIE: Floyd. Not so loud.

FLOYD: I might like to get in on that action. Think one of those mobs would consider taking on another country boy?

RONNIE: You don't look right, Floyd. Not for that. (*To* ROY.) You are handsome. You've got a profile like the magician in the comic strips. You'd look exactly like him if your hair was blue.

FLOYD: I'll show you your cot.

ROY: (*He stiffens again, grabs suitcases.*) I don't think so, Floyd. Flo and I have got to go straight back. We're just passing through this part of the country

FLOYD: But...We were going to talk. There's a pond in the back so we can swim and I was going to cook us a big supper. You've got to stay.

ROY: (*Starting toward the door.*) I've got important things cooking up there, Floyd. (FLO *is standing still, looking out the window.*) What are you looking for?

FLO: A chair. So I can...sit down. (*She crosses slowly down to the table, looking at* ROY, *selects the* U.C. *chair and sits.*)

RONNIE: (*Breaking the silence.*) Stay as long as you can. I'm dying to hear about things up North.

ROY: All right. But just for a while.

(ROY, RONNIE *and* FLO *sit around the table;* RONNIE S. R., ROY S. L., FLOYD *doesn't sit, but remains standing* U. S. R., *staring at* ROY. ROY *sits on* FLOYD's *hat.*)

RONNIE: Now. I want to hear about the clothes, and Floyd will want to know all about the new model cars.

ROY: I'll make it short. You can get anything you want up North. But you've got to think clear. When I first got there, I was confused. I don't know if I can describe it, but . . . To make a long story short, I found the right people; started hanging around the right places. In fact, I've got my own nightclub now. The Panama Club.

RONNIE: It sounds glamorous.

ROY: You should see it. You wouldn't know it if you did. It's shaped like a jungle. I hired a colored band and there's palm trees and all the waiters wear gorilla suits. Nothing up there is what it seems. It's a whole new world. You can be anyone you want. To make a long story short, I've finally found the place where I belong . . . (*Pause.*) Floyd? You going to join us? (FLOYD *sits in the chair to* FLO's *left, never taking his eyes off* ROY.) So as soon as I join the mob, I'm on my way to the top. I can't say too much more about it, but . . . my head's clear and I've got both feet on the ground. And I'm not coming back to Oklahoma again, because everything's fine now except the old things look small . . . (*Looking around uneasily.*) Everywhere I go, everything looks smaller now than I thought it should . . . I guess because now my mind is so large . . . (*He finishes, staring at* FLOYD.) You're looking good, Floyd. (FLOYD *doesn't answer. Everyone looks at the tabletop.*) Floyd? What are your plans? (*As he says "plans,"* FLO *coughs so the word is inaudible.*)

FLOYD: What?

ROY: Your plans.

FLOYD: Ronnie? What are my plans?

RONNIE: He hasn't got any.

(*As she says "hasn't got any,"* FLO *coughs so the words are inaudible. Each time she coughs, they glance at her momentarily.*)

ROY: What?

RONNIE: He hasn't got any. (*Pause.*)

FLO: There's a lot of dust in the air down here.

ROY: (*Sharply.*) That's not polite, Flo. (*Pause.*) You wrote me a postcard saying you had some plans.

FLOYD: I was going to start a cafe. Ronnie's a good cook—(*As he talks in a low voice,* FLO *coughs and continues coughing so he is almost inaudible.*) We thought we might start a short-order place. You know . . . blue-plate special . . . home-made pies . . . and . . . all that. Ronnie's a good cook. But . . . we gave it up.

ROY: So you don't have any plans? (FLOYD *nods his head "yes."*) Yes you do or yes you don't? (FLOYD *shakes his head "no."*) You don't? (FLOYD *shakes his head "no."*) I give up, it's impossible to have a conversation with you. Say what you're trying to say.

FLOYD: You're sitting on my hat.

ROY: Oh. (*He removes the crumpled hat from underneath him and tosses it on the bed. He stands, crosses around the table to* FLOYD.) You've got to understand, Floyd, the things we did in the old days . . . that was small potatoes. So you never started a cafe and you don't have any plans. I'm disappointed in you, Floyd. Can't you do anything? (FLOYD *suddenly stands and jerks the tablecloth towards him. The dishes clatter to the floor. Silence. They all stare at him.*)

FLOYD: I thought I could pull it out from under the plates . . . Sorry. I'm all right.

ROY: (*Watching* FLOYD *as he clumsily starts restoring tablecloth and plates.*) Sure. You've just been down here in the Dust Bowl too long, Floyd. (*He slaps him on the shoulder. Dust flies out of* FLOYD's *suit. He doesn't see.* ROY *and* RONNIE *laugh.*)

FLOYD: What's so funny?

ROY: Nothing.

FLOYD: Am I doing something wrong?

ROY: No, Nosir. (*He slaps him again, more dust.* ROY *covers his mouth with his hand.*)

RONNIE: (*Standing.*) Why don't you go for a swim, Floyd?

ROY: Why don't you? Cool off. Flo can go with you, and I'll sit here for a while and get to know your wife.

FLOYD: That sounds like a good idea. (*He goes to the door, takes off jacket and leaves it on the coat-rack.*)

ROY: Flo? (*She joins* FLOYD *at the door without a word. They start out.* FLOYD *stops and turns.*)

FLOYD: You won't be gone when I get back, will you?

FLO: I'm your hostage. Roy couldn't leave without me, could he? (*She bats her eyes. They exit.* RONNIE *and* ROY *are standing facing each other across the table. Silence.*)

ROY: How low you sunk. I don't believe it. Does he know?

RONNIE: No.

ROY: Four years . . . I wouldn't have thought he was your type.

RONNIE: (*Smoothing tablecloth nervously.*) He's not the man he was.

ROY: So I noticed.

RONNIE: He's got some kind of problem. I think he drinks.

ROY: He didn't drink before.

RONNIE: Well, something's wrong with him.

ROY: That's obvious.

RONNIE: Maybe you could help him out. I'd think so much of you, if you could light a fire under him.

ROY: (*Draws back suddenly.*) Please! Don't say that.

RONNIE: Why not?

ROY: Just don't. (*Smugly.*) You should have come with me. You wanted me, but you were afraid of me. So I guess you settled for Floyd out of disappointment.

RONNIE: I never wanted you.

ROY: What do you do now?

RONNIE: Play dominos.

ROY: What a waste. (*As he speaks,* RONNIE *picks up the plates and puts them in the kitchen. Then she crosses to the vanity, picks up a Flit gun and walks around the room slowly, spraying.*) I remember the first time I saw you. I walked in the Comanche Cafe and there you were, looking great in your white uniform. It was as thin as paper so I could almost see through it and you had a pencil stuck behind your ear. And you said, "May I take your order?" (*Grabbing her* D.L.) You don't fool me. You're Floyd's wife now, but you'd still like to take orders from me, wouldn't you?

RONNIE: Do you really have a nightclub?

ROY: Hell, yes. (*He lets her go, walks* U.S.C.) You should see it. A real night spot.

RONNIE: It sounds like magic. I wish I could. Before, when I knew you, I always thought I could foretell the future. Sometimes I still think I can. I believed in ghosts.

ROY: Yeah.

RONNIE: I thought there was more to the world than just what you can see. I believed someday a ghost story would happen to me. But I never saw one. And I married Floyd, and now I play dominos. (*She walks around the room spraying again.*)

ROY: Did you have a premonition I was coming?

RONNIE: Yes.

ROY: You know why I left Oklahoma, doll?

RONNIE: You were running from the law.

ROY: They could never have caught me. No, I'd gotten too smart for this place. Didn't I tell you ghost stories were a lot of baloney? Nobody believes in ghosts — not if they're smart. And I was the brains of the Hot Grease Boys. (*She walks away, spraying.*) Come back here!

RONNIE: I'm nervous.

ROY: Stand still when I'm talking to you! (RONNIE *freezes.*) You've still got a good figure. Still dream of being in the movies? (*She smiles, drops Flit gun on bed. She removes her robe, straightens her shoulders so her breasts rise, and walks across the room* S.R., *almost in a trance, the robe flung over her shoulder. Then she catches herself and stops.*) Miss! (*She freezes.* ROY *sits at the cardtable like a customer. She approaches him like a waitress.*)

RONNIE: Could I take your order?

ROY: That's more like it. (*Leaning back in chair.*) I know a lot of things you don't. I'm smart. (*Pulling her down on his lap.*) You see those flies on the ceiling? How do you think they do it?

RONNIE: What?

ROY: Walk on the ceiling. Wouldn't you like to know how?

RONNIE: (*Uncomfortably; trying to get up.*) I shouldn't have left the windows open.

ROY: But wouldn't you like to know? Why do you think they can do it and we can't?

RONNIE: Because they're smart?

ROY: (*Grabbing her angrily now, trying to kiss her.*) Forget Floyd. Come back up North with me—

RONNIE: What about your wife?

ROY: Forget Flo. Look at me—

RONNIE: No! (*She slaps him. He throws her roughly to the floor.*)

ROY: (*Dramatically.*) Hell, you don't know what you're missing. I could show you sights you never dreamed of. Picture it: you and me headed North, driving through the night. There's a star hanging over the end of the road, and I point the car at it. I'm driving faster and faster, the closer we get, and I'm telling you things that would make your mouth water. Just as the billboards going past in the dark, and the stars . . . I could show you a star that's shining so hard it sweats . . . (ROY *has found the snaps on his suitcase. It springs open.*)

RONNIE: What's that? (*He pulls out a black tuxedo.*)

ROY: That's my soup and fish—for the Panama Club.

RONNIE: You must look handsome in it. Let me see you wearing it.

ROY: (*Crossing to her.*) I might do it, doll—if you'll be nice to me. (*Their faces are almost touching.*) You have on bright red lipstick . . . (*They kiss.* FLOYD *appears in the doorway. His hair is sopping wet. He has on bathing trunks, his shirt, shoes, and socks, and there is an unlit cigar jammed in his mouth. He takes them in. Their mouths stay glued together. He comes* D.S., *sits in chair left of table, and speaks loudly.*)

FLOYD: Oh, boy. You should try that pond. Boy, do I feel good now. (ROY *and* RONNIE *have broken apart.* FLO *appears in the door.*) That's all I can say. That was a wonderful experience. Soaking in that nice warm pond water . . . I soaked all my troubles out.

FLO: Can we go swimming?

ROY: No.

FLO: I watched Floyd. It looked like fun.

FLOYD: (*He strikes a kitchen match, holds it to his cigar.*) Sure you don't want to try it, Roy?

ROY: Please. Don't hold that match so close to that table. It could go up in flames, it's only cardboard! (*He lunges forward and blows it out. Everyone stares at him.*) Look at Floyd's socks. (*They are fallen down in* FLOYD'S *shoes. He points and laughs.*)

FLOYD: (*Blowing out a cloud of smoke.*) You don't know what you're missing until you've soaked in that nice warm pond water. You should both go . . . soak yourselves.

ROY: We're going —

RONNIE: Please stay. It seems like you just got here. (*Stopping him.*) Don't leave me now, Roy.

FLO: I'm so hungry I could eat a horse!

FLOYD: Then sit right down, honey. We wouldn't dream of letting you go until you've had your supper. Ronnie? Set the table. (*He pulls back a chair for her. She sits:* RONNIE *starts restoring the plates and tablecloth.*)

FLO: Thank God!

FLOYD: Nosir. You deserve to eat at least.

FLO: I didn't want to be impolite, but I was so hungry I thought I was going to faint.

RONNIE: You look sort of pale, honey.

FLO: You don't know. A minute ago I was standing out there in the hot sun, I thought, Flo, you're going to faint.

FLOYD: No danger of that now, honey. Soup's on. You want a stogie?

FLO: No.

FLOYD: You can have anything you want here, don't be afraid to speak up.

ROY: I'm staying only if Floyd will talk about his situation man-to-man. Will you? (FLOYD *nods.*) Can you be serious about it?

FLOYD: If you want to.

ROY: You know what I'm talking about? (FLOYD *nods.*) Then let's get down to it.

FLOYD: Fine; let's talk about it. (ROY *sits.*)

ROY: You're willing?

FLOYD: It's fine with me, I think it's about time we did.

ROY: All right. Let's get to the point. Ronnie says there's something wrong with you. You've got a serious problem. (Looking at RONNIE *and* FLO.) Now I've known Floyd here for a long time, and he's a great guy. But I have noticed this one flaw in Floyd, it's that he — where you going? (FLOYD *has crossed and sat on the bed.*)

FLOYD: You looked at her, I thought you were talking to her. (*Pause.*)

FLO: We gonna eat now? (*No one answers.*) Roy's never told me about you and Ronnie. He never talks about his past; he's always talking about his plans, or the mob. I guess he wanted Oklahoma to surprise me. But now that I met you, I like you. (*To* RONNIE.) I'll bet Floyd's a good cook.

ROY: Flo.

FLO: I don't know how to cook. Neither does Roy. We're always saying we're going to learn, but we never have time, we're always on the go.

ROY: Flo.

FLO: I met Roy at the movies.

RONNIE: Sounds romantic.

FLO: He was sitting on the balcony with his feet propped on the seat in front of him. I knew you shouldn't do that. I guess I'm trying to say he had an air of danger about him. I was ushering, so I shone my flashlight in his face and asked him to please stop. He looked so handsome. He asked me to sit down and share his popcorn with him, and I couldn't believe anyone like him would be interested in me — he was so handsome, and I'm so plain. (*Pause.*)

FLO: (*Pointing at a cloud of cigar smoke.*) I saw a cloud outside. Now there's one inside. (*Not looking at* ROY.) You goin' for a dip, Roy?

ROY: Not now.

FLOYD: You don't like the water, do you, Roy? You're like a cat.

FLO: Maybe we could all go for a dip . . . after we've had lunch.

ROY: No.

FLO: But I want to go, Roy. I want to go for a dip.

ROY: No dip.

FLO: My throat's getting dry again. How about it. We can have a nice home-cooked meal, then the four of us can go for a dip —

ROY: Shut up, Flo!

FLOYD: Don't treat her that way.

ROY: I'm trying to help you solve your problem.

FLOYD: What about your problem? (ROY *stiffens, stands.*) Shoe's on the other foot now, isn't it? You know what I'm talking about. At least I haven't changed my personality. You're playing a part. Flo doesn't know because she didn't know you before, but you've got another personality now. (ROY *goes to* FLOYD, *grabs the cigar out of his mouth, breaks it and drops it on the floor.*)

ROY: What's it like?

FLOYD: What?

ROY: This so-called phony personality.

FLOYD: It's something like a fish.

ROY: Why'd you say that?

FLOYD: (*Staring at the fish on the wall.*) I don't know. That's just how it strikes me.

ROY: You'd better lay off the booze, Floyd; that's all I've go to say.

FLOYD: Did she tell you I drink? That is a lie. An absolute lie.

FLO: I believe him. I believe Floyd.

ROY: (*Crossing back to table.*) Don't you know an alcoholic can't tell the truth?

FLO: Floyd says he's not one, and I believe him.

ROY: Stay out of this, Flo, this is none of your business. He's probably got bottles hidden all over this cabin.

ROY: All I can say is, I'm mighty disappointed in you, Floyd.

FLOYD: I am not a drunk!

ROY: Ronnie says you are.

RONNIE: I never caught him at it . . .

ROY: Well, something's wrong with you. You act like you don't know me anymore, you talk like you've lost your mind, and you haven't got any plans.

FLOYD: I planned for us to stay up all night reminiscing about our days on the road and all our dreams.

ROY: Don't start that crap again, Floyd. I had no such dream about the moon.

FLOYD: You did!

ROY: I did not! (FLO *faints. Her head smashes down on the tabletop.*)

RONNIE: She's fainted.

ROY: (*Trying to revive her.*) Flo—snap out of it, Flo.

FLO: I thought we were going to eat. I had such high hopes . . .

ROY: We haven't got time for that now.

FLO: I like Floyd. Stop bothering him. Floyd's like me, he says things; he just opens his mouth and they come out . . . but not like he meant. I thought that was why you like me, Roy. I say funny things and I make you laugh. Like the other day when I was tired and I told you my feet were on their last legs.

ROY: Do we have to talk about this? The important thing is Floyd's problem. Hell, Floyd; I saw it coming a long time ago. You never could have made it up there. That's why I wanted to go it alone. You don't know how much nerve it took. (*Crossing* D. S. R.) The first night I stayed in a cheap hotel. I'll never forget looking out the window and seeing the searchlights shining in the sky—a new movie premiere or another filling station opening somewhere. Down below there were guys climbing out of taxicabs with beautiful women wearing furs. Nobody in this city ever sleeps, I thought—nobody who I'd want to know.

RONNIE: It sounds just like I dreamed it would. Wonderful.

ROY: I wanted to stay awake, but I couldn't. I kept staring at the brown wallpaper. The carpet was so moth-eaten you got drowsy just looking at it. There was a green stuffed chair and an empty glass and the lamp shade was full of dead flies. I knew I wouldn't always be staying in cheap hotels like that but I felt like if I slept I'd be . . . dirty somehow. I thought, Roy, this is not the way to get started. So I did something dangerous to stay alert. I got a box of matches and lay down in bed and lit them one at a time. I knew if I fell asleep while one was burning the bedspread would go up in smoke—hell, the whole hotel would. There's almost nothing that won't burn, you know. I've seen pictures of buildings after they've burned down and there's nothing left but shoes and old springs poking up through the ashes. Once a fire starts it can get out of control so easy, and that's why . . . (*Faint sound of a fly in the room.* ROY *snatches, catches it in his bare hands.*) You've got to stay alert! Sometimes I thought I heard footsteps in the hall—probably bellhops. But it sounded like everybody was looking for me. Don't lose your nerve, I thought. Those guys in the mobs will be looking for you soon enough. That's just your Good Angel. Everything took nerve up there. But if you just stay alert, nothing can go wrong . . . (*Sound of the fly again. He picks up a flyswatter off the vanity and crosses back to the table.* FLOYD *looks slightly confused, his eyes unfocused as if the story has hypnotized him.*) But you, Floyd, you're drowsy. You live in a dream. Look at you. (*He smacks the flyswatter down on the table.*

Everyone starts.) Pull yourself together! It's a hard world out there. They don't forgive mistakes. Have you forgotten guns, Floyd? (*He smacks the flyswatter down several more times.*) You've got to stay awake. But you — you're hiding from the world down here, living in some kind of a soft dream — because you're afraid. You've got to pull yourself together! (FLOYD *snatches the tablecloth out from under the plates. Not one falls to the floor. He stands there grinning triumphantly.* FLO *applauds.*)

RONNIE: Why don't you put on your soup and fish? Show him how good you look when you walk into your club.

ROY: (*Crossing to suitcases.*) I'm going to show you how we do things up North, Floyd. Understand? I'm going to show you how to do things in style. (*He exits.*)

FLO: Good bread, good meat, good God let's eat. We going to eat now? No.

FLOYD: Do you think I should let Roy talk to me that way? (RONNIE *gets up without answering and goes* D. S. *to the vanity, taking her chair with her; sits and starts brushing her hair.* FLOYD *looks at* FLO.) You afraid of Roy? Does he make you nervous? I know, you can't say anything. (He takes ROY's *hat and places it on the floor* D. S. *Then, while they wait, he sits in the* S. L. *chair, takes a deck of cards out of his pocket and pitches them at the hat. Some of them go in.*) I'm Floyd Simms. Roy probably hasn't told you my name. Four years ago I was as famous as him, but now . . . That's how it goes. There's no getting along with him. If you say something he doesn't like, he'll bite your head off. (FLO *gets up when he says this and crosses to the bed and sits.*) I understand. Roy thinks Oklahoma is small potatoes now. He wants to be moving on. Roy's talented, he could always talk to people . . . all sorts of people. I never could. (*Pause.*) I'm doing something wrong. I know I'm doing something wrong. Seems like nothing's ever important enough for you, so you let it go. You don't even try. Then there's all the little things that are always happening to you that make you sad. You fall asleep in the afternoon and you don't wake up until the sun's gone down. There you are in a dark room; you don't know how you got there, and it makes you sad. Or you go to a show but you don't get there until the last feature. At first it's crowded, but then people start leaving. Finally, you're almost alone. And when the lights come on you walk up the aisle real slow looking over your shoulder at the credits, showing you've got all the time in the world and you're not afraid to be the last one out of there. It makes you sad. Or you go to a store to buy clothes. You feel pretty good — then suddenly here it comes, out of a mirror in the corner, that face you don't recognize at first because you've never seen yourself from that angle before. Then you see it's you and it makes you sad and you walk out of there without buying any clothes. What am I talking about? Something about success, I think . . . Look at my socks. It just makes you sad the way you let things go, because nothing's ever . . . important enough for you. Because you're not. I'm wasting my life. (*To* FLO.) One thing: do you think I'm handsome?

FLO: You got a sad face. But it's nice. It's like those pictures you see in the
drugstore window. They're yellow and faded from being in the sun for
so long, and they look sad. But when you look closer, you see they're
really movie stars . . . (*They look at each other.* FLOYD *smiles.* ROY *appears, wearing the tuxedo. He walks slowly* D. R. *to* RONNIE; *proud,
making the final adjustments—straightening tie and cuffs.*)

ROY: I look great, don't I? Admit it.

RONNIE: (*Standing, circling around him.*) Oh, yes. Those trousers. That
boiled shirt. Those shiny black shoes.

ROY: Nothing like being well-dressed and ready to face the world. How do
you like it?

RONNIE: Won't you look, Floyd? He's just trying to help you.

ROY: You could like this if you could lick your problems, Floyd. You know
your worst enemy is yourself.

FLOYD: I got something for you, Roy. I forgot to give it to you.

ROY: (*Eagerly.*) A present?

FLOYD: (*Smiling sadly.*) I hid it somewhere in this room.

ROY: Can I have it now?

FLOYD: If you can find it. (ROY *starts looking, under the table, in the vanity.
Meanwhile, unnoticed,* FLOYD *takes a black Lone Ranger mask like his
from under the bed and places it in the hat he has been pitching cards
into. He gives* ROY *directions.*) You're getting warmer. You're getting
hot now. Hotter. No—you're cold. (ROY *goes into the kitchen, pokes
around the shelves.*) You're getting warm again. (FLOYD *goes to the
coat-rack and pulls on his pants, ignoring* ROY *as he ransacks the room.
He keeps giving him hints.* ROY *searches more and more frantically until he has turned the cabin upside down, getting now hotter and now
colder, upsetting the chairs, throwing the covers off the bed, pulling out
the vanity drawer and emptying it on the floor. The girls follow him,
trying to pick up. When* FLOYD *has gotten his pants on the room is
demolished and* ROY *has found the mask.*)

ROY: Hell, Floyd, I'm touched. Where'd you find this? (*He puts it on.*) You
know this means a lot to me, don't you, Horseface?

FLOYD: Sure, you old pisspot.

ROY: You know it's hard up there in those big cities—and you've got to be
the same way if you want to make it. Maybe I've been too hard on you
today.

FLOYD: Nobody liked you up there, did they, Roy?

ROY: What?

FLOYD: That's why you came back—you got lonely.

ROY: Lonely? No—I'm a born loner.

FLOYD: It makes me sad—another thing to make you sad.

ROY: You're wrong about that, Floyd.

FLOYD: Be ourselves, you said that day in Mound City. But you're not! You
even told me you had the same dream I had, like we were one person.

ROY: You starting that crap again, Floyd?

FLOYD: Something was chasing you in the dark, under the moon. You didn't know what, but you woke up in a cold sweat.

ROY: I don't remember.

FLOYD: You're lying. You've got to!

ROY: I never woke up in a cold sweat about anything, Floyd!

FLOYD: It makes me sad — another thing to make you sad.

ROY: (*Putting his arm around* FLOYD *patronizingly.*) What's happened to you? It's like you died. There was a time I didn't think you were afraid of anything. Look at you now.

FLOYD: Let go!

ROY: Don't you think two men can touch each other? What's the matter, you afraid of me, too, Floyd? Are you afraid to try?

FLOYD: All right, go ahead. (ROY *touches him carefully.*) Let go of me, you homo! (*He pushes* ROY *away, snatches up flyswatter off the end table.*) Try to screw my wife, will you! (FLO *gasps.*) It's true! I saw them!

FLO: It's not true, is it, Roy?

ROY: I made a pass at your wife. But she was asking for it.

RONNIE: (*Ashamed.*) He said he wanted me to run away with him, and I believed him. He told me he was going to take me to his nightclub.

ROY: You married a tramp, Floyd. If I'd been around I could have told you. (FLOYD *advances with the flyswatter.*) You've got to get mighty close to use that. (*He swings,* ROY *jumps him, forces him to let go of it like you would a gun; throws* FLOYD *down.*) I don't scare easy, Floyd.

FLOYD: I didn't scare you with that?

ROY: I don't know the meaning of the word.

FLOYD: (*Pulling gun out of his trouser pocket.*) What about this? Hold still, or I'll blow you apart! You're not the only one who can be a tough guy. This puts us on equal ground, doesn't it?

ROY: Is it loaded?

FLOYD: You want to find out? Ronnie?

RONNIE: You wouldn't shoot, Floyd. Not me.

FLOYD: Oh, wouldn't I? Get over there against that wall, both of you. *Move!* (*They do.* FLOYD *lies down casually on the bed, gun still pointing at them, hat pulled down low over his eyes, and his head propped on one hand.*) Now. I'm gonna lie here and watch you spill your guts. Do you feel like pleading for your life. Roy? Ronnie? Would you plead for him? I've been hearing about up North and I've been hearing about your bigshot nightclub ever since you got here; and now I'm fed up. You're gonna drop this phony personality — or you're gonna die!

FLO: There's no nightclub!

ROY: Flo!

FLO: Don't, Floyd. You're making a mistake, you can't shoot him!

RONNIE: No nightclub?

ROY: She's right. It's gone — burned in a horrible fire. I couldn't tell you. It's the worst thing that ever happened to me. (*Rushing on dramatical-*

ly.) I'll never forget the palm trees and the tablecloths burning, and the tinsel on the ceiling and the women's hair. The smoke came boiling down so thick you couldn't see or breathe. Flo and I are the only ones who got out alive. She can tell you—how I pulled her into the kitchen and we crawled into the icebox. When the firemen got us out the next morning, there was nothing left but ashes. So go ahead and shoot. Floyd—I've got nothing left to live for now anyway. But do you know why I really came back down here? I wanted to join up with you again. Like in the old days. Look, Floyd, I know you're still sore about your wife. But don't let her come between us. It could be like it was, Floyd—you know, the two of us driving the heat. I can almost see it now. You know, those old days were great . . . (*Suddenly he grabs* RONNIE, *holds her in front of him as a human shield.*) OK, drop your gun, Floyd; it's a stalemate! Floyd? (FLOYD *doesn't react. He advances cautiously on bed, still holding* RONNIE *in front of him.* FLOYD *is asleep.*) You shithead! (*He throws his hat down on the floor and tramples it.*) And that's for your hat!

RONNIE: It's your hat. So—there's no more Panama Club.

FLO: There never was one! You got that from that story you heard about that joint that burned down in Boston, and you're so afraid of fire and all you couldn't stop talking about it. (*She lights a match.*) The Panama Club was another one of your plans. But you'll never do it. You'll never stay in one place long enough to do anything. (*She backs him out the doorway with the match.*)

ROY: I'm going for a walk. To . . . clear my head. (*He exits.* FLO *lights a match, blows, on it, drops it in the ashtray. It doesn't go out. She blows on it and ashes fly all over the table.*)

FLO: Sorry.

RONNIE: Forget it.

FLO: I know: I'm plain. I'm not good-looking like you. But it seems to me I deserve to eat. I'm so bored with always being on the move. But I'm afraid I'll lose him. Then when Floyd said that about you and Roy . . .

ROY: Yeah.

FLO: You're not to blame. I can't keep him interested. I thought I could, but . . . something's always bursting my balloon.

ROY: Let's wake up Floyd.

FLO: Why?

ROY: He'll know what to do. (*They go and stand over him.*) Floyd? (*He doesn't move.*)

FLO: Rise and shine, Floyd.

RONNIE: He's out like a light. It's getting dark outside. Another day almost gone. You've got to learn how to deal with men. You know how to dance?

FLO: No—

ROY: I'll show you. (*She turns on the radio. They do a brisk two-step to "I Found a Dream" by Bob Wills.* RONNIE *keeps stepping on* FLO's *feet.*)

FLO: You were a waitress?

RONNIE: Yeah.

FLO: That's been my problem — restaurants. He likes to eat out, you know. Travel and eat out. Always moving.

RONNIE: Things are gonna look up for you soon, honey.

FLO: You think so?

RONNNIE: I know so. You're a good kid. (FLO *gives up. Turns off radio.*)

FLO: Look . . . maybe you could teach me how to play dominos. (RONNIE *gets dominos, turns on lamp and they sit. By now, the room is quite dark.*) See, it's not the food in the restaurants I can't deal with. It's the menu. You've got to order your food by the name on the menu or they won't bring it to you. So if you ask for breakfast, they say, don't you mean the Little Red Hen? You want a steak and they say, Oh, you mean the Panhandle T-Bone Platter. You want to cover your head with the tablecloth, but you've got to say it out loud. It goes worse and worse. Bring me your Pittsburger. Bring me your Tater Tots. If there's a number, you can say, Bring me the Number 4, thank God. But mostly, it's bring me the Chew N' Sip, bring me the Thanksgiving Turkey in the Straw. Bring me a Bromo, I'm sick. There must be more to life.

RONNIE: (*Knocking over a row of dominos.*) Yeah.

FLO: A Blue-Plate Special — that's what I ask for. Anyone can say they want the Blue-Plate Special. You've heard it asked for in the movies. So they bring it, and I eat it even if it's something I don't like. The thing is, it never is anything I like. What I really wanted was a blue plate. By now, it's the only thing I'm hungry for. A nice, blue plate. I want the food they want in movies, the food mice eat in cartoons. I wish I was in a cartoon. (*Voice breaking.*) Somebody would hit me on the head and stars would fly out . . .

RONNIE: Don't you think you could talk him into settling down?

FLO: I can give you the answer to that in two words: Im possible.

RONNIE: Don't cry honey, no man's worth it. (ROY *rushes back in. He stops just inside the door, his back pressed to the wall. He has no pants.*)

ROY: Don't go out there! There's something out there. Something loose in the bushes; it chased me back here. (*Looks down.*) Where's my pants? Flo, go back and get my pants.

FLO: Where are they?

ROY: I know: I left them on a branch. It was a dog — a big dog loose in the bushes. Flo, go out and get my pants. (*She laughs.*) That's an order.

FLO: I can't take him seriously. I never knew your legs were so white.

ROY: Somebody's got to. My keys are in them. Flo?

FLO: Why don't you get them yourself if you want them so bad?

ROY: I was down by the pond. For some reason I thought I'd like to go wading, so I took off my trousers so they wouldn't get wet. There was mud and dead leaves on the bottom. The water was cold. I was wishing I had a light so I could see if there were any fish, and then whatever it was must have heard me; because then something came rushing towards me through the woods. Something on four legs—an animal on the loose. I thought it might be a dog—a mad dog. And I lit out before it could catch me and bite me; lit out so fast I forgot my pants. I ran so hard it felt like I was floating. And the moon was shining down the whole time with this cold grin, like it had nothing to do with me. That's how I ran all the way back here, that mad dog right at my heels.

RONNIE: You sound scared.

ROY: Hell no—I'm not scared. But how can I walk around here without any pants on?

RONNIE: Pretend you're at a nudist camp.

ROY: But we've got to go. We've got to start back up North. Hit the road.

FLO: We can start tomorrow. Sit down, let's play dominos; Ronnie's showing me how.

ROY: (*Crossing to* RONNIE.) You'll get them for me, won't you?

RONNIE: You're making this whole thing up so we'll feel sorry for you, aren't you?

ROY: No! There's something out there.

RONNIE: You'll wake Floyd.

ROY: I tell you, the dog is real.

RONNIE: Like your nightclub? (*She picks up Flit gun and advances on him.*) Why'd you ever have to come back here?

ROY: Ronnie—(*She sprays him in the face.*)

RONNIE: Siddown! (ROY *hesitates. She pulls back the handle of the Flit gun threateningly; he crosses quickly and sits in the* S. R. *chair.* RONNIE *then sits in the center chair.*) Now. We've got the whole night ahead of us. Let's tell ghost stories.

FLO: Oh, good. I like being scared.

RONNIE: Let's turn out the lights so it'll be spookier.

FLO: Roy? Turn out the lamp. (*He looks at her uncertainly.*) Come on, honey, be polite.

ROY: She can turn it out herself.

FLO: You're closest.

ROY: (*He gets up, goes to the lamp and stops.*) What happens if I do and that dog comes in? (*He goes to the kitchen and gets a rolling pin.*) I'll use this to protect myself. (*He crosses back to the lamp.*) Here goes.

FLO: Nothing's going to happen, honey. (*He turns off the lamp.* FLOYD *groans, startling* ROY, *and sits up in bed.*)

FLOYD: Unnnh. I dreamed it was snowing. I dreamed I was covered with snow . . . (*He looks at* ROY.) You still here?

ROY: (*Starting toward him.*) Floyd, it's been swell, but we've got to go—

FLO: Come and sit down, honey. I'm not going anywhere.

ROY: I guess . . . we'll stay instead. (*He goes back and sits at the table holding his rolling pin. The girls are playing dominos. Without lamplight the stage is bathed in a melacholy bluish glow.*)

RONNIE: I haven't told ghost stories since I met Floyd. But it seems like tonight ghost stories might be possible. There's one about a drowned girl. That was one of my favorites. (*Standing, taking position* U. C. *to create the mood.*) You're driving by the lake one night and her ghost stops you. She's got wet hair and she asks you in a real sad voice, Can I have a ride home? You don't know she's a ghost yet. So you say, yeah, and for some reason she gets in the back seat and you start back to town. You're nervous, and you keep trying to see her in the mirror, because all the way you think you can feel her eyes staring at the back of your head. But when you get to her house, it's gone. (*She stops, thinks hard.*) Or it's a haunted house. No.

FLO: Her parents come out and tell you their daughter drowned four years ago.

RONNIE: Yeah.

FLO: I heard that one before. I didn't want to spoil your story.

RONNIE: It was my favorite one. I used to know thousands of ghost stories. Thousands. Now I'm not sure I can remember how any of them end. But wasn't it frightening? Floyd?

FLOYD: How come the lights are out? (*He gets up, goes to the lamp. But instead of turning it on, he notices* ROY *and stops.*) You're half nude, Roy. What for? (*He goes to the kitchen and comes back a moment later with a steak on a plate. He puts it on the table in front of* ROY *and stands, waiting.* ROY *looks at everyone. He prods the steak with a fork. It squeaks and he draws back, startled, dropping the fork. He looks up; everyone is smirking at him. Then he puts his head down on the table and begins to sob quietly. Coldly.*) OK, Roy. You got the part. (FLOYD *crosses to the coat-rack, puts on jacket, takes a cigar out of the pocket and puts it in his mouth.*)

FLO: You tell one now, Floyd. I want to hear a real one—about ghosts wearing sheets, with holes for eyes. Haunted houses. About somebody waiting for you by the side of the road, a hitchhiker who glows in the dark.

FLOYD: (*Sitting at table between the girls.*) In the dark old days, Roy and I drove through all those small dark towns at midnight. Not a light burning. And you'd read the signs out loud. You couldn't stop yourself. City Limits. Spark Garage. Utopia Hardware Store. Gas. Cactus Cafe. Brown Stationery. Gas. City Limits. Airport Motel. Sunset Motel. Gas. Then you're out in the dark again, moving on.

RONNIE: Where does the ghost come in?

FLOYD: Nobody saw you. You felt like a ghost.

ROY: You felt like you were dead. There was nothing to go back to, and nothing ahead but more empty towns like that. So you kept moving. How did I end up back here in Oklahoma? It's the last place I wanted to be. There must be somewhere left to go! (*Suddenly he stands.*) There's something under the bed!

FLO: I don't hear anything.

ROY: Listen! (*They do, turning out front. Nothing is heard.*) Have you got that dog under there, Floyd?

FLOYD: I think you've lost your mind, Roy. I don't have a dog.

ROY: You don't? Don't fool me.

FLOYD: Look for yourself. (*Pause.*)

FLO: Let's sing to keep our spirits up. (*Pause. Nobody sings. Nobody looks at anybody else.* RONNIE *stops playing dominos. When* ROY *starts singing, she begins again.*)

ROY: I'm gonna buy a paper doll that I can call my own . . . and not a . . . (*He falters and stops. They all look at him. When he starts singing again, they go back to playing dominos.*) I'd rather have a paper doll . . . that I could call my own . . . (*Silence.*) That doesn't sound like me. I'd never have a paper doll.

FLOYD: Like I say, that's your problem. (*He gets up, moves around the table and takes* ROY's *chair.*) Gimme a light, Flo. (FLO *strikes a match and holds it to his cigar.*)

ROY: I think I'd better have a look under that bed.

FLOYD: You still nervous, Roy? I'll look for you.

ROY: No. I'll do it.

FLOYD: Suit yourself. (ROY *goes over and starts crawling under the bed,* U. S.)

RONNIE: Sometimes you wonder where it's all gone. I know now I'll never leave Oklahoma. And Floyd and I will never start a cafe. My ghost story was a failure and I don't think I'll have any more premonitions now. I can't even remember why ghosts should scare you . . . something about the word boo. I'm sticking to dominos. They don't surprise you, but who needs surprises? Dominos is fine from now on. Except for sometimes you think you should walk out the back door and drown yourself in that pond . . .

FLOYD: (*Standing and crossing up to the door, looking out and smoking.*) I liked that pond. I was lying on my back, looking up at floating clouds. It felt like I was floating up there in the sky with them . . .

ROY: (*Under bed.*) Floyd?

FLOYD: Roy?

ROY: There's nothing under here. You were right. But a while ago I could have sworn you had a vicious dog around here you weren't telling me about.

FLOYD: There's no dog.

ROY: Good. But if there was, you wouldn't let him in here, would you?

FLOYD: Nope.

ROY: Good. (*Pause.*) But I think I'll stay under here for a while anyway. Things look pretty good under here. I'm going back up North tomorrow. I'm going alone — as Clark Gable. You know, you're all in a fog. That's what's wrong with you. Your minds aren't clear, like mine. But things look fine under here. And I'm leaving first thing tomorrow. (*Pause.*) As soon as Floyd calls off his dog.

RONNIE: In the old days, when I worked at the Comanche Cafe, everything was special. What went wrong?

FLOYD: Wind. That wind started blowing and overnight everything turned into the Dust Bowl. Wind blowing all day long and brown, blowing dust everywhere, so thick you couldn't talk or think. Overnight this country changed. It turned into the worst place in the world. Everything died. Nothing could grow. Nobody had any money. (*Coming back down to sit* S. R. *at the table.*) But worse than that, you couldn't think for blowing dust, and trying to finish a sentence was like trying to work a crossword. There was nothing more to do, and it seemed like everyone was killing time, waiting around and coughing, and everything sounded dead, like it does on a record when the music's over and there's nothing to hear but the empty part, just scratches going round . . . and round . . .

FLO: I like it here. I'm never leaving this place again. (*She takes the balloon out of her purse and starts to blow it up.*)

FLOYD: One thing was good—driving. When you were moving down the road, in the heat; and somewhere way out in front of you, you could see that water shining on the road. Those silver puddles where the centerline hits the horizon. They always made me so mad. I drove faster, trying to get there before they dried up. I drove slower, trying to keep them in sight. But before you got there, they were always gone. They were the best thing—and they weren't even real.

FLO: (*Showing him the balloon.*) Look, Floyd. (*He grins. They grin at each other, and he pops it with his cigar. Silence.*)

FLOYD: Only the sound of our guns was real. (*The stage is bathed in a bluish glow.* FLOYD *is looking out, puffing his cigar.* RONNIE *and* FLO *are bent over the table,* ROY *hidden under the bed. The air is cloudy with smoke. In the distance, a dog barks. The stage darkens slowly.*)

Author's Note

Domino Courts was inspired by several things: by the prose of Edward Anderson's *Thieves Like Us,* a forgotten Depression novel that's had two movie versions; by a reunion with some of my oldest friends in a cabin outside of Uvdale, Texas, in 1971; and by a shoebox my parents kept in the closet, where I found unfocused sepia-tone snapshots of them standing in front of a car in Tulsa, Oklahoma, in 1939—a brown decade with soft outlines, a time before I was born. It does not take place in the real Oklahoma, nor is it about the real Depression. My hometown is only ten miles south of the Oklahoma border, and as a child in the early Fifties I can remember dust storms that blew so thickly they had to turn on the streetlights at noon. *Domino Courts* takes place in my imagination; and Oklahoma, because of its physical relation to my hometown, has always been a dusty landscape without realistic detail hanging somewhere above my head.

The Vienna Notes

Richard Nelson

©1979, 1980 Copyright by Richard Nelson.
CAUTION: No performances or readings of this work may be given without the ex-
press authorization of the author's agent. For production rights contact: Ellen
Neuwald, Inc., 905 West End Avenue, New York, N.Y. 10025

The Vienna Notes was produced by Playwrights' Horizons (Andre Bishop, Artistic Director; Robert Moss, Producing Director) on January 18, 1979, with the following cast:

GEORGIA ....*Marcell Rosenblatt*
RIVERS.......................................*Kate McGregor-Stewart*
STUBBS ....*Dan Desmond*
GUNTER ....*Richard Bey*

Director: Andre Ernotte
Sets: Heidi Landesman
Costumes: William Ivey Long
Special Effects: Jack Stewart
Sound: David Rapkin

The Vienna Notes was first presented in workshop at Guthrie II, directed by Bruce Siddons; and later presented by The Mark Taper Forum Playworks Festival, directed by Gwen Arner.

Scene 1

Setting: Vienna. The sitting room of a suite in an old and intimate hotel. Upstage center, a handsome antique writing desk faces the audience. Left, a red velvet divan, laced with fringe, a potted fern, two small tables, one with a lamp, the other with a black telephone. Door to the hallway, right. Stage dark. Lights fade up. Pause. The door is opened. GEORGIA, STUBBS, RIVERS, *and finally* GUNTER *enter.* GEORGIA *(early thirties) is well and fashionably dressed. (She is the Chairwoman of the Lecture Committee for the Vienna Americans' Club.)* STUBBS *(fifties) wears a nicely fitting overcoat and a Russian-style fur hat. (He is a U.S. Senator.)* RIVERS *(late forties) wears a cloth coat, not very stylish. (She is Stubbs' secretary.)* GUNTER *is the porter and he carries in the suitcases.*

GEORGIA: *(Entering.)* Well? What did I tell you? Just what did I tell you? Was I right? Or was I right? *(She looks for a reaction, but gets none.* STUBBS *has begun to take off his coat, loosen his tie, etc., all the while taking in the room.* RIVERS *just stands for the moment and looks around.)* It's everything I said it was, isn't it? *(She looks for a reaction, but gets none.)* And you can't believe your eyes, can you? *(No response.)* Vienna! City of mystery. City of ambiance. City of Mozart. City with that old world charm. That musty charm. You can just breathe it. Breathe it!

RIVERS: *(Who wasn't listening.)* What?

GEORGIA: Breathe! *(*RIVERS *breathes.)* Vienna! City of intrigue. City of cafes. City of wine. Of singing. Of glittering chandeliers. And it's all right here before us. All of it. The best part. You can just see it all right here. And feel it. Go 'head!

(No response; short pause.)

GEORGIA: And that lace. Just look at that lace. And that velvet. Incredible. And look at that craftsmanship in that desk. Do you believe that? Do you believe that!

(Short pause; no reaction)

Well, I can't. I've lived here almost two years and I still can't. I mean, you don't find three-hundred-year-old rooms like this in America, unless they're carved into the side of a cliff. Am I right? Or am I right?

RIVERS: *(Taking off her coat; not really paying attention.)* You're right.

GEORGIA: I knew you'd say that. I just knew it. Because you know why? Because that's exactly how I felt. I felt the same way. When Winslow and I arrived here. *(Smiles to herself; almost laughs.)* Boy do I remember that. *(As she continues talking, she opens her purse and looks for a handkerchief. But before she finds one, she has to first take out a few items—a compact, an address book, and a snub-nose revolver. RIVERS notices but is not terribly surprised.)* Brother. Did you know I was disappointed at first? It's true. I was. My first glance. We got off the plane and God only knows what I was expecting to find. But it certainly wasn't just another airport. An ordinary old airport. Winslow says my face dropped a good foot. And I'll bet it did. 'Cause all I was thinking, see, was: Georgia, girl, you could be anywhere. This is just an airport. I thought that. Admittedly the jet lag didn't help. But I. I'll admit it. On first glance I was terribly disappointed. Isn't that crazy? *(She looks around and realizes no one is listening.)* Gunter, take the bags into the bedrooms.

STUBBS: *(Who has been looking over some scraps of paper he had in his pants pocket; without looking up:)* Not the brown one. That oughta stay out here.

(GUNTER leaves the brown bag and exits left with the others. Pause. GEORGIA looks around, waiting for someone to say something.)

GEORGIA: *(Finally.)* And then we took a taxi. A Mercedes. At least that's a difference, I told myself. But the ride, itself. Well it wasn't much. Was it? It wasn't anything really. Anything to write home about, that is. I mean, the same city sounds, you know. The same sort of smells, you know. The same chuck holes you could find anywhere. Maybe there was a bit more police around. You know, checking cars. That kind of thing. But that isn't something you'd jump for joy about, right? *(Short pause. No reaction.)* So I guess you could say — are you with me?

(STUBBS and RIVERS have opened the brown bag and are rummaging through it, taking out notebooks, files, thumbing through these, sorting them out and piling some on the desk.)

GEORGIA: So I guess you could say. That by the time we pulled up in front of the hotel. As a matter of fact this same hotel. *(No reaction.)* You could say, I wanted to go home. I was nearly in tears. I'd expected something mysterious. Something, you know, Viennese. But all I'd got was, well, you know. And then we got into the lift. And I remember feeling so tired and so resentful, but thinking in utter disbelief, mind you, that Winslow —

and that meant me too — that Winslow had a contract to stay put here for three years. Three whole years! Do you believe that? (*No reaction; feeling more and more self-conscious.*) And so on that note. I remember this so well. Listen. We walked into our room. It wasn't this room. But the effect is the same. And I saw the antiques. And my mouth opened. And I saw the fringe on the lamps. And I got a lump in my throat. I felt the velvet. And it was velvet. And all of a sudden. I found myself shaking. I *was* shaking. I was! I found myself almost spellbound. I had to pinch myself. Pinch, I said! Pinch! And I turned to Winslow. And tears began to roll down my cheeks. I stretched out my arms. This is wonderful, I wanted to say. But the words wouldn't come out. But I guess he knew what I was thinking. Because he smiled. And I remember laughing. Just laughing, you know, as the tears, they just streamed down my face.

(STUBBS *has unplugged the lamp on the table and has taken it over to the desk.*)

STUBBS: (*To* RIVERS) You see a socket?
RIVERS: (*Still going through the bag.*) There's gotta be one somewhere around the desk, Stubbs.

(*Pause.* GEORGIA *now very self-conscious, very confused, tries to get ahold of herself. She goes to* RIVERS *and taps her on the shoulder.* RIVERS *looks up.*)

GEORGIA: So you like it? The room, I mean.
RIVERS: (*Looks around.*) It's nice. (*Returns to the bag.*)
GEORGIA: You mean that?
STUBBS: I can't find one.
RIVERS: Just a sec. I'll look.

(RIVERS *goes to the desk, leaving* GEORGIA *alone.*)

GEORGIA: I knew you would. I knew you'd like it. So I guess all the trouble I went through was worth it, right? (*No response.*) With my club, I mean. In talking it out. In coming to an agreement. There's alot that had to be taken into account. It wasn't all that easy. Believe me. Alot. In choosing a hotel for a guest speaker. Especially for a Senator. Especially for a Senator who'd been a whisker away, right, from being a President. There's a whole lot. Isn't there?
RIVERS: Here's a socket that cord would reach.

(STUBBS *unravels the cord, plugs it in.*)

GEORGIA: But do you know what finally made us decide? On this hotel? It was something *I* said. Do you want to hear? (RIVERS *returns to the bag.*) Do you really? I said. Listen to this. I said, if he is going to visit Vienna. If Senator Stubbs is going to be our guest in Vienna. Then, damn it, he should *visit* Vienna. Do you see what I meant? (*No response;* STUBBS *at the desk, looking through papers.*) You do? (*No response.*) Well, was I right? (*No response.*) Or was I right? (*No response.* GEORGIA *is upset, though making a great effort to control herself.*)

STUBBS: (*Without looking up.*) I got a few notes in my coat, Rivers.

RIVERS: I'll get 'em. (*She does. Pause.* GEORGIA *doesn't know what to do.* GUNTER, *who returned a few moments ago, has been standing left waiting.*)

GUNTER: (*To* Georgia.) Now?

GEORGIA: (*Almost yells.*) What?! Oh right. I'm sorry. I nearly forgot. Sure, Gunter. Go ahead and tell your story. God knows, maybe they'll be interested in that.

(GEORGIA *sits on the divan;* GUNTER *moves center, clears his throat. Every so often,* STUBBS *and* RIVERS *pick up their heads for a second and listen to* GUNTER, *but for most of the time they ignore him and continue what they've been doing.*)

GUNTER:: It was a winter's evening, one hundred and twenty years ago tonight. The crowd lining Kartnerstrasse was three deep as Franz Josef's white carriage rattled along. Peasants in red scarves cheered. The gypsies rang bells. Others waved and bowed. The wheels of the carriage made a clapping sound over the cobble stone. And the breath of the horses created small clouds in the air.

At the Opera House, the carriage door was opened by an attendant dressed in gold. He held his hat and bowed. All in one movement. And the Emperor walked out. "Oh!" gasped the crowd. Then absolute silence, except for the scraping noise of Franz Josef's sword against the Opera steps. The mammoth wooden doors opened seemingly by themselves, and the Emperor slightly tilted his head to acknowledge the crowd. Which then went wild.

Once inside, the Emperor took his royal box. The opera that evening was *Faust*. Ambassadors stood and raised their plumed hats to the box. Women hid their faces, though not their eyes. The orchestra stood and saluted the salute they had practiced earlier that day. And then the overture began. And the music sounded heavenly.

While Faust was singing his doubts, Franz Josef scanned the audience with a pair of opera glasses. They had been a gift from the Dutch Ambassador. In return, the Emperor had given Holland a very fine harpsichordist. Everyone was satisfied. The conductor was nervous and drops of perspiration formed like beads on the top of his bald head. And Faust sang his heart out.

Suddenly, a woman, not in a box, but in the loge, caught the Emperor's eye. He twitched. He felt his stomach tighten. He examined her closely through the glasses. He could not take his eyes off her. Franz Josef consulted with his ministers. But no one knew her name. Ushers went scurrying to other boxes. The French Ambassador thought she might be French. The Opera House was filled with whispers. Even the singer playing Mephistophilis glanced her way. Finally, the curtain for the interval came down.

Attendants rushed to the woman's seat. But only to find her gone. Hallways were quickly searched. Carriages which lined the streets were examined. Franz Josef was beside himself. "Find her!" he yelled. And ministers hid behind each other. Then just as the Emperor was about to give up hope, a small young man brought to him a white glove. It had been left under her seat, he said. And the Emperor handed the man a coin. Franz Josef held the glove loose in his hand. He tried to smell it. He held it up to the light. He played with it as if it were alive. Then. A card fell out. Franz Josef screamed at his ministers to stand back. There was an address on the card.

Franz Josef gave his driver the address. The horses were whipped. The carriage lurched back. A beggar was nearly run over. "Faster!" shouted the Emperor. "Faster!" he continued to shout, until the driver had finally replied, "We're here."

And so Franz Josef found himself standing before this very hotel. My great great grandfather almost fainted as he bowed. The Emperor took two stairs at once. He appeared almost to fly. His heart obviously was racing. He found the door without much trouble. He checked the number with that on the card a third, and then a fourth time. It matched. It matched. He smelled the glove which he still held loose in his hand. And then. Then he pounded. He pounded harder. And the door creaked as it opened. And Franz Josef, Emperor of the Austrian-Hungarian Empire, was heard to sigh. And the door swiftly closed behind him.

(*Short pause.*)

Three hours later, the Emperor left this hotel.

(*Pause.* GUNTER *exits right.* GEORGIA *waits for a reaction.*)

GEORGIA: (*Finally.*) Well? (*No response.*) Isn't that incredible? Can you believe that? Doesn't it just make your skin crawl? (*No response.*) See, it was this hotel. This same hotel. Right here. That happened right here!! (*No response; she explodes.*) GOD DAMN IT! HERE!! HERE!! WILL YOU PAY ATTENTION!! HE DOESN'T TELL THAT TO EVERYONE!!! THAT WAS SPECIAL!! THAT WAS SUPPOSED TO BE A TREAT!!! I PAID HIM TWENTY BUCKS TO DO THAT!!! LISTEN!!! LISTEN!!! (RIVERS *looks up.* STUBBS *has 'snuck' a glance, but keeps writing in a notebook.* GEORGIA *tries to calm herself, to put on a 'better face.'*) I'm sorry. I don't know what got into me. Did I tell you how much I've looked forward to this? I have. Really. Meeting you? Greeting you? I must have imagined, you know. In the mirror. Before falling asleep. I must have imagined a thousand times what I'd say to you. To make you comfortable. To get you to enjoy yourself. Give you a good time. But I never really imagined. Not this. (*Short pause; erupts again.*) LOOK! I'VE

GONE TO A FUCKING LOT OF TROUBLE FOR YOU!!! (STUBBS *and* RIVERS
watch; short pause; then nearly out of control.) Look. I may be a nobody.
Okay. Georgia nobody. Granted. Fine. I will buy that. But it seems to
me. It just seems to me. Am I wrong? Tell me if I'm wrong. But it just
seems to me that don't mean you couldn't have. You couldn't have. Well,
does it? DOES IT!!! (*No response.*) DOES IT!!!! Okay, Jesus, maybe I'm not the
smartest. Maybe I'm no big shot. But you could have. DAMN IT, YES YOU
COULD HAVE PRETENDED!!!

(*Pause.* GEORGIA *goes to the door, opens it, looks back, no response. She exits, slamming the door.*)

RIVERS: We'll see you tonight then? Nine thirty, wasn't it? (RIVERS *returns to
her work.*)
GEORGIA: (*Quickly re-entering; hopeful.*) What? What did you say? (*No re-
sponse.*) Were you talking to me? (*No response. She turns slowly,
defeated, and exits, closing the door gently this time. Pause.* STUBBS *remains staring at the door, obviously thinking.*)
RIVERS: (*Notices he isn't working.*) What's the matter, Stubbs?
STUBBS: Oh boy.
RIVERS: Hey, I thought you couldn't wait to knock off this entry? Come on.
(*Short pause.*) What's wrong with you? You said you couldn't concentrate
on the plane so as soon as we could get set. Well, we're just about set.
Stubbs, we're set. (*Finally notices he's thinking, has that look which she
has seen so many times before.*) Oh. I get you. I think I'm with you. But
when the hell did that happen? When did you get another one? About the
girl? Is it about the girl?
STUBBS: Maybe. We'll just have to see, won't we? See if it plays.
RIVERS: Then you want me to get ready to write?
STUBBS: What? Yeh. That's a good idea. Get yourself ready. 'Cause this
kinda thing you gotta get while it's hot. 'Cause it's gonna be all detail. All
in tiny bits. Now sit on the couch and give me some room for this. Some
breathing space. (*Still staring*). Okay. Okay. It might just be nice. You
got a notebook?
RIVERS: I had to get a new one. The last was about full.
STUBBS: So what's the number?
RIVERS: The last was eighty three.
STUBBS: (*Still staring.*) So then it's notebook number eighty four. Put it
down. (RIVERS *writes.*) "The Memoirs of Henry Stubbs, United States
Senator." Put in the date.
RIVERS: (*Writes.*) Done.
STUBBS: (*Still staring.*) Good. Very good. (*Suddenly he breaks his stare and
begins; getting into what he says;* RIVERS *writes.*) My hotel suite. Vienna.
I had just flown in from the U.S. Still with that taste. That stale airplane
taste in my mouth. Uncomfortable. With aching legs. Feeling tired.
Weak. Not quite all there. Not quite solid. The jet-sound still inside me.
Still echoing. Drumming. Pulsing. So, feeling first, that I had better get

down to work. And second, that I wanted to stretch out. Relax. Maybe a hot bath would be nice.

So as I walked in. Off went the coat. The tie was loosened. The file case unpacked. A place of work set up. To get cracking. To get to the point where I wouldn't feel guilty about stretching out. And unwinding. And taking it slow and easy. So all this while I looked around. Took things in. Not bad, I thought. This suite. Got a certain. Je ne sais quoi. A feeling to it. A certain charm. That I like. That pleased me.

So all this while my hostess. From the Americans' Club. Where I'm to deliver a lecture that night. (*Quickly turns to* RIVERS, *snaps his fingers.*) Name!

RIVERS: (*Writing.*) Georgia.

STUBBS: By the name of Georgia. So all this while I heard her talk. About this and that. About Vienna this. Mozart that. Even something about Mercedes. I heard only fragments as they cracked my concentration. I heard only the strain. The tone of the voice. And this, for an instant, concerned me. Something odd. Something out of wack. It nicked at me. I rubbed my eyes. I wondered, what kind of talk is . . .? But before I could finish the thought, the voice became silent. Still. And the porter . . . (*Turns to* RIVERS.) The porter? (RIVERS *nods.*) He took over for a while.

So there was a calm. In retrospect, I would probably say, a calm before the storm. But then, there was just a calm, in which I turned back to my work. Back to the desk. Back to my fingers which I watched move silently across the piece of paper. Back to urging myself. Telling myself, concentrate. Concentrate. And 'hot bath.'

But soon. How long? I'd lost touch. Lost a feel for the time. Like maybe a rash one first feels before it turns red. Just a hint. Just an itch. I felt this sudden. This growing sensation. Tension. Around me. In the room. It seemed to be pressing up against me. Nudging me. It seemed to have somehow changed the complexion. Of the air. The atmosphere here. Blurring it. Confusing it. Just a general fuzzy sensation that something was about to. On the very verge of. What is going . . .?

But before I could even get the words into my brain. The sensation, it was past that point. Past the point of dealing with. Way the hell past. Because this woman's voice. It was back. Like gangbusters. This Georgia. I was hearing her now shout: "GOD DAMN IT! GOD DAMN IT!" So what I'd felt to be growing like an itch, was now, well now it was building. It was crescendoing. Her words, gaining speed. Faster. What is she . . .? FASTER! Too god damn fast. Getting run together. Sounding to my ears more like emotions now. More like tiny little screams: "ATTENTION!!" "SPECIAL!!" "FUCKING TROUBLE!!"

I listened. I craned my ears. If that's possible. If that is feasible. But no sense. Found nonsense. So I'm just telling myself, these things. These annoyances. These obnoxious annoyances. They happen. They can't be. No help. They just come with the position. Of being powerful. Of being well-known. So what is the use. What's the. Just gotta tolerate it, that's all. Just gotta live with this sort of. TOLERATE!! I scream at myself. And I jam my finger into the paper, trying to doodle a circle. What can I do? So I draw a crowd. So people stare at me. So I'm just shown to my hotel suite and a woman. This woman, she is screaming: "I'M NOBODY!!" SO WHAT THE HELL CAN I DO?!!! THAT'S YOUR PROBLEM!! I want to scream. I want to shove my face at her and scream.

And then. As I am shaking my head and thinking, not much more. There's not much more of this I can take. Well, she is just hitting her stride. What had come before. What had come out before sounding like a last-breath-effort. Well now, now, it sounds like an off-hand comment compared to. With this. "THAT DOES IT!!!" I'm thinking the same thing. "THAT DOES IT!!"Then: "DAMN IT!!" Then: "YOU COULD HAVE!" I'm biting my lip. BITE! Then: "YOU COULD HAVE!!!" I'm rubbing my face. I'm thinking: hold back. Hold back. Then, finally: "YOU COULD HAVE PRETENDED!!!!"

(*Short pause.*)

Then calm. A couple of heart beats. What next? I loosen my grip and drop my pen. Like a pin dropped. That quiet. Then. BANG!! And I jump as the door was slammed shut. And I'm thinking. Boy am I thinking: "hot bath. hot bath. hot bath."

(*Short pause.* RIVERS *writes.* STUBBS, *out of breath, though suddenly now business-like, out of the story.*)

Okay. That's it. Not bad. Not half bad. Maybe a little rough in spots. But what the hell. We can fix that. (*To* RIVERS.) Mark my thoughts for italics.
RIVERS: Right.
STUBBS: Maybe a bit slow here and there. Can't tell yet. It felt okay. Not wonderful. But okay. (*To* RIVERS.) You done?
RIVERS: (*Writing.*) Just about.
STUBBS: Well, check *her* words. Make sure you have 'em all in quotes. I don't want any confusion 'bout who the hell said what.
RIVERS: I always check, Stubbs.
STUBBS: The opening. Definitely. The opening was sluggish. I could feel that. I remember feeling just that. Loose. Very loose. "I did this. I did that." I mean, Jesus, if people are really gonna get this into. I mean, go through it themselves. If they're gonna be empathizing themselves blue. If they're really gonna *get* the picture of the kind of stuff I go through. Or, depending. Depending on when the hell they read this, of the kind of stuff I *went* through in my life. Then, Christ. Playing loose. Playing loose, especially early. That won't do. You gotta let 'em in. And let 'em in fast.
RIVERS: Done.

STUBBS: What? Oh great. Let me see that. Who knows, maybe I'm wrong. Maybe I'm wrong and it just *seemed* loose at the time.

(STUBBS *looks over the notebook. The door opens.* GEORGIA *enters with great hesitation.*)

GEORGIA: I. I got half way home. And I. Well I suddenly remembered that I'd forgot to tell you. (RIVERS *looks at her;* STUBBS *ignores or doesn't really hear her.*) You won't say no, will you? It's not that far. Just a few kilometers. (*Short pause.*) Winslow's home getting ready. (*Short pause.*) If you're worried about getting back. If that's it. Well, you shouldn't. That shouldn't be a problem. (*Short pause.*) You really won't say no, will you? (*Short pause.*) But if you'd rather not . . . If you have other plans. (*Short pause.*) If you're tired. (*Short pause.*) If you want to be alone. (*Short pause.*) If you would really rather not.

RIVERS: Rather not what, Georgia?

GEORGIA: Uh. Come to *my* house. For dinner.

RIVERS: Well, Stubbs?

STUBBS: (*Looking at the notebook, suddenly.*) GOD DAMN IT!!! (*Looks up, notices both* RIVERS *and* GEORGIA *are looking at him.*) It is sluggish. (*Short pause.*) Well what? I wasn't listening.

(*Blackout.*)

Scene 2

Setting: GEORGIA *and* WINSLOW'*s rented converted farmhouse. The living-room. Upstage left and angled center—door, paned windows with drapes on either side of the door. This on a platform, so there is a step down to the livingroom proper. Center: sofa, table with vase, wooden bench, coffee table, telephone, oriental rug, etc. Stage dark. Lights up. Door opens.* GEORGIA, RIVERS *and then* STUBBS *enter.* RIVERS *writes in her notebook.* GEORGIA *listens fascinated.*

STUBBS: (*Entering; he is 'into' his story, feeling almost everything he says.*) And the hum. Drone. Soothed me. Almost massaged. For moments, I felt myself almost encased by the sound. Like in a bubble. Like in a cell. And the lights, they jarred. First, the street lamps. While still driving through the city. Then the oncoming cars. Their lights flickered quickly across my face. It felt almost like I was blinking.

GEORGIA: (*Taking off her coat; quietly, to* RIVERS:) He said, this is for his memoirs?

RIVERS: (*Writing.*) Sh-sh.

GEORGIA: I'm sorry.

STUBBS: So I closed my eyes. An effort. The window had been rolled down. I stuck my face. Almost shoved it. Into the rush of night air. At first, the urge. The impulse to hold my hair. Keep it out of my eyes. But eventually. Finally. I let it blow. There was conversation in the front seat. That much I knew. But just 'conversation.' Because the wind. The drone. All combined. It sounded like a foreign language.

GEORGIA: This is exciting. (*Loud whisper.*) Winslow! Come and hear this!

STUBBS: A reach for a cigarette. The explosion of the match. The glow. I felt down the side of the door. Where's the ashtray? Georgia had to tell me where it was. I can find it, I thought. I CAN FIND IT!!!

GEORGIA: (*To* RIVERS; *trying to be quiet.*) He's gonna use that? What *I* said?

STUBBS: I felt old. My hand on the leather seat. Never that smooth. My skin was never that smooth. I looked around me. The blue dashboard light. The red glow. The oncoming cars. A landscape. A landscape of dreams.

GEORGIA: Could you hold it a minute. Just until I got Winslow. You couldn't imagine what a thrill he'd get. (*She exits left.*)

STUBBS: And then I saw myself. Don't be sentimental, I wanted to say. Don't be indulgent. But I saw myself like this. Like here. Other cars. In other back seats. Other cities. Countries. Drivers. All blurred. All stuck together. I wanted to reach into my brain and pull them apart. I saw a Spaniard with medals pinned to his chest. The two of us. Back seat. But where? Then I saw papers. Briefs for 'eyes only.' Piled across my lap. My head buried. My head hidden. Now I'm alone. And now police cars both front and back. Where is ... And now there. THERE! DID YOU FEEL THAT?!!! That was the thump as we drove across a median. Because this is urgent. See, this. Essential. This. What is this?

GEORGIA: (*Off.*) Winslow!

STUBBS: And now my arms. Outstretched. The top down. And a beauty queen both left and ... And right. And we're smiling. We're. This a parade of. Marking what? For what ...? But the sunshine. I can definitely feel the ... But now it's blurred. Now it is in the middle of the. It's pitch. It's. I can't see a thing. Just my driver. We're waiting for. This, an Army airstrip. We're waiting for an important. For some. And he and I. We're ol' buddies. We are. We're shooting the bull. Talking good ol'. Football. And smoking. We were smoking. We were.

GEORGIA: (*Off.*) Winslow!

STUBBS: Then I coughed. As I rubbed out my cigarette. And I could feel the veins. The forehead veins. Pulse blood. Straining. Knew my face, now beet. Now bright red. And my chest. My chest, it aches. And I rubbed at my brain. Almost. Wanted to. Nearly kneaded it. Until I could finally. Just close my eyes. Shut them. Without it hurting.

GEORGIA: (*Entering; concerned.*) I even looked on the porch. (*She exits right, to check out the bedrooms.*)

STUBBS: (*After a brief pause.*) And when I finally woke. Because the light overhead had come on. Because Rivers' voice, I heard it now. It was outside the car. She's out there tapping on the window, and saying. What's she saying. That I'm old? That I'm feeble? That I get things sometimes mixed up? Is she saying where we ...? What city? What country? What's she telling me? What am I supposed to know that she's telling me! Speak up! Rivers speak up! WHAT!! WHAT!! TELL ME!! TELL ME!! I DON'T KNOW WHERE I AM!!! (*Short pause.*) But Rivers. When I finally can make it.

Understand. All she is saying. She's just saying, "we're here." (*Short pause.* STUBBS *suddenly breaks out of the story.*) That's it. What did you do with my cigarettes?

RIVERS: (*Writing.*) You had 'em in the car, Stubbs. You want me to check?

STUBBS: You got that down?

RIVERS: (*Writing.*) I will in a minute.

STUBBS: Then you finish. I'll go hunt them up.

GEORGIA: (*Off.*) Winslow!

(STUBBS *opens the door; then turns back to* RIVERS.)

STUBBS: What did you think? It wasn't what you'd call loud. Not in fucking neon. But the old guy just remembering. There's a built in thing in that. The situation itself, I would think, oughta be enough to grab 'em and hold them in. Don't you?

RIVERS: (*Writing; sincerely.*) It was nice, Stubbs. Really. Just real nice.

STUBBS: Good. You know, it was just so easy, you begin to get doubts.

RIVERS: Well you shouldn't.

STUBBS: Thanks. (*Turns to exit, stops.*) Who the hell is that?

RIVERS: (*Writing.*) Somebody out there?

GEORGIA: (*Off.*) Winslow!

RIVERS: (*Writing.*) Must be her Winslow. (*Calling.*) He's outside!!

STUBBS: (*Looking out.*) Boy, what a fucked up place this is. I heard it was bad, but shit. Look at that, Rivers. You gotta carry a gun just to go out-side your own house. That's somethin'.

RIVERS: (*Writing.*) He's got a gun?

STUBBS: Which one is Winslow?

RIVERS: (*Stops writing, looks up.*) Which *one*?

STUBBS: Yeh, there's at least ... And what the hell do they have on their faces?

(*Suddenly, off,* GEORGIA *screams at the top of her lungs.* RIVERS *sets the notebook down.*)

STUBBS: What is wrong with her? (*Returns to looking out the door.*) It looks like ... They're in a shadow. I'll be able to tell when they get closer.

(RIVERS *looks toward where* GEORGIA *screamed from, then back at* STUBBS — *something frightening begins to dawn on her.*)

RIVERS: (*Forced calm.*) Stubbs. Close the door.

STUBBS: Huh?

RIVERS: Just close it.

(STUBBS, *confused, does so.*)

RIVERS: (*Screams:*) NOW BOLT IT!!

STUBBS: What are you talking about?

(GEORGIA, *enters in shock, blood stains on her hands and dress.*)

RIVERS: (*Seeing her.*) Oh my God! OH NO!! NO . . .

GEORGIA: (*Screams.*) THEY KILLED HIM!!!!!

RIVERS: Please, Stubbs. PLEASE BOLT THE FUCKING DOOR!!

(*Very confused,* STUBBS *bolts the door, and moves in front of the window.*)

RIVERS: A gun. Where's a gun? A GUN!! Think. Think. Okay. That's right.
I saw one in her purse. Now where's her purse. (*Sees* STUBBS *at the window.*) Stubbs, get away from the window. (*He doesn't move.*) Where's the
purse? (*To* GEORGIA.) WHERE'S YOUR GOD DAMN PURSE!!! (GEORGIA *moves
her hand.*) Over there? Over where? I don't see it. Stubbs, do you see it?
WHERE OVER THERE!!

STUBBS: (*Confused, but calm.*) It's on the couch. You want me to get it for
you?

RIVERS: (*Seeing that* STUBBS *has not moved.*) I WANT YOU TO GET
DOWN!!!

STUBBS: Okay. (*Starts to stoop.*)

RIVERS: DOWN!!!!!

(STUBBS *ducks down. Gun shot off, the window over* STUBBS *shatters. He
freezes.* GEORGIA *screams.* RIVERS *has found the revolver, runs to the window, ducking down, raises the gun over her head.*)

RIVERS: (*Running to the window.*) DON'T COME ANY CLOSER!! DON'T
COME ANY CLOSER!! (*She shoots four times.*) STOP! STOP! STOP! STOP!!!!
(*Then she freezes, out of breath. Pause.*)

STUBBS: (*Picks up his head, peeks out the window.*) They're gone. Or at least
they're out of sight. (*He closes the curtain; to* RIVERS.) They had ski
masks on, didn't they?

GEORGIA: (*Screams.*) WINSLOW!!!!!!!!!!!

(*Everyone is still. Long pause. Slowly, very slowly,* STUBBS *and* RIVERS *relax,
breathe easier. They get themselves together.* GEORGIA, *in shock, does not
move.*)

STUBBS: (*Brushing himself off.*) Not bad. Not bad at all. (*Short pause.*) But
not perfect. (*Short pause.*) I know what could have been alot better.

RIVERS: What do you mean, Stubbs?

STUBBS: What do I mean? I mean her. (*Nods toward* GEORGIA. RIVERS *is
confused.*) I mean when we've got a situation thrown at us like we had
here. Just had thrown at us. Well . . . her just coming in here and screaming her lungs out. Well, that doesn't add much, does it?

RIVERS: I'm still not following, Stubbs. (GEORGIA *watches with growing
disbelief.*)

STUBBS: Well, what I'm suggesting is, is that this could have been, well, what
it almost was. And that is one of the most interesting. Most exciting. Most
dramatic moments of my life. See, it *could have* been. But it wasn't.

Now that doesn't mean it wasn't any good. 'Cause it was. That's obvious.

But great? No. No way. 'Cause, see, you don't do great by coming in here and screaming your lungs out. That could work, sure. But it'll work like the shockeroo that it is. Like the stick in the spokes. Like the tack on the chair that it is. Call it what you want. But whatever you call it, it's gonna come out meaning 'slick.' Meaning 'easy.' And meaning 'cheap.' You see what I'm saying now.?

RIVERS: Yeh, I think so.

STUBBS: 'Cause, Jesus, where is the build there? In screaming like that. Where's the subtlety? God only knows. I mean, if you're gonna do it right, you gotta pluck it for all that it's worth. Like we did. Like you running around. Like you getting this. Getting that. Like me. "It's all slowly dawning on me." That kind of stuff. That subtle stuff. But screaming? Doing shit but scream your lungs out? Tell me, where's the build in that?

RIVERS: Yeh. I see what you mean. But what do you think she should have done?

STUBBS: What do I think? Shit. There's a thousand. There are possibilities. By the. There are millions. You really want to know? (RIVERS *nods.*) Well. Let me think. She could have. Maybe. Like maybe, she could have come in. You know, without saying anything. No words. Nothing. But maybe holding something. Like. (*Sees the phone book.*) Like a book. (*Picks up the phone book.*) Okay? Like a book. So she's holding a book. And. I haven't really thought this out. And, she suddenly drops it. (*He drops the book.*) And she doesn't pick it up. Doesn't even look down. Like she didn't even know she did anything. So that's odd. That's peculiar. It's obvious *something* is up, but nothing's been given away. Okay?

RIVERS: Okay.

STUBBS: And then. Maybe she plays with that bracelet. Fasten it. Unfasten it. Her fingers tense. That's how you notice they're shaking. First the bracelet, then the tenseness. Sense of her holding back something. Repressed. Ready to explode. But you don't really know that yet. Just her nervousness, right?

RIVERS: Right.

STUBBS: Then. How about tears down her face. But no sound. No crying. Just the tears. That's very powerful. Very upsetting. And now a comment. She's saying something. One thing. Something off the wall. Something that is definitely gonna register, gonna click a little "uh-oh" in the brain. A little, "what is going on here?" Something like . . .

RIVERS: "I keep seeing my father's face"?

STUBBS: What? Yeh. That's not bad. And her face blank. No expression whatever. And then she starts to take a step forward. One step. And as if just that little movement brought her back to. Back to her situation. Her hands quickly cover her face. She bends down, trying to remain tough. Remain self-possessed. But can't. Just can't. And then. At that time. Now she can explode. Now. Damn it now, she can scream her lungs out.

RIVERS: Yeh. That's pretty good.

STUBBS: So what do we have. (*He plays 'Georgia.' He drops the book.*) The book.
RIVERS: (*Nodding.*) The book. Yes.
STUBBS: I don't look down. (*He fiddles with his 'bracelet.' His hands are shaking.*) No expression on my face.
RIVERS: Right.
STUBBS: "I keep seeing my father's face."
RIVERS: Good.
STUBBS: And tears. And . . . (*He starts to take a step. Covers his face, lowers his head slowly and suddenly screams.*) Something like that. It *could have* been just great. (*Shakes his head.*) You sure you don't have my cigarettes in your purse?
GEORGIA: (*Screams.*) WINSLOW!!!!!
STUBBS: See? See? That's just the kind of thing I've been talking about.

(*Blackout.*)

Scene 3

Setting: The same. Stage dark. Lights fade up. RIVERS, *on the couch, holds her notebook.* STUBBS, *near her, standing and thinking. Pause.*

STUBBS: (*To himself.*) Okay. Maybe. Then: door. Then: duck. Then: bang. Then: okay. Right.
RIVERS: You ready?
STUBBS: Just a sec. I'm running it over. Then: yeh. And I'm feeling? Right. Uh-huh. I won't be long.

(GEORGIA *enters right. She carries a rifle, an automatic revolver, and an ammunition belt. She is still quite 'dazed.'*)

GEORGIA: (*Entering.*) I found these in a closet. (*Holds them up; to* STUBBS.) Which do you want? The pistol or the rifle?

(RIVERS *puts a finger to her lips, to 'sh-sh'* GEORGIA. *Short pause.*)

GEORGIA: There's also this ammunition belt.
RIVERS: Georgia, not now.

(GEORGIA *just looks around, doesn't know what to do.* STUBBS, *thinking, sighs.*)

GEORGIA: I'll give you the rifle. (*She sets the rifle and belt on the bench and sits.*)
STUBBS: (*Snaps his fingers.*) Okay, Rivers. I *think* I'm set. So what the hell. Let's give it a go.
RIVERS: (*Set to write.*) I'm right with you, Stubbs.
STUBBS: Right. Now just stay with me. (*'Envisions' the scene.*) Farmhouse. Country. Outside Vienna. Somewhere. God knows where. I didn't. I'm sure I didn't. I'd just completed an entry. Not bad. Not half bad.

Nothing loud. Nothing in neon. And I was thinking, that was easy. That was maybe too easy. So doubts. So concerns. So I was going back over it and thinking and reaching for a cigarette. But the pack's in the car. Rivers tells me. So I was half way out the door, still fretting, when: who the hell is that? I said, who the hell? Somebody's out there. Oh that must be, Rivers said. Her. Her husband. Okay. So my mind, it moves back a moment. Back a beat. Back to. To maybe it was too god damn easy.

So then. Coming slowly into focus. A gun. Not a whole gun. But the light on the porch reflected itself say, as a spec on the barrel of the gun. And that appeared to bounce. The spec, that is. As the gun was moved. Boy oh boy, I said. You gotta carry guns in this place. And then. Suddenly there are three. Not just guns, but men. But not really men. But noses. Their faces, see, were dark. Black. But their noses? Why? They were white. Maybe they, I'm thinking. Maybe wearing what? Mufflers? Beards? I even thought, maybe a native costume. I did. How ridiculous. Do you believe that? See how the mind can play tricks? SEE!!

So three noses. Three specs of light. And there is a scream too. Behind me. From way the hell behind me. And Rivers is saying, close the door. And I'm thinking, but I don't feel much of a breeze. And she's saying, bolt it. And she's screaming, get down. GET DOWN!!!

And so I'm down. Why? I didn't ask. Just did it. No reason. Why the hell argue. But I'll admit to feeling a touch foolish. When: BANG!!! Then: CRASH!!! The two sounds as simultaneous as two sounds can be. Can get. And now I'm covered with glass. A rain of glass, I think. All fast. One one hundreth of a second, maybe. That's all. That is it. The time it took. But I felt it all happen. As in steps. Bang-crash-rain. And I smelled it too. Get this. Don't forget this. The smell of a sudden, almost immediate, discharge of my SWEAT!!!

And my hair, get this. That was the next thing. The next object of my attention. My hair standing up. But can you believe this. What I noticed. Not head hair. Not neck hair. But the hair on my knuckles. What an odd sensation. What a strange. The knuckles. Of all places. Of all stupid places. Then. Then I look up. And above me. On the sill tottering. One piece. One small jagged piece of glass. On the edge and tottering. That made me shudder. Really. I want to knock it off. I want to push it back. Anything. Either. It's un-nerving. Just as long as it stops tottering on the god damn brink!! I said to myself, something like, "oh no."Not appropriate. Not enough. My hands don't move. Won't budge. Like stumps. Like they had roots. My heart racing. Banging. Like a berserk. Like a berserk something. REACH!! REACH!! DO SOMETHING!! DO SOMETHING!!

(*Suddenly, the telephone rings interrupting the remainder of* STUBBS' *entry.* STUBBS *and* RIVERS *almost freeze for an instant. Then they turn to* GEORGIA.

Short pause, as the phone rings.)

GEORGIA: The line was dead just a minute ago. (*Finally,* GEORGIA *picks up the phone.* STUBBS *and* RIVERS *watch. Into the phone.*) Hello?

RIVERS: (*Quietly, to* STUBBS:) Stubbs, do you feel it? The sudden interruption. Everything stops. Then the sense of anticipation. And the mounting tension. Don't you love it?

(STUBBS *nods, but motions for her to be quiet.*)

GEORGIA: (*To* STUBBS.) It's them. (*Into the phone.*) Yes . . . Right . . . I see . . . Right . . . Uh-huh . . . Uh-huh . . . Uh-huh . . . Yes . . .

RIVERS: (*In a whisper.*) There's sort of a built-in suspense 'bout hearing just one side, isn't there? Maybe I should make a note of that. We could use that sometime. What do you think?

(STUBBS *nods, but again motions for her to be quiet.*)

GEORGIA: (*Into the phone, hiding her face from* STUBBS.) Yes . . . Right . . . I understand . . . We won't try to call . . . Right . . . I will . . . I said, I will . . . I'll tell the Senator . . .

(*Short pause. She hangs up. Can't look at* STUBBS *or* RIVERS. STUBBS, *scared, begins to slowly back up.*)

STUBBS: (*Finally.*) Tell the Senator what? (*No response.*) Tell me what?!

RIVERS: (*Looking through her purse.*) All I got is maybe. Maybe eighty dollars at best. The rest's in traveler's checks.

STUBBS: Georgia, please.

RIVERS: And Stubbs has. I'll bet he's got less than I do. But if they want it so bad they can have it. (*She reaches for* STUBBS, *wallet.*)

STUBBS: FORGET THE MONEY!!! (*He pushes* RIVERS *away, she falls to the floor. To* RIVERS.) I'm sorry.

GEORGIA: They want you.

STUBBS: They what?

GEORGIA: They said something about an exchange. How you could be real useful to them. But I didn't really understand much of that. (*Short pause. To* RIVERS.) They don't want us. We'd be let go.

RIVERS: (*Getting up.*) Stubbs, I thought it was a robbery.

GEORGIA: They gave you an hour. I guess, 'cause they know we have guns. They said, maybe if we thought about it for a while we wouldn't do anything dumb. (STUBBS *looks down, he fiddles with his watch.*) And. And they said one more thing. (*No one looks at her.*) They said. They said that killing Winslow. They said that had been a mistake. (*Short pause.*) I guess he must have surprised them. Maybe heard them outside or something.

STUBBS: (*Trying to get control of himself, rubs his eyes.*) Oh boy.

GEORGIA: What do you think we should do? There's only one neighbor. And they're away for the month. I know, 'cause I'm supposed to be taking in

their mail, (*She looks for a response, but gets none.*) Except for them,
there's nobody within at least a kilometer. (*Short pause.*) Did you hear
me?

STUBBS: (*Quiet.*) What? Just hold it a minute. Just give me a sec to think. Sit
down.

(*She sits on the bench. Short pause.*)

GEORGIA: (*Stands.*) The milkman's due around six. But that doesn't help
much does it?

RIVERS: Sh-sh. Just sit down.

(*She sits; short pause.*)

GEORGIA: (*Stands.*) The lecture's in. In less than two hours. Maybe someone'll get concerned enough and drive out here. What do you think?

(RIVERS *suddenly and violently grabs* GEORGIA *and throws her back down.
She falls over the bench. For a moment she is dazed, then begins crying.*)

GEORGIA: (*Screams.*) WINSLOW, THEY SAID IT WAS A MISTAKE!!!!!!
(*She is crying.* STUBBS *suddenly turns to* RIVERS, *who gets set to write.*)

STUBBS: (*Bellows and pounds his fist in the air.*) "THEY'VE GOT THEIR
NERVE!! THEY HAVE CERTAINLY GOT THEIR NERVE!!!" This almost the first.
Almost my initial reaction.

(*Blackout.*)

Scene 4

Setting: The same. Stage dark. Lights fade up. GEORGIA *is on the couch.*
STUBBS *stands center.* RIVERS, *with notebook, stands right watching* STUBBS.
Long pause.

STUBBS: (*Finally.*) I'm feeling . . . I'm feeling angry. Yes! (*He takes a bowl
from the table and smashes it on the floor.* GEORGIA *screams.* STUBBS *is
suddenly calm. He shakes his head.* RIVERS *crosses out in her notebook
what she had just written.*) No. No. That's not what I'm feeling. (*Pause.
He paces and thinks.* GEORGIA *confused.*) I'm feeling . . . I'm feeling sentimental. Yes! (*Slowly with tears almost in his eyes, he approaches* RIVERS
*and tenderly moves his hand across her cheek. Then he looks down,
wipes a tear away, reaches up and rustles her hair. Then suddenly moves
away.*) No. No. That's not right. (*Pause. He paces and thinks.*)

GEORGIA: (*Quietly.*) Rivers . . . ? Rivers . . . ?

RIVERS: (*Watching* STUBBS.) What?

GEORGIA: What is he doing, Rivers?

RIVERS: (*Notices that* STUBBS *has stopped pacing.*) Sh-sh!

STUBBS: (*Suddenly smiling, arms raised.*) I feel happy! I feel full of love! I feel
joyous! I do. Yes. I want to wrap my arms around everyone and
everything! I do. I do. I feel majestic. Yes. I feel like I've lived a full life. I

feel at peace with myself. Yes! I feel . . . (*Breaks out of it.*) Nope. Nope. I
don't feel like that. Nope. Cross it out. (RIVERS *does. Short pause.*)

GEORGIA: Rivers . . . ?

STUBBS: (*Quickly.*) I see my life passing before my eyes! (*Breaks out.*) Uh-uh.
No way. Who am I kidding? (*Paces and thinks. Short pause.*)

GEORGIA: (*Quietly.*) Rivers, do *you* know what he's doing?

RIVERS: (*Watching* STUBBS, *to* GEORGIA.) Come again?

GEORGIA: I mean, what he's doing, does it make any sense to *you*? (*No
response; explodes.*) DOES IT?!!!!

STUBBS: (*Suddenly begins backing up toward the door.*) I'm alone. And I'm
forgotten. I feel small all of a sudden. Small. And unwanted. And un-
needed. I feel like a dark speck of something against a white space. (*He is
against the door, folding himself, becoming smaller.*) A speck. Just a faint
speck. Getting smaller. Dimmer. Fading fast. Going out. Being extin-
guished! (*Suddenly shouts.*) HELP ME!!!! (GEORGIA *is frightened, starts to
scream.* STUBBS *breaks out of it. Calm.*) Shit. That's not right either.
(RIVERS *crosses it out.* STUBBS *shaking his head, thinks. Short pause.*)

GEORGIA: (*Stands; obviously on the verge of tears, on the verge of screaming.*) Would it be. Uh. Uh. Would it be stupid of me to. To ask, see, just
what you are. What exactly you are up to. I mean. I mean are you . . . ?
See I can't really. I can't tell myself, see. Do you see? Just what it is you
are. Your feelings. Your thoughts. What you are planning on. What you
are going to do about. It just doesn't seem to make any. To me. Though
maybe that's just me. Maybe 'cause I'm so. So, you know. Maybe 'cause
my head, see. My head is sort of spinning. So I don't hear too. All that.
MAYBE BECAUSE WINSLOW IS UP THERE DEAD!!! I DON'T KNOW!!!

(STUBBS *has been watching her with interest.*)

STUBBS: (*Snaps his fingers at* RIVERS *to get her attention, to get her to watch*
GEORGIA. *She nods. To* GEORGIA.) Go on.

GEORGIA: I DON'T KNOW!!! (*Hears* STUBBS.) What?

STUBBS: That's very nice. Now keep going. "Maybe because Winslow is up
there dead. I don't know."

GEORGIA: Uh. Uh. (*Self-conscious.*) Uh. He is up there dead. So. So maybe I
don't see things all that clear, maybe. Maybe after all it's my fault that I
don't know what's going on. What you are doing. Maybe. It probably is.
It's real simple. Real obvious, even. Logical, even.

STUBBS: Never mind. (*Turns to* RIVERS *shakes his head.*) I shouldn't have
stopped her. She's forcing it now. (*Continues his own thinking.*)

GEORGIA: Huh?

STUBBS: (*To himself.*) I'm feeling . . . ? I'm feeling . . . ? What?!

GEORGIA: (*Very lost, watches* STUBBS, *then* RIVERS, *then* STUBBS.) Maybe.
Maybe it is the most common thing to do in the whole world. I don't
know.

STUBBS: I'm feeling . . . ? Mmmmm.

GEORGIA: Maybe I'm the strange one. For *not* understanding. Maybe that's it.

RIVERS: Sh-sh.

STUBBS: (*Suddenly triumphant, to* RIVERS.) I'm worried! I'm worried!

GEORGIA: You're what?

STUBBS: I'm really upset.

GEORGIA: No you're not.

STUBBS: I'm scared shitless.

(RIVERS *is set to write now.*)

GEORGIA: I know you're not. No.

STUBBS: I don't know what to do. There doesn't seem to be a way out. (GEORGIA *shakes her head, and mumbles 'no.'*) It just don't seem fair. It don't seem to make any sense. So I'm scared. Yeh.

GEORGIA: No. I don't believe you. No.

STUBBS: (*Sits on the couch and is suddenly into his story.*) Like a bubble. A bubble rising to the surface. A bubble of cold.

GEORGIA: I said, I don't believe you. Uh-uh!

RIVERS: (*Who is writing.*) Shut up!

GEORGIA: WHY DON'T YOU SHUT UP!!!

(*Short pause.* STUBBS *stands; looks at both* RIVERS *and* GEORGIA. GEORGIA *walks to the far end of the room, her back to them.*)

STUBBS: (*To* RIVERS.) For a second I thought we had something exciting beginning there. But I guess not. Anyway . . . (*Sits, starts again.*) Like a bubble. A bubble rising to the surface. A bubble of cold. Of chill. Beginning in my legs. That's what it feels like.

I notice this as I sit on the couch. By this time, it has been maybe fifteen minutes since the phone call. Since Georgia had said, her voice dull, her voice somber, "You. They want you."

So by now, there has been time for it to sink in. To soak through. And now like a bubble in my legs that is rising, I feel afraid. I'm scared. I don't know where to turn or what to do next. I can only think — 'bad luck' and 'why me?' And I can only feel the throbbing in my knees. Which I think I can shake off. Maybe just walk off.

(*He stands;* GEORGIA *turns, slowly her attention is caught.*)

So I stand. But instead, the pressure. Instead of going away, it's begun to relocate in my eyes. Yeh, my eyes. So I touch myself. My eyelids. My face. Cheeks. Mouth. So I wonder out loud — 'what am I doing? With these entries. This talk. With a life down on paper when there is a life here that breathes. That is afraid.' So I wonder: 'shouldn't I really be. Be doing anything. Some other thing. Rather than this hiding behind some lousy memoir that no one will bother to read. Bother to get to know. Bother to love. Bother to save.' I wonder out loud, why I am not bothering to save me. And what does this say about the kind of. That I am. About what is wrong with me? Am I a man? Am I human? Am I? I said, AM I?!!!

(GEORGIA *watching with sympathy now.*)

Areas of the room once, before, only lit bright by a lamp, now appear as in pools of harsh light. And the colors, they have faded visibly till now everything is bleached white or sucked black. Objects. A simple chair. Even my own feet go out of focus, then quickly back in. Then out again. Jesus, I don't even know if I am breathing or just twitching. If I'm crazy. If I'm alone. Or if I'm lost.

My ears are ringing with sounds. All kinds of sounds. It's deafening. But each distinct. Very individual. I keep hearing myself as I scream: SHUT UP! But I don't even know if I've spoken out loud. At all. I don't even know if that was me speaking.

GEORGIA: (*Quietly.*) He's shaking.

STUBBS: So I'm listening to myself. That's all that I am doing. This constant listening and watching and revealing. Don't I care about me? Have I no feelings? If not for anyone else, then how about for me? This life, doesn't it matter? Doesn't it move me? I guess not, because all I do is listen. How disgusting. Just listen to a voice. This voice which sounds like it's a mile away. "Mine? Is that mine?" Deep in a hollow. Out there. Or in there. Somewhere. Crying its guts out now. Damn it. Wailing. Like a god damn bubble exploding. And screaming. Screaming: WHY ME?! WHY ME?!! WHY ME?!!! (STUBBS *is crying.*)

GEORGIA: He's crying. He's really crying.

(*Pause.*)

STUBBS: (*With tears down his face; to* GEORGIA.) Did you like?

(GEORGIA *freezes in shock, staggers a few steps back, looks at* STUBBS, *then* RIVERS. *Suddenly, she runs to the door and begins pounding.*)

GEORGIA: (*Pounding; screams.*) Help me!!!! Help me!!!!!

(*Blackout.*)

Scene 5

Setting: The same. Stage dark. Light fade up. RIVERS *sits on the couch, going through her notebook, making corrections, additions, etc.* STUBBS *stands behind the couch, he pounds its back, thinking. Pause.* GEORGIA *enters with a tray—coffee cups, coffee pot, bottle of milk.*

GEORGIA: (*Entering.*) I couldn't find the sugar. And I thought it'd just be asking for trouble to turn on the kitchen light to look for it. (*Short pause. She sets tray down on the table in front of* RIVERS. STUBBS *goes to the window and peeks out.*) I guess I could have pulled the blinds. But I just couldn't face going anywhere near the window. You know what I mean?

RIVERS: (*Without looking up.*) What?

(*Short pause.* STUBBS *returns to behind the couch, continues pounding on its back, thinking.*)

GEORGIA: (*Pouring herself a cup.*) It isn't fresh. I just warmed it up. (*Short pause; no response.*) We keep the sugar in the counter cabinet. But, you know, when I felt for it, it wasn't there. (*Pours in some milk, picks up her cup.*) I guess, I'll have to ask Winslow where he put it.

(*Suddenly,* RIVERS *looks up at her, and* STUBBS *turns toward her, both waiting for her reaction.* GEORGIA *realizes what she has just said, freezes for an instant, then drops the cup which shatters. Short pause as* GEORGIA *just stares.*)

STUBBS: (*To* RIVERS.) Better. No doubt about it. Much better than screaming her lungs out. She's catching on.
RIVERS: (*Nods.*) Very nice, Georgia.

(STUBBS *returns to his thinking;* RIVERS *to her notebook.* GEORGIA *sits on the bench, and stares. Pause.*)

STUBBS: (*Suddenly, without expression.*) I feel aggressive. I've been pushed too far. I've taken just about all I'm gonna take. I want to fight.

(RIVERS *quickly turns to him. She rifles through the notebook until she finds the first clean page. She gets set to write.*)

STUBBS: Where's the rifle?
RIVERS: (*She tries to write this. Stops. Shakes her pen.*) Hold it a second, Stubbs. (*She gets up, goes to her purse.*)
STUBBS: (*At first, not hearing her.*) Where's the ri. . .?! (*Sees* RIVERS *is not writing.*) Where are you going? Why aren't you writing?
RIVERS: I'm getting another pen. The other one was running out.
STUBBS: Wait a minute. Tell me something. And what am I suppose to do while you're looking for this pen?
RIVERS: It'll just take a second.
STUBBS: How long it'll take doesn't change the fact that *you* are holding *me* up.
RIVERS: I'm sorry, Stubbs.
STUBBS: Sorry for what? Your stupidity? Your incompetence? Your arro- • gance? Just who the hell do you think you are?
RIVERS: (*Nearly in tears.*) It's just that the pen was running . . .
STUBBS: Look, I don't pay you for excuses. I pay you to write. SO WRITE!!! (*Turns away, looks around.*) NOW FOR THE LAST TIME, WHERE IS THAT GOD DAMN RIFLE?!!

(RIVERS *begins to desparately search her purse.*)

RIVERS: (*Without looking up.*) It's next to Georgia.
STUBBS: (*Without moving; to* GEORGIA.) Give it to me.

(*Short pause.*)

RIVERS: (*Without looking up, to* GEORGIA.) Give it to him. (*No response; looks up.*) Give it to him!!! . . . I'll get it, Stubbs.
STUBBS: No! She is going to have to learn just who is in charge here. . . . Georgia, the rifle. Hand it to me. That's an order.

(RIVERS *continues to dig through her purse.* GEORGIA *slowly reaches for the rifle, then stops.*)

STUBBS: I said, that is an order.

(GEORGIA, *very hesitantly, picks up the rifle and hands it to* STUBBS. STUBBS *suddenly grabs it away from her; he begins to bounce it in his hands, looking it over, nodding and smiling.*)

RIVERS: (*In a panic.*) Stubbs, I can't find another pen.
STUBBS: (*Explodes.*) GOD DAMN IT, WHAT ARE YOU TRYING TO DO TO ME?!! Do I have to do everything myself? You want a pen? (*Yanks one out of his shirt pocket and flings it across the room.*) There's one!!! Now shut up and write!!!!

(RIVERS *chases after the pen, finds it, and hurries to get set to write.* STUBBS *plays with the gun, trying to get into the 'mood.'*)

STUBBS: (*'Into' his entry now.*) I find a rifle. And for an instant I wait. Expecting. In fact listening for it to somehow bark orders back to me. Into my brain. Back through its barrel. Like Bouganville. With the palm trees. The huts. The steam jack-hammers slashing away at the coral. Like my sergeant. Up to his thighs in mud, but still barking. Still in control. Still telling me what to do. Now. Next. Now. (*To rifle.*) SO TELL ME!!!!!!
RIVERS: Stubbs, you won't believe this, but this one doesn't . . . (*Makes a writing movement.*) . . . either.
STUBBS: (*Doesn't hear her; to* GEORGIA.) JAM THAT BENCH AGAINST THE DOOR!!! (*Smiles.*) I'm surprised by the strength of my voice. The bark of my voice.

(RIVERS *is now up and searching through her coat.*)

GEORGIA: (*Tapping* RIVERS *on the shoulder; trying to remain calm and above it all. She holds the coffee pot.*) Rivers, more coffee?
RIVERS: Leave me alone. Can't you see I'm busy?!!
STUBBS: (*To* GEORGIA.) DO IT!!
GEORGIA: (*Ignoring him; pours herself a cup; to* RIVERS.) Don't hesitate to help yourself, if you change your mind.
STUBBS: (*To himself.*) This same voice. From the same brain. Which had been. Well, it had been shaking. Almost breaking, in fact. Almost ranting. Maybe this now just another form of ranting. Maybe. Maybe. This taking charge just another way of giving up on myself. Trying to locate a more comfortable spot somewhere else. Inside someone else. Something

else. Maybe. Maybe.

(GEORGIA *suddenly discovers a pencil near the telephone. She waves it at* RIVERS.)

GEORGIA: Rivers, look what I found.

RIVERS: (*To herself as she searches.*) I don't believe this. What are the odds against this sort of thing happening?!

STUBBS: WHERE IS THAT AMMUNITION BELT?!!!

GEORGIA: (*With pencil.*) Rivers. Yoo-hoo. Rivers.

RIVERS: It's just not fair. One pen going dry, maybe. But two!

STUBBS: I find it. I find it myself on the arm of the couch. I throw it over my shoulder. I pat it as if it were alive. (*Pats the ammunition belt.*)

GEORGIA: (*With pencil, insistent.*) Rivers...!!

RIVERS: Will you get off my back!!!!

STUBBS: (*Yelling at* GEORGIA.) I TOLD YOU TO MOVE THAT BENCH!!!!

RIVERS: (*Seeing the pencil, screams.*) WHERE DID YOU GET THAT?!!! (*Grabs the pencil and begins to write.*)

STUBBS: (*To himself.*) I'm screaming now. That's just what I'm doing. But shit, maybe I need to scream to shift gears. To move myself onto another thought. To think of what to do next. Now.

(GEORGIA *sits on couch. She tidies up the coffee table, fluffs up the pillows, etc. She ignores* STUBBS *and* RIVERS.)

STUBBS: Look, I'll keep the rifle. Rivers, you take the revolver. And Georgia, you will be our extra pair of eyes. (*Turns away.*) So that is what I'm thinking, is it? Not bad. Not half bad. I had no idea I had such a plan worked out. No idea. Jesus, I wonder what I'm gonna say next.

(GEORGIA *hums quietly to herself.* RIVERS *has picked up the revolver and holds it under her arm as she writes.*)

STUBBS: (*To* RIVERS *and* GEORGIA.) We'll stay at the window. Rivers, you take left. I'll stay right. And Georgia. Over there. OVER THERE! Get the fuck over there and keep one eye on the kitchen and scream your fucking lungs out if you hear so much as a peep. NOW DAMN IT! DAMN IT, GET INTO POSITION!!!!

RIVERS: (*To* GEORGIA.) YOU HEARD HIM, MOVE IT!!!

(GEORGIA *hums and doesn't move.*)

STUBBS: And now I sigh. Now I step back. Step back and look around. Now I expect to find myself somehow feeling as if I'd finally climbed into a skin that will *not* shudder. Will not shred. But instead. Yeh. Instead. Get this. I find I can't help smiling *at* myself. Can't help wondering if all I am really doing now is just a fair. Just a decent. Just a pretty good impersonation. NO! NO!!!

(STUBBS *and* RIVERS *at their respective windows.* RIVERS *continues to write.*)

So. I. Now. As if to try to prove myself wrong. To prove I have indeed
been well cast. That I fit. Fit! That I belong in this skin. At this time.
Under these conditions. Fit. I WANT TO. I WANT TO FIGHT!!!!

(He suddenly breaks the window with the butt of his rifle. Pause.)

But no. Oh shit. No. No. Instead of cementing. Instead of proving. Get
this. The breaking glass only makes me shudder. Draws me back. And
now. Now even worse I get it into my head. You won't believe this. I get it
into my skull. Where first I'm wondering if it had really been necessary to
break the window. I think that. Really. I think, how expensive a window
is. Incredible. I don't believe it. How stupid. And now, second, I begin to
see myself as small. As downright out of place. Out of my element. I begin to feel my age. And feel awkward. And I begin to see this whole thing.
With the gun. With the window. With the barking. I begin to see it as a
charade. And myself as embarrassing. As pointless. As sad.

And now I stand. Pull my rifle back. 'My' rifle. What a joke. I stand.
Very alone now. Very much alone. Very red in the face. Very ashamed of
myself. WHAT AM I DOING?!! WHAT THE FUCK AM I DOING WITH THIS?!!!! *(He
throws the rifle down. Covers his face. Short pause. Then, suddenly 'out
of' the entry, he takes a pack of cigarettes out of his pocket. To* RIVERS.*)*
You want one? I found them in her purse. (RIVERS *nods, finishes her
writing.* STUBBS, *breathing heavily, lights their cigarettes. They smoke.
Short pause.)* Good scene. (RIVERS *nods. Pause.)*

GEORGIA: *(Suddenly screams twice.* STUBBS *and* RIVERS *turn to her.)* You
know what *I'm* doing? Do you? Huh? I'll bet you don't. I'll bet you haven't
the faintest. Well am I right? Or am I right? Well I'm trying to shake it all
up. All up in here. *(Points to her head.)* Figure it couldn't hurt. No. No.
Maybe the pieces will begin to fall into place. Up here. Couldn't hurt.
Couldn't be worse. Could it? Huh? Huh? *(No response.)* DO YOU KNOW
WHAT IT FEELS LIKE?!!! *(To* RIVERS.*)* Do *you*? To be standing here. And
you. Him. He starts up. He starts crying. He starts shoutin', do this. Do
that. *(To* STUBBS.*)* And her. She's right with you. The two of you. And
me. I keep thinking. Brother, I sure missed something. Brother am I
stupid. *(Stops. She screams.)* Nope. Still doesn't work. Still didn't shake
nothin' into place. But as I was saying. Brother am I. Am I. What was I
saying. WHAT THE HELL WAS I SAYING?!!!!!

STUBBS: *(Quiet, soothing voice.)* Go on. Go on.

GEORGIA: *(Screams again.)* That's better. That's much better. So. Maybe it's
because I'm not seeing things so good. What do you think? Possible? Is
that possible? Maybe 'cause everytime I close my eyes. See, I've closed
them. And all I see is: bedroom. Is: blood. So maybe because my mind is.
Is what? TELL ME!!! Maybe because of that. You. And her. It all seems so
very very odd. Maybe that's why I'm feeling so. Right? Right? Do you
think that explains it? Do you? Do you? Please, do you?! TELL ME! TELL
ME! PLEASE SOMEBODY TELL ME!!! *(She covers her face. Short pause.*

STUBBS *applauds.* RIVERS *joins in.*)
STUBBS: Bravo. Bravissimo. Bravo.

(GEORGIA *looks up, crying.*)

GEORGIA: Huh?
STUBBS: (*He walks over to* GEORGIA, *pats her on the shoulder.*) Georgia.
    Nice. That was tremendously moving. (*He returns to his thinking.*)
RIVERS: (*Walks over to* GEORGIA.) I'm touched. I'm deeply touched. (RIVERS
    hugs GEORGIA, *turns, returns to her notebook.*)
GEORGIA: It . . .? (*No response.*) It was . . .? (*No response.*) It was really good?

(*Blackout.*)

Scene 6

Setting: The same. Stage dark. STUBBS, *in black, begins to laugh, almost
uncontrollably. Lights up.* STUBBS *stands center.* GEORGIA *and* RIVERS *are
on the couch watching him.* RIVERS *no longer takes notes.*

STUBBS: (*Continuing with a 'story'; trying to hold back his laughter, though
    not succeeding very well.*) And so. So for some reason. (*Laughs.*) Some
    God knows why reason. I start to. Because the entire situation here.
    Them out. Out. This whole fucking picture. (*Laughs, giggles.*) With
    Rivers there concerned. Looking very prim, see. With Georgia almost in.
    Almost in. In anguish. (*Laughs.*) And the window. Let's not forget the
    window! And with my own face. No doubt. Very stiff. Yes. Very serious
    face. This face. My face. (*Laughs; wipes the tears from his eyes.*) So for
    some reason. It just all becomes hilarious. I don't know why. Just one
    great big. Big joke, see. That now. That now I'd somehow just been let in
    on. You see? (*Laughs.*) Even though. One side of me. Angry. Yeh. Pissed
    as hell. Yeh. One side telling me: shut up. SHUT UP! But I can't. I can't.
    No way. Not for a million bucks. It's too. It's just all too. Why the hell
    not? It just all too funny now!!!! (*Laughs out of control. Suddenly stops.
    Calm. Out of his 'story.'* RIVERS *and* GEORGIA *applaud.* STUBBS *sits on the
    couch,* RIVERS *stands, thinking, she clears her throat. She takes center
    stage. Short pause.*)
RIVERS: I'm confused. Or maybe. Better. I'm sort of at odds with myself. On
    the one hand, see, I want to try to figure out what there is that we *can* do.
    You know, maybe run for it. It's pretty dark out there. Or go out
    shooting. I don't know. Whatever. Something like that. But on the other
    hand, I feel like I should be doing just what I have been doing. Right here
    with you, Stubbs. Helping you. You know? After all that is my job, isn't
    it? (*Short pause.*)
STUBBS: Start again. More . . . immediacy, I think. Know what I mean? It
    sounds like you have it all figured out.
RIVERS: Immediacy. (*Nods.*) Okay. (*Clears her throat, throws back her*

hair.) I'm scared. That's here alright. My hands have been shaking so hard it's been difficult to write. Really. I keep hearing those gun shots. And somehow my fingers keep feeling for that revolver. I feel a chill. A chill that's so solid, so physical, it feels like a hit. A punch. A constant banging. Like a heavy cold shower. I can't seem to get comfortable. I want to work. I want to concentrate. After all. After all that's my job. That's very important to me. But there still is this fear. I guess because of shooting. *Actually* firing. Because I really *did* pull the trigger. I guess 'cause I got started. And then. Then just stopped. Stopped and started waiting. So there's the sense of conclusions, you know, not yet having run their course. Not yet completed their cycle. That sense of an uncompleted motion. A half-step. Start-stop. And all too sudden. And the waiting makes it worse. Like the action is still right there, I just gotta grab it. The action is just waiting forme to finish it. So the sense of being pulled at. Tugged at. This way. And that. Well, it sometimes has even felt like I was splitting apart. Like, see, I'm breaking in half. Then. Then it's real bad. What I'm feeling. Then, it's terrible. Then it's real bad. What I'm feeling. Then, it's terrible. Then it's real bad. What I'm feeling. Then, it's terrible. It's a nightmare. Then: Jesus. JESUS CHRIST. STUBBS, IT'S SO GOD DAMN AWFUL, I CAN'T STAND IT!!!! (*Breaks down. Short pause. It takes* RIVERS *a little while to get calm. Applause.* RIVERS *returns to the couch.*)

STUBBS: (*Takes* RIVERS' *hand and winks.*) Better. Much better. (*She sits.* GOERGIA *stands, nervous.*)

GEORGIA: Well. I guess I feel, you know. Well, sort of privileged. In a way. After all, you're a Senator and I'm. Well, who the hell am *I*, you know?

STUBBS: (*He has been listening intently; snaps his fingers;* GEORGIA *stops; he goes to* GEORGIA, *almost whispers to her.*) Look Georgia. It is always obvious when one is faking the emotion. Do you understand? And when it is obvious, there is no interest. When there's no interest, no point. No point, then why do it? You understand? (*She nods,* STUBBS *returns to the couch.*)

GEORGIA: I am feeling . . . (*Short pause.*) I guess I'm feeling, you know . . . resentful. (*She looks for a reaction;* STUBBS *nods.*) I mean, well. You come into here. My house. This *is* my house. Where *I* live. And. And mostly you. But also her. You come into here and you keep doing this stuff. And I'm made to feel like I'm the one who is intruding. That I'm the one butting in. That I don't belong here.

And then. When we realize what's happened. When I'm frightened. When I keep thinking and I can't get it out of my mind, and I feel guilty even trying. Thinking that Winslow is dead. When, as you know too. When what happened to Winslow will probably happen to us, too. That all this isn't over. Not by any means. Not by a long shot. When all this has happened in my house. And in my head. And I turn and look for what? Maybe just a little tiny bit of concern. Of consolation. Not only because of Winslow. But also because we're all in this together. Stuck together, almost. No choice. Well, there should be, I keep telling myself. There should be some mutual concern. A certain togetherness. A 'let's help each other' spirit. But you. You not only don't put your arm around me. Give me a shoulder to ... but you make me feel like I'm fucking butting in. Like I should go away. Well, where should I go? WHERE THE HELL SHOULD I GO?!!!!!!

I don't know. See. It's all become like a dream. That I can't remember anymore. Nothing specific. Just this feeling. This after-taste. But still. But I know it's still not over. So I keep pricking myself. Keep thinking, you are not really there. No. 'Cause if you were. If you were there, I wouldn't be feeling so much hate and disgust for you. So much resent-ment. I wouldn't be feeling like even though I'm in my own god damn house, I'm stuck somewhere else. Some place I've never been before. Somewhere. Where I'm all alone.

(*Short pause.* GEORGIA, *close to tears, closes her eyes, not knowing what to expect.* STUBBS *claps loudly.* RIVERS *applauds and whistles.* GEORGIA *opens her eyes and smiles, pleased. The applause stops.* GEORGIA *sits,* STUBBS *stands, thinking. Pause.*)

GEORGIA: Can I try one more?

(*Blackout.*)

Scene 7

Setting: The same. Stage dark. Lights fade up. STUBBS, GEORGIA, *and* RIVERS *are waiting. Each is doing something idiosyncratic, like clicking their nails, jiggling a foot, etc.* GEORGIA *also reads a book.* STUBBS *and* RIVERS *on the couch.* GEORGIA *is on the bench. Pause. Gun shot, off. The vase on the table explodes. They are startled, jump.* GEORGIA *stands slowly. She drops her book. The others watch her. She does not look down. She fiddles with her bracelet. No expression on her face. Her hands shake.*

GEORGIA: (*Finally.*) I keep seeing his face. I keep seeing Winslow's face up there. (*She starts to cry. She begins to take a step toward center, but stops, covers her face, lowers her head, then raises her head slowly and suddenly screams.*)
STUBBS: (*Stands; angry.*) Oh fuck, I'm getting real tired of this. SHUT UP!!
RIVERS: (*Holding him back.*) Stubbs, she's upset.
STUBBS: Oh she is, is she. Well what do you think I am, huh? I'm upset too. ME TOO!! But least I make the effort to control myself. Make the effort to keep a lid on this. Keep myself together. LEAST I'M NOT SCREAMING EVERYONE'S BRAINS LOOSE!!

(GEORGIA *screams.*)

STUBBS: I SAID, STOP THAT!! (*He grabs at* GEORGIA's *arm, she turns toward him, and spits in his face.* STUBBS *is taken aback, but very angry now. He wants to hit her.* RIVERS *jumps up and grabs* STUBBS.)

RIVERS: Don't touch her, Stubbs! (*She pushes him away. To* GEORGIA.) You shouldn't have done that, Georgia. (*Puts her arm around* GEORGIA.) Hey, take it easy. Come on. Come on. It's all forgotten. There. There. (*Comforts her;* GEORGIA *stops sobbing. Short pause. Suddenly, everyone calm, they all nod at each other and return to their earlier positions.* STUBBS *and* RIVERS *on the couch, etc. Pause. Explosion, off. Everyone turns to the door.* RIVERS *gets up and peeks out the window.*)

RIVERS: (*To* STUBBS.) Georgia's car's on fire.

GEORGIA: (*In shock.*) What?! *My* car?!! (*She gets up and charges toward the window.*)

RIVERS: (*Trying to stop her.*) Don't get too close. (GEORGIA *fights to get away.*) I said, don't get close!! Stop kicking! (GEORGIA *bites her hand.*) She bit me!! She bit me!! (RIVERS *slaps her across the face,* GEORGIA *falls to the floor.* RIVERS *walks away, rubbing her hand.*)

STUBBS: (*To* RIVERS.) Let me see. (*Looks at her hand.*) You'll live. (*Smacks her on the fanny. He goes over to* GEORGIA.) Georgia . . .

GEORGIA: (*Pointing toward the door.*) But *my* . . .

RIVERS: (*Rubbing her hand.*) She broke the skin.

STUBBS: (*Giving* GEORGIA *his hand.*) I know. I know. (*She takes it. He pulls her up. Short pause. They all 'break,' become calm, nod pleased with each other, and return to their former positions. Pause.*)

GEORGIA: (*She starts to wipe her hands on her dress, then notices the blood. She tenses, and mumbles.*) Those bastards.

STUBBS: What did you say, Georgia?

GEORGIA: Never mind.

STUBBS: Georgia, if you have something to say, you should say it.

RIVERS: Stubbs is right. Get it off your chest, Georgia. You'll feel better.

GEORGIA: (*Holding up part of her bloody dress.*) I said, 'those bastards.'

STUBBS: And how do you feel about those bastards? Do you hate them? (GEORGIA *nods.*) Then say it like you do.

GEORGIA: (*With hate.*) Those bastards!

STUBBS: You want to strangle them with your own hands, don't you?

GEORGIA: (*Nods; with more anger.*) Those bastards!!!

STUBBS: You want to tear their eyes out!

GEORGIA: (*Standing, yelling.*) THOSE BASTARDS!!!!

STUBBS: That's it!

GEORGIA: (*She grabs a pillow from the couch and begins punching it and shouting.*) THOSE BASTARDS! THOSE BASTARDS!

STUBBS: THAT'S IT!! THAT'S IT!!

GEORGIA: (*Screams.*) THOSE GOD DAMN BASTARDS!!!! (*Short pause. They all 'break,' become calm, and return to their former positions. Pause.*)

RIVERS: (*Finally.*) It's still your turn, Stubbs.

STUBBS: (*Suddenly angry.*) DON'T YOU THINK I KNOW THAT!!! (*Calm.*) That felt nice.

(*Pause.*)

GEORGIA: Did I tell you about what I was feeling in the car? When I was driving you two here?

STUBBS: (*To* RIVERS.) Did she? (RIVERS *nods.*)

GEORGIA: Oh.

(*Pause.*)

STUBBS: I feel nothing. Nothing. Not a thing. As if my emotions, so stretched. So strained. Have not bent, but broken. And so now, like maybe snapped ends of a wire, they lay limp. Unable to make any connection. . . . That's a possibility. (*He thinks.*)

(*Pause.*)

GEORGIA: Did I tell you about how I felt at your hotel? My frustration? My confusion? My pent-up anger?

STUBBS: Did she?

RIVERS: Yes.

GEORGIA: Oh.

(*Pause.*)

STUBBS: I feel . . . everything. All at once. A mess and a blur of feelings. Wires crossed. . . . That's also a possibility. (*He thinks.*)

(*Pause.*)

GEORGIA: Did I tell you how *I* was feeling when those men out there called? (STUBBS *turns to* RIVERS *as if to say 'did she?'*; RIVERS *nods.*)

GEORGIA: Oh. (*Pause.*) Did I tell you about how I felt when I found Winslow?

STUBBS: Did she?

RIVERS: No.

GEORGIA: (*Slaps her hands together and takes center stage.* STUBBS *and* RIVERS *watch.*) Well. Well, see, I guess you could say I was already worried. See, I hadn't admitted it to myself, you know. The kind of worry that you only feel but don't allow yourself to think. I mean, after he wasn't in the kitchen. After I'd seen the roast still in the sink. I felt, well, I guess I even thought — 'heart attack.' I think I even said to myself: 'heart attack.' So, see, I was already pretty anxious when I started up the steps to the bedroom. I was already holding my breath and jumping for explanations. I was already seeing, you know, expecting to see a note on our bureau telling me he'd got a call from the office. And I was already angry at him for leaving and forgetting about the roast.

So, when I tried to open the door, and it was jammed. Not locked. But jammed so I could only open it a couple of inches. I had no thought.

Nothing. This just didn't fit. What the hell could this have to do with that
note on our bureau I kept 'seeing.' So I pushed. With all my strength. I
pressed my shoulder against and pushed. And then.

And then — a foot. Only a foot. PUSH! PUSH, GEORGIA! HEART ATTACK!!
PUSH!! Then — blood. Then as the door inched open. Then — (*Suddenly
gun shots rip a line of holes across the door. Everyone turns to the door.*
GEORGIA *steps upstage.*)

STUBBS: (*Quietly.*) Here they come.

RIVERS: It won't be long now.

GEORGIA: I guess not.

STUBBS: (*Taking center stage.*) Now, let me think — my last words. I am
going to need some appropriate last words. (*He thinks. Short pause.*)

RIVERS: Now that you mention it, Stubbs, I guess, so will I. (*She takes
center. Short pause.*)

GEORGIA: Me too. (*Takes center. Short pause.*)

RIVERS: What about . . . ? No. No. (*Short pause.*)

STUBBS: I've got mine . . . No. No. (*Short pause.*)

GEORGIA: How does this sound . . . Nah. (*Short pause.*)

RIVERS: Uh. . . . No. Too maudlin. (*Short pause.*)

STUBBS: Yeh: . . . Too clever. (*Short pause.*)

GEORGIA: I have mine!. . . Wait. I just lost it. . . . Shit, it's right on the tip
of my tongue . . . (*Short pause. Gun shot blast — the door is shot off its
hinges and crashes to the floor. They all turn and look..*)

(*Blackout.*)

Scene 8

*Setting: Vienna. Sitting room of a hotel suite. Same as Scene One. Two years
later. Stage dark. Lights up.* RIVERS *sits on the chaise.* GUNTER *stands
center.*

GUNTER: It was a winter's evening, two years ago today, when a black
American limousine sped through the narrow side streets of Vienna. In
the backseat, the American Senator thumbed through an issue of *The
Herald Tribune*. He read the football scores first. And then the news. As
he pressed his face to the window, he saw a cathedral. He noticed that the
breath of the pedestrians created small clouds in the air. As they passed a
Coca-Cola sign, he smiled to himself. The Senator sat back as the car
lurched forward, headed for an intimate Viennese hotel. This hotel.
Where upstairs, in Suite 812, a bald headed man paced his room,
avoiding every squeak in the floor.

Suddenly, this man stops and pulls back the lace window curtain. He
looks down on the street below. He keeps the light off and one hand over
part of his face. He turns the yellow knob of the radio and listens to a
Strauss waltz. He smokes American cigarette after American cigarette.

He waits.

The limousine glides up in front of the green awning of the hotel. I hurry outside and bow as a porter is trained to bow. That is, without much to do. The Senator grips my shoulder and winks. The elevator jerks and squeaks, but the Senator calls the ride smooth. His bags are of the softest leather. Other guests on the same floor have left their doors open just a crack. They wish to get a peek of the famous American Senator. An inconspicuous peek.

One door, however, remains closed. The door to suite 812. Where, inside, the bald headed man is practicing putting a drinking glass against a connecting door. The one which connects his room with suite 814.

A couple of guests now find excuses to wander the hall. One says she is looking for her shoes. The Senator slaps everyone on the back. He shakes two different hands at the same time. He retires to his suite. Number 814.

I return to the lobby. I find myself humming. Something by Liszt. I catch my reflection in a mirror which has a pattern in gold leaf. I wink at myself. I practice shaking two hands at the same time. I whistle, 'O Susannah.'

But upstairs. The man in 812 has grabbed for a phone. He is dialing. The call is answered on the first ring. "The country!" He wants to scream, but forces out a whisper. "Yes, the country." And he hangs up. He lights the last of his American cigarettes. He pats the spot on his chest, making sure the bulge made of metal is still there. Weeks later, it would be learned that this man had been trained in the Middle East. That he was an expert with explosives. That his father was a retired schoolteacher from Burgenland. That his aunt writes poetry. And that his mother had died when he was twelve.

And so the course of events, which were soon to be played out in a farmhouse. With terrorists. With death. With fear. That course of events which would dominate the headlines and gossip of Vienna for weeks. Had been set in motion. It had begun. It had begun here. In this hotel. Right here! In suite 812. And in suite 814. Just two years ago today. (*Short pause.* GUNTER *looks for a response.*)

RIVERS: (*Nods.*) Thank you, Gunter. Very charming. I will have the Senator call you when he wakes up. (*Short pause.* GUNTER *doesn't move.*) Is there something else, Gunter? (GUNTER *gestures with his head toward the pile of books on the desk.*) Oh, of course! Of course, the book. How stupid of me to forget. By all means, Gunter, take a copy of the Senator's Memoirs. I'm sure he'd want you to have one. The top copy, yes. I believe that one is already signed. (GUNTER *takes a copy and checks to see if it is signed.*) And thank you again, Gunter, for that very lovely story. The Senator will be thrilled to learn that he has become part of the history of this hotel.

(GUNTER *exits with book.* STUBBS *enters from the bedroom. His hair disheveled; he wears a smoking jacket; he holds a large new book — his published memoirs.*)

RIVERS: Stubbs, don't you think Gunter is cute?

STUBBS: Who?

RIVERS: Gunter. The porter. He just told me the cutest little story.

STUBBS: Forget Gunter, and tell me what you think about the election night story.

RIVERS: About the what?

STUBBS: I'm thinking of giving it for the lecture tonight. You think there'd be interest in that kind of thing?

RIVERS: The election night story? But I thought you were going to do our rescue story. I even think that's what they're counting on, Stubbs.

STUBBS: Forget that. And just tell me if you think they'll go for this. (*Opens the book.*)

RIVERS: But Stubbs, they have even named the lecture series after Georgia. You know, as sort of a memorial. Wait a minute, I think I've got the flyer here somewhere.

STUBBS: Look. I know what happened. You know what happened. They know what happened. I'm tired of that story. You're tired of that story, and, damn it, I'll bet they're just as tired of it too. So let's just forget it, okay?

RIVERS: Tired of it? What with us having given up hope. What with guns blazing. And bullets everywhere. And fire and smoke so you couldn't see your hand in front of your face. What with the two of us behind the couch. You patting my head. And me. I'm shaking like a. And Georgia! Georgia! Where the hell is she?! Georgia! We're screaming. We're choking. When suddenly, outside we begin to hear . . .

STUBBS: (*Cuts her off.*) Rivers, come on, I'm sick of telling it, okay? Come on and listen to this.

RIVERS: Sure, Stubbs. If that's what you want.

STUBBS: Well that is what I want. Now just tell me whether you think they're gonna go for this. . . . Where the hell are my glasses.

RIVERS: I'll check the bedrooms. (*Gets up.*)

STUBBS: No. Why the hell don't you read it. That might be interesting. Maybe I can hear it better that way, and be able to tell myself where it'll play or not. Here. (*Hands her the book.*) Where it's marked.

RIVERS: "Election night. I was in my suite"?

STUBBS: That's it. I'll stand back here. So it's more like it'll be. You ready? (*She nods.*) Then, let's hear it. And for God's sake take your time. This ain't a race, okay?

RIVERS: Okay. (*Short pause; she clears her throat; reads.*) "Election night. I was in my suite at the Hotel Pierre. Three televisions were set in front of me. One for each network. I lounged with my shoes off on the couch. Friends, supporters, news people made a steady stream past me. I felt like I was holding some sort of court. I remember laughing to myself at the thought. I stretched my legs out, but just couldn't get comfortable. I tried to eat, but my stomach already felt full. That's how tense I was. Trying to relax, I took a shower. But still felt dirty. I felt like I smelled as soon as I toweled myself off. I put my shoes back on so I'd feel like I didn't have to relax. That I wouldn't feel pressured to relax.

"The first returns had come hours before. A small town in Vermont. I won the town by twenty three votes. And made a joke about it. Something like, 'Now we just gotta run even.' Everyone laughed. Real hard.

"As the East Coast states started to come in. I surprised everyone by going to bed. I'm playing this cool, I thought. I wondered if I'd wake up the President. Or a loser. When I did wake up I thought I'd been asleep for hours, but it'd been only seconds. My sense of time was all warped. I felt a little bit foolish when I returned to the televisions so soon. But we all just laughed about it. Real hard.

"As the network projections were being flashed state-by-state, I got into the differing graphics of the three stations. One gave the precentage inside an American flag. Another within a group of stars. And the third had the map of the state that was in question. I thought about what I'd have chosen if the graphics were my job. I didn't come up with much.

"By midnight we were neck and neck. It was becoming obvious that California would be the big casino. One roll. One very big roll of the dice. It'd come down to that. I tried to name all the cities in California that I'd visited. I gave up after thirty. That's enough, I thought. You should have no regrets. So we all relaxed because we knew California wouldn't be final for a couple of hours. We all breathed easy. Getting ourselves set to start that slow move to the edge of our chairs as the minutes began to tick away. For the first time that night, I took a drink. I told myself I'd just sip it slowly. Make it last until California.

"But then. I never even had the chance to take a drop. Because. Because suddenly it was flashed! Ohio had changed hands! We'd lost it! We'd won it and now we'd lost it! There'd been a mistake. A big mistake. It was suddenly. What happened? WHAT HAPPENED?!! IT WAS OVER! IT WAS OVER! California wasn't enough. WE NEEDED OHIO!!!!!

(*Short pause.* RIVERS *is very 'into' the story. Almost has to fight back tears.*).

"I couldn't think of anything to do. I couldn't think of anything I wanted to do. Except *not* cry. Not cry like *they* were. Like everyone around me was. My actions, then, they became *not* actions. Do you see what I mean? I was *not* going to give up. I was *not* going to bed. I was *not* going to break down. I was *not* going to win." (RIVERS *shuts the book; takes a handkerchief and wipes her eyes. Pause.*)

STUBBS: (*Half-smile.*) I. I really do feel for that man. And so will they. It will play. It will play. It will play.

(*Blackout.*)

Author's Note

There is nothing inherently false about acting. We all to some extent are in control of how we express our feelings and emotions. Drama, or the dramatic, lies in our veins. Given the most heated argument, we gesture, increase volume, punctuate our tears and sighs in order to produce the desired effect upon *our* audience. The dramatic, or the art of acting our feelings, is a civilized means of getting ourselves across, understood, and empathized with.

Some of us are better and more practiced in this art than others. There are amateur actors and professionals, subtle actors and histrionic ones. A man of few outbursts can create a tremendous effect upon his audience with a single outburst. Those prone to outbursts (that is, those who have gone to the well too often) must seek more complicated means to create their desired effect. The impact of one's acting is in direct relation to how one has portrayed oneself to one's audience beforehand. To constantly get attention and empathy, one must constantly change tactics.

To act out an emotion is not to lie about that emotion. The Senator of *The Vienna Notes* never lies about what he feels or what he is experiencing. The emotions he expresses do in fact exist within him. His concern is never to find a "better emotion," only to find a better way of expressing his emotions.

The *lives* of our politicians, as well as those of our celebrities, have become the focus of our interest in them. (Biographies of writers abound, while their works remain out of print.) The politics of personality are the politics of our time. Political personalities (which are the characters created by the performance of public figures) are more important to us than are political acts. A "liberal" action (i.e., the ending of the draft) can become "conservative" when made by a "conservative personality" (Nixon). A "conservative" action (i.e., the Bay of Pigs) can become "liberal" when made by a "liberal personality" (Kennedy).

The notion of HISTORY has become what the notion of HEAVEN once was. Whereas a public figure may have once sought "his place in Heaven," now he seeks "his place in History." And just as one once struggled for his soul's immortality by doing good works, one now struggles for the immortality of his characters in History by attempting to create as good, exciting, and empathetic a personality as he can. We should not underestimate the desire of Senator Stubbs to have his character live and be experienced by future generations. This obsession is as great as another man's struggle for his soul's immortality.

Finally, plays are played, not written. And for a play which in part is about performance and self expression and audience reaction this is doubly true.

So in reading *The Vienna Notes,* try to keep in mind that the laughing, the sighing, the snarling and the booing of a live audience are as much a part of this play as are the words.

———————

Boy on the
Straight-Back Chair

Ronald Tavel

©1969, 1980 Copyright by Ronald Tavel.
CAUTION: No performances or readings of this work may be given without the express authorization of the author's agent. For production rights contact: Helen Merrill, 337 West 22nd Street, New York, N.Y. 10011.

Boy on the Straight-Back Chair was first performed on February 14, 1969, at The American Place Theatre, New York. It was directed by John Hancock, and the cast included:

TOBY . . . . *Kevin O'Connor*
STELLA . . . . *Katherine Squire*
DELLA . . . . *Doris Roberts*
SINGER . . . . *Christopher Stoeber*
STRIPPER . . . . *Gloria LeRoy*
MARY . . . . *Martha Whitehead*
ROMEO . . . . *Clark Burckhalter*
MAY . . . . *Nancy McCormick*
RAY . . . . *Ernestine Mercer*
MAUDE . . . . *Jacque Lynn Colton*
LYNN . . . . *Lori Shelle*
BAD BUTCH . . . . *Norman Thomas Marshall*
MUSICIAN . . . . *Richard Vos*
THE SOUND MAN . . . . *John Lefkowitz*

Sets/Costumes: Robert Lavigne
Music: Christopher Stoeber
Lighting: Dennis Parichy

Years ago when I was living in Wyoming and such things were not yet understood, Charles Starkweather and Caril Fugate began their shooting saga that was to end in the deaths of eleven innocent persons. For seven terrorful days and nights the states of Nebraska and Wyoming were virtually an armed camp. The couple was finally apprehended near the town in which I was living.

The fictional character Toby in this play is derived from a composite of various accounts of uniquely American killers such as Charles Starkweather, Richard Speck, Charles Whitman, and the murderers of Theresa Genovese and Jane Britton.

In the northwest spring comes quite late and May is actually the month of thaw, the month that must decide.

Act I

SCENE: *A semi-circle of chairs, its ends curved toward downstage. Several chairs scattered upstage with dummies in them. An enormous disc, painted as a vortex, is behind the centermost chair in the semi-circle. A girder runs from the base back of this chair to up and over the vortex disc. A platform is at its highest point. A second girder runs diagonally across the stage, from downstage right to upstage left, criss-crossing the platform of the first girder. Sun and moon move along this diagonal. The floor may be inlaid with mirrors, sand mounds and cactii scattered here and there.*

TOBY *stands on the centermost chair of the semi-circle.* DELLA *sits to his left,* STELLA *to his right.*

A BALLADEER *with guitar emerges from the dark downstage right and begins to sing a country-blues song. As he sings he strolls diagonally upstage directly under the path of the girder. A spot follows him.*

BALLADEER:
    WELL, I AIN'T GONNA SING MY HONEY NO MORE MASTERPIECES
        I'M GONNA WAIL TILL I PREVAIL WITH NOTHIN' GREAT:
    BLUES WHAT LET 'EM KNOW WHERE IT'S REALLY ACHIN',
    TELL ALL THE REASONS WHY YA KNEES IS SHAKIN',
        GET YA LITTLE LOVIN' AN' A AWFUL LOTTA HATE.

    I'LL SING MY HONEY NO MORE MASTERPIECES
    CAUSE THAT JIST AIN'T WHAT MY HONEY WANTS TO HEAR:
    SOME BALLAD SHORT 'N SWEET
    AND ON THE REAL EMOTIONS CHEAT —
        WELL THAT OUGHTA WIN THE LOST LOVE OF MY DEAR.

        MY HONEY WANTS TO DANCE TO EVERY COUNTRY SONG

CRY ABOUT THEIR SERMONS ON WHAT'S RIGHT 'N WRONG,
HOW THE SUN GO DOWN IF THE MOON COME UP
AN' THE WHOLE WORLD'S TASTED FROM THE TINIEST CUP:
BUT THE BIG, BIG THING WHAT'S BREAKIN' UP INSIDE
AN' GONNA GET DRAGGED OUT IN THE NEXT FLOOD TIDE
NEVER HAD A LINE FOR MY HONEY ALL ALONG,
IT NEVER HAD A LINE MY HONEY'S HEARD ALL ALONG.

SHE'S GOT A HEART, I'M TOLD, 'N A WILLIN' EAR
   BUT SOMETHIN' DEEP DOWN IN HER JIST DON'T CARE
AND THOUGH A LOT GOTTA HAPPEN FORE THE HURTIN' CEASES
YET I'LL SING MY HONEY NO MORE MASTERPIECES
   CAUSE THAT JIST AIN'T WHAT MY HONEY WANTS TO HEAR.

(*The* BALLADEER *reaches the other* MUSICIANS *upstage left. A light has brightened on* DELLA, *surprising her at her knitting; she is humming the melody.*)

DELLA: Oh! You fellas finished? It was real short tonight. (*To audience.*) Sorry, but I never know when them boys is gonna be done. Sometimes they like to tack a extra sentiment or two onta the end of that ballad. I been rushin' here to get done with this sweater; it's fer ma little girl, name's Rita. I expect her along any minute.

(*A light brightens on* STELLA, *finding her in an agreeable mood.*)

STELLA: (*Standing, going to the footlights.*) We got lots a little girls.
DELLA: Stella!
STELLA: Kids, dogs, mothers with baby carriages 'n whatnot crossin' back 'n forth on route 30 runs right up the middle a town so when ya come through our town, 35 miles a hour please.
DELLA: 'N ya might pass it up if ya go any faster.
STELLA: (*Ignoring her.*) Our town's fabulous far west affair. We got quite a strip.
DELLA: Beg ya pardon.
STELLA: Della! This here's a clean place to live 'n raise up yer kids. People are doin' it all the time. Nice clean western affair. Boys got crew cuts, school girls wear skirts in this here town they do, not like over in Vegas. But we got a strip like Vegas even if it ain't but route 30. Plumb full of gas stations 'n hamberg joints, chop suey parlors, wash 'n dry, electric neon, general motors, used car lots the Cocktail Rendezvous and general provisions notions 'n sundries, everything provided at 35 miles a hour. Nice clean all-American town bring yer kids up right straight around these here parts ya can. (*Darkly.*) What's more, people round the route thinks pretty much alike 'n we sticks together too case yer thinkin' 'bout makin' any trouble, folks.
TOBY: (*Till now with his back to the audience, pivoting about fiercely on the chair.*) *My* face is my own creation. Most folks are born with faces. Cow

folks, sheep folks, town folks, squares; squares settle for their faces. Not me. I made my face. Spend four minutes a day, religiously, under a high-powered electric sun lamp. Capped my teeth, nervously moisten my lips and embroider them with the consummation of a large, well-placed mole. But my beautiful sea-blue eyes are my own, all my own, as is the wine-dark anger vein that throbs like a unicorn horn in my high and handsome brow. I keep lookin' for the action!

DELLA: Wonder what kinda action he means. Always gotta be one maverick in the crowd, don't there, Toby?

TOBY: Don't always gotta be.

STELLA: Now that there boy worries me. He's short. Toby Short. We like our men-folk big, big, ya know what I mean? But Toby's short, *he keeps lookin' fer the action!!*

(*The* BALLADEER *and* MUSICIANS *strike up a blast of western acid rock that borders on uncontrolled madness.*)

BALLADEER:
ACTION! ACTION!
TOBY'S LOOKIN' FOR THE ACTION!
HE DON'T 'LLOW NO DUMB DISTRACTION
QUICKLY MULTIPLY SUBTRACTION
IN THE MANHUNT FOR THE ACTION!
  ACTION! ACTION!

TOBY'S SHORT, SHORT, SHORT!
AIN'T NO WAY HE CAN CONTORT,
AIN'T NO CAP OR SHOE SUPPORT
GONNA MAKE HIM LOOK LESS SHORT —
  SHORT! SHORT! SHORT!

TOBY: I have burnt my motto into a semi-circle over my heart. It reads: "Born To Raise Hell." I bare my mottoed chest to only the most intimate of my guests — for surely it is a sign of the selected few to be born, as I, to raise hell!

DELLA: Wonder what kinda "hell" he means.

BALLADEER:
TOBY'S SHORT, SHORT, SHORT!
AIN'T NO WAY HE CAN DEPORT,
MUSCLE BUILD OR BOAST HIS FORTE
GOIN' IN ANY WAY DISTORT
FACT THAT HE IS JIST PLAIN SHORT —
  SHORT! SHORT! SHORT!

TOBY'S LOOKIN' FOR THE ACTION! ACTION! ACTION . . .

STELLA: In school, Toby's an indifferent scholar and a different ath-e-lete. By which I mean to say, he can play ball but he's dumb.

TOBY: Wadda ya mean dumb?? I am famous fer ma highfalutin' lingo. I have read 'n reread the Gospel Accordin' To St. John, committed it to heart, I tore it to tatters 'n swallowed it. It has filtered down to the squeeze in ma lower intestine 'n from there been osmosed everywhere. Ma frame is racked with the Word that was God and the same in the beginnin' racked God. Therefore, ma speech is peppered *par force* with the piety 'n intellect of a poet's apostle ask any chick in our town.

DELLA: It's boring in our town.

TOBY: I'm bored.

DELLA: Toby's bored. I think he has cancer.

STELLA: Must have somethin'.

TOBY: (*Crying.*) Probably, probably . . .

DELLA: Don't cry, Toby, your mole will run. We all feel sorry for you.

TOBY: (*Consoled.*) I'm glad fer that — cause even though I'm a hero figure, and I am nothin' if not a hero figure, still I thrive on feelin' sorry fer myself. Ma pa was a skid row habitué in gin-mill Denver 'n ma ma a Vegas stripper, so ya all can feel plenty sorry fer me if ya want to.

STELLA: Ya ma's a *Vegas* stripper?

TOBY: Stella, do ya feel sorry fer me?

STELLA: Yeah.

(*A* STRIPPER *appears singing and dancing to a ballad with a burlesque beat.*)

STRIPPER:
  NEVER MARRY A BLONDE, BOY,
  NEVER GET FOND OF A BLONDE, BOY,
  NEVER ABSCOND WITH A BLONDE, BOY,
  NEVER MARRY A BLONDE, BOY!

  WHEN YOU GET TO BED WITH A BLONDE, BOY,
  'NOUGH SAID, 'NOUGH SAID, 'NOUGH SAID!

  BLONDES'LL EAT YA — LOTS O' HEAD!
  NIBBLE ON YOUR GINGERBREAD,
  STUFF YOUR SHORTS WITH THOUGHTS O' BED,
  MAKE YA HUNGER TO BE WED: —
  BUT THEY'LL MILK YA, SORE-MISLED,
  AT AN ALTAR NEVER RED: —
  SON! THEIR CHERRY'S LONG SINCE DEAD!
  AND HOW THEY'LL CHEAT YA, UNDERFED,
  TO A BANQUET OVER-SPREAD!
  AND HOW THEY'LL CHEAT YA — AIN'TCHA READ? —
  AT A BANQUET OVER-SPREAD!

  NEVER MARRY A BLONDE, BOY,
  NEVER GET FOND OF A BLONDE, BOY,
  NEVER ABSCOND WITH A BLONDE, BOY,
  NEVER MARRY A BLONDE!

  SO DON'T YA NEVER MARRY A BLONDE, BOY,

LESSON, TAKE A LESSON FROM A BLONDE, BOY!

STELLA: Like I said, nice respectable town. Wanna bring yer kids up here, ya do. Don't ya, Della?

DELLA: I ain't married.

STRIPPER: Never marry a blonde boy.

DELLA: There goes yer ma, Toby.

TOBY: So long, ma.

STRIPPER: (*Exiting.*) So long, son.

STELLA: What ya do last night, Toby?

TOBY: (*Swinging a yo-yo, slowly, ominously.*) I looked fer the action.

DELLA: What ya find, Toby?

TOBY: Nothin' much. Jist ma cat. Tied a string around his tail 'n swung him up against the wall a couple a times.

STELLA: I feel compassion.

TOBY: You feel compassion — why?

STELLA: It's a warm, sweet feelin'! (*To audience.*) Hard to have a good come-back to questions like that. Yes sir, a warm, sweet feelin'. Soft, furry, warm.

DELLA: (*Lifting up her knitting-work and putting it aside for the moment; we see that it is a great fine spread of blue, much more like a cloak than a sweater.*) Our kids say Sir and Madam, play stick ball, eat strawberries and cream, they cream, they stick, they go to bed at ten out here in the great West, that's how the West was won, that's how it often was goin' west, they're good to their folks, have nice table manners, good leanin's, fine learnerments, got respect, they are flowers all of them, cactus flowers. Toby, would ya stop swingin' that yo-yo! Ya gimme the chills. What's a nice boy like you goin' 'n wantin' to swing that yo-yo fer?

TOBY: (*Ominous.*) Gettin' nervous, Della?

DELLA: What me nervous? Never been nervous a day in mah life! What's there to be nervous about in a nice western town like this, eh Stella?

STELLA: (*Her sense of stage-competition renewed.*) Good, clean dry Utah air. Best air in the country. Folks with asthma come out here to die. Got them stock piles here, too.

DELLA: Whatcha say about piles, Stella?

STELLA: Ranch-type houses, green-sprayed concrete lawns, sprawling super-markets, fresh fish frozen and powdered, shiny chrome, home sweet home, yes sir, this is the land of the big rock candy mountain, the land of powdered milk and honey, the promised land, get along little doggie, yip-pie aie eh! aie eh!

DELLA: Now _____ . . . (*Using the actor's real name.*) I asked you to stop swingin' that there yo-yo! You deef or somethin!?

TOBY: (*Furious.*) Better close yer trap, old girl, better close it up like yer eyes 'n yer ears, if ya know what's good fer ya!

DELLA: Old girl!

TOBY: Missed yer appointment at the beauty saloon this week, didn't ya, _____? (*Using the actress' real name.*) It shows.

DELLA: But you didn't miss yers, did ya? Notice ya got that there streak a white dyed real bright right up the middle of yer black head.

TOBY: A crescent of white sets off the night of black same's a perfect quarter-moon.

DELLA: That right? Guess I jist don't cotton to two-faced hair. Specially on scene-stealers.

TOBY: (*Struggling to remain in character.*) Shows what taste ya got. What do you know anyway? All yer good fer is doin' — *our town's* dirty laundry.

DELLA: (*Feeling nervously for the cloak.*) Nice town, nice clean town, got nice clean laundry. — Acourse, the dressin' room could use a little airin' out.

STELLA: (*Trying to make peace.*) Why don't ya get yerself a different job, _____ . . . (*Using the actor's real name.*) . . . 'n stop swingin' that yo-yo like Della tells ya? She tells ya good, Toby Short.

TOBY: What job? Ain't no jobs fer us kids: the coast-come semi-retired asthmatics pick up all the part-time work at minimum wages. Chicken feed. The old gizzards are crowdin' us out. There's too many ancients around, not to mention you two old birds, 'nough to open up a museum specialize in fossils.

STELLA: Ya hear!

DELLA: Who listens?

TOBY: There's a school a course, the schools out here are strickly boss, up ta date, up ta daisy-pushin', streamlined, shiny home-chrome mod-Mormon architecture — but *small*, ya dig, small!!!

DELLA: Short.

TOBY: Us kids are on split-level session, we're on the loose 'n in the noose from noon on, some from four till noon next day. Lots 'n lots a time. Idle hands are Edgar Allan Poe's workshop. He wrote somethin' about a swingin' cat once, didn't he, Stella?

STELLA: Poe was never really my favorite.

TOBY: I get a lot of ideas from what I read —

DELLA: University studies show that even the most salacious readin' matter has no adverse effect on innocent —

TOBY: I'm a salacious, voracious reader. A voracious reader and the leader — the leader of the high school set.

DELLA: But yer forty-two years old.

TOBY: And I know how to *hump* a hundred different ways.

STELLA: Get that in school in them new courses on marriage, did ya?

TOBY: Get it on ma own, ma own experimentin', ladies —

DELLA: Knit, one, pearl two; my weddin' girl's gonna wear jist blue.

TOBY: Yer weddin' girl's gonna wear jist plain ol' quotidian white same's the rest a them dumb-dumbs gits hitched up round the route. And, speakin' a the quotidian:

(ROMEO, *a very tall, painfully awkward and diseased-scarred young hood, emerges jauntily from the upstage entrance, over-prepared and over-anxious to do his thing.*)

ROMEO: At Motel Mama's, "M" over "M" in electric neon light, ya can dog, monkey, hamilton, swim, or jerk the night away. Me 'n Motel Mama prefer the snake shake or the moribun'-Mormon knee-high paten' after the adobe dizzy rain dance. Makes ya dizzy ... At the malted milk drive-ins 'n round the pizzerina parlors our cars endlessly circulate, suped-up cylinders, mufflers rumbling, we check each other out. We check each other out. We are out of work, out of line, out of combat, out of pity, and bored. Man, we're bored. Nothin' to do in this here town. Less to do in life.

TOBY: Lookin' fer somethin' to do, Romeo?

ROMEO: Lookin' fer the action. A-lookin' fer the action. No action in this town. Less in life. (*Quickly deflated, taking a seat.*)

TOBY: No action, eh? What say we bring out —

DELLA: Rita! (*Singing.*)

> NOTHIN' COULD BE SWEETA
>
> THAN TO SEE
>
> MY PRETTY RITA —

(*Standing, looking back with expectation.*)

TOBY: (*Slamming hard.*) *Mary*!! What say we bring out Mary?!

(MARY, *a high school girl with hard facade, appears from the darkness upstage. It is difficult to make her out at first and* DELLA *peers into the darkness with the cloak in hand.*)

DELLA: Rita? That you, Rita? Pretty girl, that you? No, that ain't Rita: that's Mary, Stella's girl ...

STELLA: Hi, hon.

TOBY: (*Triumphant, sneering* DELLA *back into her chair.*) Mary! Mary! Quite Contrary, how does yer garden?

MARY: Needs some rakin', rake.

TOBY: What wit.

MARY: Shit.

TOBY: Come here, Mary, 'n give us a kiss.

MARY: (*Strutting up to his chair, her head on a level with his crotch; she stares at it blankly.*) Where?

TOBY: Wise guy, huh? I could flatten yer Nevertitti bee-hive head into a flunky Nubian's brillo from here.

MARY: Lotta pretty tall talk fer a greasy fried shrimp. Talk, Toby, talk, and no action.

TOBY: But lots a soul, eh, Mary?

MARY: I can soul-kiss.

TOBY: That's an upstart — I mean, it's makin' a move anyway.

(TOBY *bends down and they soul-kiss, long and sexy, in this peculiar position.* MARY *keeps smoothing down her beehive hair-do. The others half watch, stirring uncomfortably.*)

STELLA: Fine, right, up-standin' kids.

DELLA: Up-standin' kiss. Tongue-kiss. Della-catessen.

ROMEO: Up-standin' kicks. Tongue-kicks: — Words; no action.

TOBY: Yer quite a gal, Mary, too bad yer so short.

MARY: Well, I ain't growed up yet. So.

DELLA: (*Trying to change the subject, trying to get involved.*) Where ya been, Mary Lamb, sista to Charlie Lamb?

MARY: Jist come from a boondock, Dell. Rode out in Charlie's damn one-cylinder cramped jalopy. Five 'n fifty kids layin' around in the damp sand. Five 'n fifty kids swillin' beer out in the desert. Kids' stuff.

TOBY: Lookin' fer some growed-up fun, eh, Mary?

MARY: Lookin' fer anything, Toby, anything, I'm hair to heel bored.

TOBY: Jist about anything, eh? Try Pickup-Palace?

MARY: Yeah, it's a come-down. Hey, why don't ya come down?

DELLA: Down . . .

STELLA: Down . . .

TOBY: Oh, no, not me, I'm always high, on a par with the star the angels set upon. Try the pizzeria parlors?

STELLA: Try the open air the-a-ters?

DELLA: Try the malted milk drive-ins?

ROMEO: (*Sudden enthusiasm.*) The birds pulls up to us in the malted milk drive-ins, they checks out our car, they check to see who's out every evening.

MARY: If the boys look bitchin', we pull up next to them in our cramped ramshackle jalopy, roll down the window 'n yell: "Hey you studs got a dollar for gas?"

ROMEO: Then we slip the birds a bill. Nothin' to do.

MARY: So the studs slips us a buck; and we let 'em take us to Cookie's for a Coke.

ROMEO: . . . Some of us kids got problems. Sad problems.

TOBY: Sad, deep, intricate, unravelable problems. The mirrors of my eyes. These are my people.

STELLA: The steeples of our churches are . . . lovely, lonely things.

DELLA: Oh yeah. I think churches are . . . beautiful. Specially when yer first walkin' into them.

TOBY: (*On a sudden upbeat.*) But me, myself, Toby High, I'm in the chips! I got bread — bagloads a bread from my folks the jokes. I got a car, right? — a *groovey* car. And a wardrobe would turn Elvis green with envy. And I'm willin', jist killin', to spend my greens, spend rolled-up wads of it —

MARY: On anyone that'll listen to him.

ROMEO: Jist so long as ya listen to Toby.

TOBY: Y'all better be listening to me. My words could move masses — turn, like Joseph Smith, the tide of Western history.

DELLA: Yup, that's how the West got won.

TOBY: The Mormon West. Someday, babies, someday soon I'm gonna be heard.

STELLA: He's a bird, he's a high bird, he's a bird dog.

DELLA: Oh, yes, real town fer pets this is: birds, dogs, black cats . . .

TOBY: 'N I got a pad all my own . . .

STELLA: Furnished Hollywood style . . .

DELLA: Potted palms 'n zebra rugs . . .

ROMEO: Iron decanters 'n Arabian veils . . .

MARY: Throws parties at his pad, Toby does. Interminable parties.

TOBY: Like to party, Mary?

ROMEO: Like to party, Mary?

MARY: Toby's got impeccable manners.

ROMEO: Does swashbuckler things.

MARY: Bows, kisses yer hand as well as yer tongue. He's always anxious to
help out a friend, do in a foe.

STELLA: Went up to the hospital to see her when she had the chicken pox.

MARY: Dribbled all over the sheets, he did.

TOBY: Cute nurses in the hospital. Nurses know a lot about life, about death.

ROMEO: 'Bout life, 'bout death. Gee, nothin' to do in this town. Bored, baby,
bored, anxious.

TOBY: Notice somethin' funny about people, funny-peculiar: everybody ya
meet seems a wee bitty bit nervous, a little afraid, jist a little afraid . . .

STELLA: Little afraid, everybody's jist a little afraid.

DELLA: Nervous. Anxious, ya might say.

ROMEO: Yeah, ya might say anxious.

TOBY: My people.

MARY: Toby's more mature than most of our set. Got hair on his back.

STELLA: He's also older than you kids. He's in his twenties.

TOBY: I'm twenty-five years old, look twenty-six, and feel forty.

MARY: He *feels* like a man pushing forty.

DELLA: Pushing!

ROMEO: And if he wears make-up — well, Dell, at least he's different.

MARY: Yeah, Toby's different. Ya couldn't get more different. I mean, start-
in' with jist his git-up. 'N the way he gits it up. I'll go to Cookie's fer a
Coke with anybody jist so long, as long as he's different.

TOBY: You'll go further than Cookie's.

MARY: Yeah, I'll go far.

DELLA: I think Toby's a creep.

MARY: He is a creep. But to us kids, bored, lonely 'n lost, he's a kind of hero.
A hero creep. To the ne'er-do, Dell, the good time Charlie Lamb, the
delinquent, the dropout, the drop in, the dead, the chick with the Mary
Antoinette hair-do . . .

ROMEO: . . . the cats with acne and long, awkward, lanky legs . . .

MARY: . . . he's a creep hero.

TOBY: A hero sandwich to you, babe, you swallow it!

DELLA: Anxious, everybody's anxious. 'N a little overwrought, Tob.

TOBY: Creep?? That's what people say about somebody who's more stagey,
who's more dramatic, who's more Byronic, who's more intriguing than
they are.

DELLA: Trash, well done.

TOBY: Yeah, trash well done. People always say that about something they love, and can't understand their love for.

STELLA: *I'm* bored now.

DELLA: Ditto. And annoyed. Gettin' restless jist sittin' here. (*To* TOBY.) Plain to hear you ain't got nothin' new to say tonight.

STELLA: Don't wanna mis ma show now, favorite TV show of all, jist about ma favorite. "Dorian Grey, or the Psychological Face Lift." On every weekday night jist about now . . .

ROMEO: (*To* TOBY.) Hey! Loud mouth, doncha ever get bored sayin' the same ol' brainless things every night? The same ol' lies? Have a heart.

TOBY: Nothin' new to say tonight?! brainless things?! same ol' lies?!

ROMEO: Aw, Toby, have a heart.

TOBY: Heartless to those who are small of heart; brainless to those who have no brains; a lie to them who've never heard a truth — 'n jist the same ol' things to —

ROMEO: It's the same ol' things to us _____. (*Using the actor's real name.*) After all . . .

TOBY: Listen, Romeo, do me a favor, will you? 'n hand me that rock like a good rock.

ROMEO: (*Going back and picking up a huge rock.*) Rock of ages . . . (*Carrying it with some difficulty to* TOBY's *chair.*) What a weight to bear. Rock of ages . . .

TOBY: (*Taking the rock, weighing it, seeming to find it serviceable.*) Stock of piles. Hero Creep.

ROMEO: Wanna stand on it, do ya, Toby? So's ya won't feel so low down 'n out at the heels?

TOBY: (*Calmly.*) Not exactly, Romeo, not exactly . . . Wanna do me a favor encore? Bring Mary over here.

ROMEO: We gonna party, maybe the three of us, huh, Boss?

DELLA: We're gonna have a cast party after the show. For all of us.

ROMEO: Oh, Mary, wanna come with me fer a space, like a sweet bird, like a sweet little winged thing.

MARY: Got a buck for gas?

ROMEO: Er, sure, anything, Mary.

MARY: My achin' back you do!

TOBY: My achin' foot. My bow-legs. My itchin' fingers. My weighted palms . . .

MARY: Well, er, first I gotta ask my mama if it's O.K.

STELLA: It's O.K., Mary, you can go with Romeo.

MARY: (*Anxious.*) Ya sure, ma, ya sure I can go with Romeo?

STELLA: Of course, I'm sure, dear. Why wouldn't I —

MARY: But ma —

STELLA: Don't be botherin' me now — m' show's on. Go with the boy.

MARY: But mama, I'm afraid! What time should I be back?

STELLA: Silly, child, what's there to be afraid of? I can't pay no tension if you keep botherin' me like this. Mary —

MARY: Mama, please! please!

STELLA: Hush, child, hush . . . go with the boy.

ROMEO: Come on, Mary.

STELLA: Good-bye, Mary . . . Such a nice quiet town. Very quiet. Little too quiet at night . . . bye, Mary.

TOBY: Mary Lamb.

MARY: Lamb? — Ya like my Mary Antoinette hair-do?

ROMEO: Will do.

TOBY: Engineer her over here, Romeo, where I can reach . . . Hold her hands behind her back, will you . . .

ROMEO: Like this?

TOBY: Will do. Er, move her over a little inch more. Fine.

(ROMEO *holds* MARY's *arms helplessly behind her back, imprisoning her directly under* TOBY. TOBY *lifts the rock and brings it down cruelly on her head. Again and again. The women are looking the other way, staring into the tube of the audience; neither notices a thing, each is as blank as the dummies.* MARY *drops lifeless to the floor.*)

TOBY: (*Calmly.*) Wanna get a shovel, Romeo, 'n bury the broad behind my chair, like a nice boy?

ROMEO: Yer kinda extreme, ain't ya, Toby?

TOBY: Romeo act good like a sidekick should.

ROMEO: What kinda kicks is this? I was with ya when —

TOBY: Are you with me?? You are with me. Yer as much a part of this as I am. Yer as much a part of this as Mary's mother.

STELLA: Quiet town. Real quiet town. Been real quiet since Mary run away . . .

(ROMEO *drags the body behind* TOBY's *chair and we can hear the evil sound of shoveling.*)

Sometimes, now and again, I think of my little girl, my little girl who run away . . . wonder where she is, Mary, where are you, little girl, late at night, middle of the night, Mary, Mary? — Is that you? Is that you, Mary? Keep, thinkin' I hear Mary comin' up the front steps, keep thinkin' keep thinkin' . . . guess I jist think too much these days, think too much at night, but, ah, the night is lonely since my little girl run away. I had such plans for her. You shoulda seen the graduation dress I had picked out for my little girl, pretty thing it was, with flower . . . with a bright little flower emblem, you know the kind, a flower paisley design, a green center with a thin red border running around in a . . . in a . . . yes . . . You know the kind . . . had nice buttons, simple buttons, sham pearl they was I think . . . in a . . . I used to love pearl when I was a kid . . . always dreamt of having a graduation dress with pearl buttons when I was a kid . . . Course, we couldn't afford real pearl buttons for Mary, wouldn't have been practical anyhow, you know how kids are, always pullin' a but-

ton, gettin' it caught in somethin' and then before ya know it, pop, and
it's lost, gone, gone forever, lost, jist like that ... nothin' easier, nothin'
easier than losin' a button on a dress, pearl button or what have ya ...
pearl buttons get lost easy as plain ones, sure they do, ask anyone, anyone
knows that, why any fool knows that ... Quiet town, real quiet around
here. Don't hear a sound. Not a sound. Nary a sound. Hard to hear.
Hard to hear things around here, hard to hear a sound. Course, I'd be
complainin' if there *was* noise, somebody'd be complainin' if there was
noise, still, ya know, it's not bad to hear a, a little sound once and again,
now and then, keeps, gets lonely ... sorta lonely without even a little, little ... little? ... small? ... my baby ...hmmmmmmmmmm ... Mary?
That you, Mary?

(RITA, *a dark-haired beauty, emerges from the shadows upstage and crosses
very slowly toward the vortex behind* TOBY. DELLA *rises with the cloak in
hand and moves toward her.*)

DELLA: Rita? Is that you, Rita?

(RITA *crosses behind the vortex and* MAY *emerges from its other side, a tall
blonde carrying books.* ROMEO *stares at her, enthralled;* TOBY *has returned
to swinging the yo-yo like a slow, ominous pendulum.*)

STELLA: No, that ain't Mary: that's the neighbor's girl, May.
MAY: I have a premonition that when I come back, and am justly reincar-
    nated, it'll be as a cat.
DELLA: Honey, I coulda sworn ya *was* reincarnated, but as May, not a cat.
ROMEO: Ya smell good, May, ya wearin' perfume?
MAY: No, silly, it's just me. I don't fool with perfume.
TOBY: Romeo's a lover boy. Didn't think we call him Romeo fer nothin', did
    ya?
MAY: Tomorrow's a big day for me. Big exam tomorrow morning, impor-
    tant. Gotta be up a step ahead of dawn.
DELLA: May's a better than average student. She takes school seriously. Sweet
    girl. Everybody likes her.
ROMEO: I like her.
TOBY: I had her.
ROMEO: Don't say that, Toby, don't say that if ya don't mean it.
TOBY: How do ya know I don't mean it? How do ya know I didn't have her?
    Sure, I had her.
MAY: Sure I have a good time in school. Why not? I plan on goin' ahead to
    college as well. They say that archaeologists are just underpaid publicity
    agents for dead royalty, but I'd like to be an archaeologist anyhow, I'd en-
    joy that.
TOBY: I enjoyed her.
MAY: I dig around a lot in the desert outside of town —
TOBY: Hope she doesn't dig around too close to me.
MAY: It's absorbing. Fossils, tyrant-osaurs, ferns 'n all. I want to work in a

museum like Margaret made, a block-long "C" shaped museum like the ones they got in New York.

DELLA: (*To audience.*) New York's quite a place, babies! all seven nights of the week.

MAY: Once I visited New York with my parents during Easter recess it was fantastic. The whole Easter week, fantastic week!

ROMEO: Ya smell sweet, May, yer like a sunflower what counteth the steps a the sun.

MAY: I'm sensitive, too: I can handle a lot of romantic novels: — Dumas, Bronte, the Brontes, Charles Lamb, and Sir Walter Scott, Hot Shot, and Walpole 'n them.

TOBY: And "My Secret Life" and "Fanny Hill" and "The Child's Traveller's Companion."

MARY: And Ladies' Home Colonel, Woman's Night, and the diary of chambermaids.

STELLA: And chamber music, I love chamber music, what do you think about chamber music — Romeo, I'm talkin' to you!

ROMEO: (*Absorbed in* MAY, *dancing.*)
WHILE WALKING THROUGH THE PARK ONE DAY
IN THE MERRY, MERRY MONTH A MAY —

STELLA: I loved them novels when I was a girl, used to sit up all night in bed a-readin' them. Nothin' like a good book late at night . . . May nights, too . . .

MAY: And I take scary walks through the park of the Utah desert at night, the May night . . . Most marvelous month of the week, er, year, May is.

TOBY: Didn't think we call her May fer nothin', did ya?

DELLA: (*To audience.*) Lemme save ya time, folks, she could go on like this about herself all night: — May suffers from melancholia —

MAY: They call it adolescent melancholia —

DELLA: She thinks about death, suicide, outer space, empty desert air and the stairway to the stars, and hopes to die real soon and be reincarnated as a cat.

MAY: People around here don't seem to know what I mean when I express that premonition. Cats are — And desert cats. Man, desert cats! Mountain lions. — There's a lot to be said for them.

TOBY: Sure there is, May, lots to say fer cats — swingin' 'em. Original. I want to be original.

ROMEO: You *are* the original, Toby. You sure are the original.

DELLA: No, he ain't, Romeo.

STELLA: Nearly, but not quite.

TOBY: Not quite, no. But that's what I'm workin' fer. To be original, Toby Original . . .

DELLA: . . . first . . .

STELLA: . . . the starter . . .

TOBY: . . . the coxswain, fugleman, the cocksman — preferable one of a kind!

DELLA: Our kids is ambitious.

STELLA: Because us elders sets the good example.

TOBY: That is true. We abide by the example our elders sets.

MAY: *I* tried to teach my parents the Monkey. I tried relating to them.

ROMEO: She is related to them. What was it like when you had her, Toby?

TOBY: Same as any other crevice, same as any other burrow.

MAY: Indeed!

ROMEO: Gee, she's intelligent. So pure. 'N sensitive. — Everyone says she's sensitive.

MAY: Everyone says I'm sensitive.

TOBY: Yeah, she *is* sensitive. She bathes herself at night, slipping her alabastard body into the sunflower oil of her oil bath — the hot water turns her sensitive skin a slightly painful pink. And she washes her hair, her long, straight, yella hair . . .

ROMEO: What do you think about Toby, May?

MAY: He's a creep; he makes me feel itchy; but he can be gentle — I mean — I —

ROMEO: What do you think about me?

MAY: Who thinks about you.

ROMEO: Aw, come one. Tell me. Please?

MAY: You're weird, Romeo, everybody knows that. Every single body in town. They say you had some kinda affliction when you were little that scabbed up yer whole body, scabbed it up like a Grunewald paintin' a Christ 'n turned ya inta a Quasimodo a least, a half-way thing between human 'n animal, between heaven 'n earth, 'n that to stop ya from scratchin' the accursèd pocks the doctor had to tie mittens to yer hands, mittens tied to yer hands the livelong day 'n at night they had to tie you to yer bed or else ya would had scratched yerself till ya bled to death in yer tormented sleep. Eech!

ROMEO: Don't that make ya feel sorry fer me?

MAY: You nuts? Why, that's like being a leper. Should *I* love a leper?

TOBY: Ya oughta, May.

MAY: Why oughta I? I can't even figger out what the symbol of his scabs is supposed to be.

STELLA: I think they're in the real life story that they based this here play on.

DELLA: That's right. It's foolish to look fer symbols.

MAY: (*Unenthused.*) Really?

ROMEO: (*Sitting beside* MAY.) Please, Maytime, date me. Jist once. Huh? We could go to the pizzerina.

MAY: (*Sudden enthusiasm.*) Which one? (*Suddenly turned off.*) Oh, besides, ya gimme the crawls. They say yer so conditioned that even now ya have to put on them mittens 'n be tied to yer bed in order to sleep each night. Think I'd be caught dead with someone like that? What if ya got sleepy? I'd have to tie ya up.

ROMEO: Don't make fun a me, May. Bein' tied up by you would be a pleasure, it would be a dream-fulfitment.

MAY: I'll bet. Beat it, buster, you bug me. They say you beat it in yer mitten.

I'm sensitive.

ROMEO: That's what I thought them mittens was for.

TOBY: (*Laughing.*) You scratch her the wrong way, Rom. You lack grace — the state of Grace.

ROMEO: Maytime, how come ya think so much about suicide? 'N about killin' yarself?

MAY: Gets me attention. Talk like that snaps people to attention.

STELLA: 'Nough tension around here to keep a cat "asleepen all the nyght with open eye."

ROMEO: But don'tcha wanna live a long time to grow up 'n work in that there museum with all them dinahshores?

MAY: Ya ever think about Mary Lamb, Rom, sista to Charlie Lamb? She killed her mother. Knifed her. Knifed her in the night. What a way to relate to your parents.

TOBY: Got results.

MAY: Yeah, they locked her up. In the upstairs bedroom I think, all her life. Charlie took care of her. Got results. — How would ya like to lock me up in my bedroom, Romeo? 'N would ya like to tie me up, tie me up to my bed at night?

ROMEO: Why? ya got them scabs too?

MAY: What a dud! What a insensitive well-behaved dud! Must be somethin' wrong with his kidney or liver to make him so well-behaved. — I mean, *you* are right, Rom. Maybe yer totem's in the wrong place.

ROMEO: Meanin', May, you may need me one day, huh?

MAY: (*Exhausted.*) I may. I may . . .

TOBY: Aye, May. You may. One day. But I rather think not.

ROMEO: Why would you rather not think that, Rom, er, Toby?

TOBY: Cause May's stuck on me. I kin levitate durin' a lay, big bull, treat a chick to that jist once 'n she's spoiled, anythin' less ain't gonna satisfy.

ROMEO: (*Standing, angry.*) How do you mean?

TOBY: I mean I kin straddle a gal —

ROMEO: Straddle a gal, huh? I bet you could you bow-legged, black-headed woodpecker! Why, a pig could run between yo' legs without touchin' the sides 'n —

TOBY: Guys bigga bully you and you bully guys littler: that's dated, man, scram, I mean outta mah May afore I stamp on yo' head 'n leave mah imprint fer archaeologists t' come!

ROMEO: Don't threaten, Toby, remember what I got on you!

TOBY: What, buster scab, what? Who'd believe it? Who'd care? Who'd dare to care?

ROMEO: That's a dumb thing to say!

TOBY: Is it? Nobody cares, man, nobody downstage cares what the hell anybody upstage does. You could do Gog 'n Magog's business up here against the vortex and the whole home-bound audience would be bound to go home all the same. The same. The same. The same. Nobody looks to listen, nobody keeps the watch, nobody patrols the soul, and ain't

nobody, nobody double cares. I'd do anything to get a rise, to goose the
squatter rights to attention at my wrong. I've already done it —
everything. The worst. The absolute worst, right? And who cares? And
who wing semicircle over to wing cares? Who knows? Who looks? Who
books me at the station for my action?

ROMEO: (*Carried away.*) Speak to yer people, Toby!

TOBY: (*Shouting to* STELLA, DELLA, MAY, THE MUSICIANS, *etc.*) Listen, you
people out there!!!!! I killed somebody! I killed a girl! I killed Mary! —
That's Mary! Mary! I killed her!! Listen to me, look at me, turn around
and look at me, won't you! Won't somebody? (*Screaming.*) Hey, hey,
help!!!!! Oh! Take stock in what I say!

(*No one turns.* STELLA *files her nails,* DELLA *reaches for her knitting,* MAY
flips through her books.)

DELLA: There's that talk about them stock piles again, keep bringin' up
them stock piles all the time. (*Picking up her knitting.*) Won't be long
now afore I finish this here sweater. Gonna have it jist the right fit fer ma
weddin' girl. Cause she's the sweater girl. Name's Rita . . . or Lana?
Lana.

MAY: Yes, her name is Rita. Exotic dark-haired girl. But is she your daughter, Della . . . (*With blatant malice.*) . . . or jist one a yer relative slips? I
thought —

DELLA: Stella, didja know my brother was one a them pilots that flew over
Hero-shoe-ma and Nugisaki, Teriyaki, whatever ya call them places, I
forget names easy now . . . 'n dropped . . . they dropped . . . he . . . a, he
was one a them what dropped . . .

STELLA: Yer brother was shot down over Japan wasn't he, Della?

DELLA: Yeah. He took off his shoes as soon as he knew the plane was goin' to
crash. The floors of heaven are made of sandal wood. They who would
walk there must go so on their soles.

STELLA: We was all right fond a yer brother. A good boy.

DELLA: Never went to them meetin's to vote on how much to put up fer his
memory . . .

STELLA: The stone's right pretty, real work a art it is. 'N them wreaths every
August — don't ya —

DELLA: I don't give a damn to see what it looks like. I never did see it. Never
want to, not that there stone, not anythin' around it, not anythin' near it,
not anythin' . . . not anythin' . . .

MAY: I wish they woulda cut out some of her long speeches, ya know?

DELLA: Ya know ya got a pretty big mouth for a bitch who can't even field a
line, girlie.

MAY: Young enough to still learn, though, which is more than I can say for
some sentimental old bitties I know.

DELLA: Sentimentality is protesting the putting of a monkey into a rocket
shot to the moons of our misbehavior, honey, don't you ever forget that,
and with the same breath yeasaying the annihilation of Injins, Amerinds,

Blacks, Wetbacks, Yellow —

MAY: (*Taking out a cigarette; using actress' real name.*) Miss _____, ya got a match?

DELLA: (*Icy pause.*) Yes. My husband.

TOBY: Husbandry 'n hope have held me in the chorus you all comprise for long enough! Why should I account for any of yer lives who have cut me out of that collective understanding keeps you sitting in yer seats?

BALLADEER: (*Interrupting* TOBY *with a hill-billy type ballad.*)

"WHY DON'T YOU SING US THE REST OF YOUR SONG?"
    THE SINGER COMPLAINED TO HIS HEART.
HIS HOT HEART REPLIED: "I COULD EASY HAVE LIED
    AND SUNG ON WELL AFTER MY START,

"BUT THE SIMPLE TRUTH IS MY SONG'S FIRST NOTE
    FINDS LISTENERS THEN OR NEVER
AND WHO HASN'T HEARD MY SONG'S FIRST WORD
    TO MY WHOLE SONG'S DEAF FOREVER.

"SO LOOK TO TRANSCEND FROM YOUR URGE TO DEPEND,
    O SINGER, LOOK TO TRANSCEND:
FOR HAVING MADE LISTENERS ONCE YOUR NEED
    EXPECT SINGING FOREVER TO END.

    "EXPECT SINGING FOREVER TO END
    OR, SINGER, LOOK TO TRANSCEND . . . "

TOBY: Hate to get carried away that way. Inexcusable outbursts from a guy what kin look to transcend.

DELLA: Wonder what kinda transcendin' he means?

STELLA: Some folks always gotta be lookin' around to change things. Oughta let hell be.

MAY: (*Her bid for exclusive audience attention having finally exhausted itself, examining and taking in fully her fellow actors for the first time.*) Ya know, things are pretty weird around here, you people are jumpier than a cat, and that's exactly what makes me feel like I'm coming back as a cat.

TOBY: Good thing ya got plans to come back, May.

ROMEO: Whatcha mean, Toby?

TOBY: You thick or something'? Whatcha think Ah mean by sayin' good thing she's comin' back? Obviously, because she's goin' first. May got plans fer comin' back 'n Ah got plans fer May's goin' away.

DELLA: How pinpointed his eyes is when he says that!

TOBY: Wonder how she sees that, facin' so squarely downstage as she is. Hey, Dell —

STELLA: Pinpoint eyes, piercin' eyes, looks right through ya. Seems to be seein', seems to be searchin' through the secrets of yer cookie jar. Beautiful eyes. Deep set they are, very blue. Ocean blue. Wish I was by the ocean, wish this town was by the ocean, seems things wouldn't seem so bad then, not so bad at all if we was by the ocean. Miama maybe.

ROMEO: (*His overwhelming boredom giving vent to song.*)
  THE MOON OVER MIAMA BEACH
  AIN'T BRIGHT ENOUGH TO REALLY REACH;
  WHAT WISDOM IT COULD HAVE TO TEACH
  IF THE MOON WERE NOT THE EARTH'S LIGHT LEECH!

MAY: And he sings too!

DELLA: What a bargain.

TOBY: Lightless waves crashin' the beach, spittle ridin' the brackish breakers 'n sprayin' the landy shore. More 'n more. Washes everythin' clean, white-washes. Not like here in the desert, Dell, Stell: things preserve here in the desert, don't budge, stay stuck up right where ya bury them; don't even have to bury merry them: — nobody'll be to see— be by to see, *be* to see . . . no one stare to care, even care to stare for a second . . . second girl . . .

STELLA: Really pushes, don't he? 'n fer nothin'.

DELLA: Guess he's jist conscientious.

MAY: (*Stirring.*) I sense a strange conspiracy in the desert air—a room for doom in all things called, a calling, it's my calling in life . . .

TOBY: (*Reaching for the rock; singing.*)
  "WHEN I'M CALLING YOU-OO-OO-OO, OO-OO-OO
  TANGOING TAKES TWO-OO-OO-OO, OO-OO-OO..."

MAY: The windy whisper of the saguaro and cholla slipping over the stated line inta Colorada as ever woman for her demon-lover wailed . . .

(MAY *begins to wander toward the desert upstage. She moves voluptuously beneath the line of the girder, comes dangerously close to* TOBY. TOBY *raises the heavy rock in his hands as* MAY *slips about him. The others tense up with a horror they are unable to feel or hear accurately and, therefore, express themselves. They become riveted to their chairs with ever-mounting inarticulate anxiety and guilt.*)

ROMEO: May, hey, May, May hey, where ya goin'?

TOBY: Here, I'm here, my moving backward demented beauty . . .

STELLA: What's she wanderin' around out there on the desert fer?

DELLA: She must have wanderlust, wanderlust I call it . . .

ROMEO: May, ya wanna sausage sandwich, fried onions 'n peppas, let's get somethin' to eat, May, May, hey . . .

TOBY: My wife your life . . .

STELLA: May is maddening in the Utah desert: other places, other Mays have rigorous riots of violets to boast, this state has only the steady, hiatusless evergreen of the neurotically water-hoarding cactii to—

DELLA: Time was a body could detect the difference in the seasons here. But now I get confused, it's much on a May-December affair, time rushes and returns, autumn miscengenates with spring and winter abbreviates the vaguely sprawling limits of the central summer mon—

STELLA: Where is Ray, where the hell is that woman? Doesn't she give a hoot in the dell about her daughter? Shoot! Ray, Ray, ya shoppin' on Main, shootin' fer jackrabbits, a-gamblin' at cards? Deal yerself out this dealin', Ray! ah, Ray!!

MAY: Wonder what blocks the nothing of night? — like a giant opuntia spanning the stretch twixt heaven 'n earth — (*She is standing directly under* TOBY, *touching him and trying to reach around him and beyond him into the space being drawn up into the vortex.*) O blissful dawning!

TOBY: One gambol more my cat, paw me now and leap to heights!

MAY: (*Taking a step back.*) What is it seems to alter now I'm near, alter form as the I of cat to something other, something not —

ROMEO: (*Grabbing a large bouquet of sunflowers.*) May, I got a present for ya — wanna see it? Wanna? Here! Here, I got —

MAY: Romeo?

ROMEO: (*Rushing across the stage at her.*) I got some —

MAY: Whatcha got?(*Stiffening into a near paralysis as* ROMEO *shoves the bouquet up into her face.*) Sunflowers?!!

TOBY: (*Hysterical.*) Romeo, you scum!!!

(ROMEO *grabs* MAY; *she struggles with him as the rock hovers back and forth over her head, crying out in fear and confusion and pulling on* ROMEO's *"fashionable" suspenders. The suspenders snap and* ROMEO's *trousers fall to the floor.*)

MAY: (*Starting back.*) What's that??

(TOBY *smashes the rock down into the empty space.*)

ROMEO: (*Hesitantly; humiliated.*) A present? . . .

MAY: Idiot! Let me go! I'll tell my moth —

(*As both turn to look down at the rock,* MAY'S *mother,* RAY, *suddenly appears in the dark upstage.*)

RAY: May, child, where are you? I told you never to go out!

(ROMEO *lunges at* MAY, *pulling her to the ground; he tries to cover her, awkwardly entangled, as he is, in his trousers.*)

ROMEO: Be still will ya, don't make a sound.

MAY: Get yer scabbed paws off me —

STRIPPER: (*Entering behind* RAY.) Toby, child, where are you?

ROMEO: Lay still! Ya jist can't go runnin' around gettin' guys all horny 'n all 'n think nothin's gonna hap — ya awmost got killed by —

(ROMEO *and* MAY *freeze as the* STRIPPER *comes slowly downstage.*)

TOBY: I eat mostly outta cans, ma, when yer away. Don't even bother to heat 'em up eat everythin' cold, chili 'n soup 'n such.

STRIPPER: That's bad, Toby, growin' boy oughta get somethin' warm in his tummy. That cold stuffs ain't a-gonna do ya much good.

TOBY: (*Filling in his anger vein with a purple crayon.*) Bothers ya, does it, ma, that the level a ma eatin's hit rock bottom?

STRIPPER: Sure it does, son. Bothers me a whole lot. Whatcha wanna go 'n give extra care to yer workin' ma fer?

TOBY: Git booked for any action in Denver lately?

STRIPPER: Had one or two dates up there. Why?

TOBY: See paw?

STRIPPER: Now, son, I don't play that side a town. Class stuff, club dates, that's what I get.

TOBY: See paw?

STRIPPER: I don't —

TOBY: See paw? see paw?? see paw???!

STRIPPER: Now you go ahead 'n keep that kinda questionin' up 'n I ain't gonna come about here no more.

TOBY: What makes mah paw come about?

STRIPPER: Paws jist don't come about. They're what we makes 'em.

TOBY: But maws is different, right?

STRIPPER: That's right, son. Maws makes.

TOBY: Ya make a lotta men on the road, ma, between yer club dates, that is? Y'all fool around a lot?

STRIPPER: My, but you was a teeny stranger in the manger when you come. Never did see a wee crumb like that afore. Ya come afore yer time, a whole month, maybe two. Hard time I had Caesarean. Doc thought ya wouldn't make it thru that night, let alone that whole long cold winter. Winter's no much fun in Denver fer them what's layin' in. It's a pretty city, though, the downtown's like the downtown nowhere else, all neat 'n compact 'n clean. 'N the residential part, oh most a Denver *is* residential, runs out in straight avenues away from that downtown which I say is very perfect, a very model kinda place itself. Why, it's all as pretty as any pitcher ya seen a Washington! —Didja know I'm a little far sighted? That's right. Always was. Even in school. See real far into most anythin' happens down in our town. So I kin see real far down them avenues runnin' away from the downtown . . .

TOBY: Spend a lotta time on them avenues, huh? Them streets?

STRIPPER: I'm your mother, Toby. You can't hide anything from a mother.

TOBY: Why don't ya jist keep walkin', huh, ma, jist keep walkin'.

STRIPPER: Never had no beat-up customer ever seemed quite so defeated as —

TOBY: Hit the road!!

MAY: (*Breaking the freeze.*) Let me go now! Help! Help! Ma!

STELLA: (*Startled.*) Oh! God, where are our daughters?

DELLA: (*Rushing downstage.*) Give to "Save The Children Fund"! Save Rita! Oh, poor Rita, how is she? This is "Save Our Younger Souls Week"! Give, give, good people!!

TOBY: (*Singing a hymn that grows to Bible-belt fervor.*)

GIVE, GOOD PEOPLE

WHAT THEY THINK THEY WANT:

PERCHED UPON THE STEEPLE

WAITS OBLIVION!

GIVE, GIVE GOOD PEOPLE,
NOW OR NEVER GIVE
TO THOSE NEAR THE STEEPLE
STILL GOT HOPES TO LIVE.

GATHERED 'NEATH THE STEEPLE
EVERY FEARFUL SOUL,
GIVE, GIVE GOOD PEOPLE
SAVE THEM FROM THE TROLL!

RAY: (*Rushing downstage to* MAY.) I'll give you hell! May, a-comin' out here all alone without yer ma! Why, they got them mountain lions out here!

MAY: (*Yanked up by* RAY, *pulling away.*) I ain't afraid of cats, ma, I'm a cat, a cat, a cat!!!

RAY: You ain't alone neither! That freak is with you!

ROMEO: (*Pulling up his trousers.*) Now wait a minute, Mrs. Mixer, I ain't no freak.

RAY: Fiend! Freak-face! Double trouble! Triple trollop pocked-faced acne covered sex maniac! Child molester! Assault! Battery! Bombast! Billygoat! Belligerence! Bellicose!

DELLA: Bad, plain bad!

STELLA: Bad! Buxom! Blossom! Bloom! Boom! Doom! Death!

ROMEO: Yis is got me wrong — yis is a mixin' me up with old toad stool — why, if it wasn't fer me, May would be —

TOBY: (*Singing to a Country rhythm.*)
IF IT WASN'T FER ME
MAY WOULD BE
DUE IN JUNE —
CROON, GARDNER, CROON!
YA'D RUN AROUND DOUBLE
TO BUST MAY'S BUBBLE,
FIND A SUCKER TO PAY
HER ABORTION TROUBLE!

AH'M A TOP A MAH STOOL
BIGGEST TOAD IN THE POOL,
GONNA WAIT IT OUT COOL,
JIST A-SET IN MAH STOOL.
O, LITTLE POOL WITH A BIG TOAD!
LITTLE POOL, YER DONE NEAR OUTGROWED:
AH REPRESENTS QUITE A AWESOME LOAD
FER A LITTLE POOL WITH A BIG TOAD!

(*The* STRIPPER *steps down wildly discarding her housecoat and adding new disorder to the scene; singing, dancing.*)

STRIPPER:
DOES YER ENGINE NEED A BATTERY?

YER ACCELERATOR ACTIVITY?

DOES YER CARBURETOR RUN ON GAS?

AND SLOW YA DOWN AT HYMAN PASS?

IF I JACK YER FENDER UP FOR FREE,

WILL YA SCREW THE RUBBER ON FOR ME?

EASE THE BRAKE, WAX THE BRASS,

SLOW DOWN DRIVIN', SAVE MY—

RAY: I know your type, Romeo Rancor, and you don't have to fib with me! I'm calling the police. The trouble around here is that too many folks let trash like you run around on the loose and have their way.

ROMEO: What way?

TOBY: This is the Way.

RAY: This is your way to waylay innocent girls who don't know the facts of life out here on the prairie!

STELLA: It's pretty scary, it's scary, scary!

STRIPPER: (*Resuming her singing after the rude interruption.*)

YEAH! THE FACTS OF LIFE

ARE MANY AS THE DAYS IN MAY,

MERRY MAY! YEAH! MERRY MAY!

MERRY MAY YOU MAKE YOUR LIFE!

NOW A HUSBAND MAY BE HARD TO HOLD,

A GAL WITH A GUY GOT MORE THAN GOLD:

BUT SOME OUT THERE AIN'T GOT NO WIFE,

AND SO I'LL LIST THE FACTS OF LIFE

IN A STARTLING EXPOSE

IN THE MERRY MONTH OF MAY!

THE MERRY MONTH OF MAY!

THE MERRY MONTH OF MAY, etc., etc.

MAY: (*As the music suddenly aborts.*) Oh, ma, stop embarrassing me. Of course I know the facts of life. I'm fifteen. 15, 14, 36. 'N 98 pounds. 'N 98 on every exam this semester.

ROMEO: Yer daughter needs protection from that—

RAY: You in the shakedown business too, sonny?

STELLA: (*Motivated merely by* ROMEO'S *movement.*) Grab him, grab the pervert, the childless molester, don't let him bound outta sight quick as a quarter moon drops from the night!

TOBY: (*Indicating his dyed streak of hair.*) Hear that, Dell? —quarter moon's minded yet, never quite outta eye shot!

RAY: Hot shot! Let's go, Tonto!

ROMEO: Now jist a second! —hold yer horses.

STELLA: (*Rising to the occasion.*) Make our town safe for democracy!

RAY: Let's war to end all war!

DELLA: Keep the home fire burning! fire up, ladies, fire up!

RAY: Seize the scrubby tumbleweed!

(STELLA, DELLA *and* RAY *rush at* ROMEO *and a chase and struggle ensue; they beat him with their pocketbooks, jab him with their knitting needles, pull his hair, tear at his shirt and kick and punch and pinch him.* ROMEO *tries to elude them but never strikes back. The* STRIPPER *strips and sings during this capture scene, her song being simple enough: she keeps presenting various aspects of her body to the audience and declaiming, "This is the first fact of life! This is the second fact of life!" etc., etc. (she also points out and underlines the injustice of the action), until she reaches the "twentieth fact" at the time that the three women are preparing to drag* ROMEO *upstage "outta sight a the younguns.")*

RAY: (*Ramming her rifle into him.*) Take the jut of my butt!

ROMEO: But—

DELLA: Stick, prick, knit up his ravelled sleeve!

STELLA: Shake, shake, shake! Shake him up, shake him down!

RAY: Deal the dingo double trouble!

DELLA: Douse the dullard duely round!

STELLA: Sound the cry to curfew caution; meet the monster, match for scratch.

DELLA: Have fun, be done, the fun's begun!

ROMEO: I'm done fer!

STELLA: Make more of futile Mormons mum,

DELLA: By hacking *to* his parts his sum,

RAY: And pasting the pieces back with aplomb!

DELLA: Kill, crush, mix, mush!

RAY: Squeeze, tease, please yerself!

STELLA: Fix with tricks, confuse, abuse! Lust and dust, strike, hike the rents, rent his shirt!

ROMEO: Wait, wait! Leave us not get carried away now.

RAY: Carry him away upstage—outta sight a the younguns!

(*The music stops. The* STRIPPER *is pointing to the savage group with her line "This is the thirtieth fact of life!" The women pause in their violence and stare icily at her.*)

TOBY: Stella, Della, Ray, let Romeo go!

STELLA: Never! We're sick a his Mormon immorality!!!

STRIPPER: *This* is the thirty-first fact of life!!

TOBY: But he is innocent. I am the cul—

DELLA: Whadda ya mean innocent? He was caught in flagrant delecto!

STRIPPER: Toby, child, come down from that chai—

TOBY: —Della, let me see your daughter!

DELLA: Wha—

TOBY: Let me see her *now*!!

DELLA: But she ain't come by yet, Tob. You askin' the impossible.

TOBY: Let me see Rita now!!

STRIPPER: Toby, child, come down from that chair!

(The BALLADEER *suddenly emerges into the midst of the crowd, singing a furiously paced hill-billy romp addressed directly to* TOBY.*)*

BALLADEER:

RITA'S A PRETTY GAL 'N SHE'S A-COMIN' SOON,
NOW WE'RE IN THE MONTH A MAY BUT THAT'LL MAKE IT JUNE:
FLOWERS ARE GONNA GROW, THEY GOT BUT NINETY DAYS—
RITA'S A-COMIN' SOON, HALLELUJAH! PRAISE!

TOBY: Let me see Rita *now*!!

(The BALLADEER *turns his tune to a southern gospel of highly refined melody. The crowd responds with a chorus that seems to argue liturgically with the* BALLADEER, *but they finally are won over and all join him for the final stanza.)*

BALLADEER:

WAKE THE PREACHER, TOLL THE BELLS
    RITA'S COMIN' FOR TO WED:
LIKE SWEET LAUGHTER SHE DISPELS
    IMAGINED DREAD.

ALL:

CHOOSE 'N LOSE,
CHOOSE 'N LOSE,
IF LIFE IS HIS,
DEATH IS WHOSE?
CHOOSE 'N LOSE!

BALLADEER:

CALL THE PEOPLE TO THE TEMPLES,
    LEAVE THE SHEAVES TO BIND THEMSELVES,
RITA WILL REPLACE OUR SANDALS
    LIKE GRACE-FULL ELVES.

ALL:

CHOOSE 'N LOSE,
CHOOSE 'N LOSE,
IF LIFE IS HIS,
DEATH IS WHOSE?
CHOOSE 'N LOSE!

BALLADEER:

DRESS AS FOR THE FINAL FAIR
    WHERE WE'LL BRING OUR STOCK TO TEST,
ROUSED TO STAND BY TRUMPETS' BLARE
    BEFORE THE REST.

ALL:

CHOOSE 'N LOSE,
CHOOSE 'N LOSE.
IF LIFE IS HIS,
DEATH IS WHOSE?

CHOOSE 'N LOSE!

(*Leaving the stage through various exits, except for* TOBY.)

LOOK AWAY TO WHERE THAT BRIDGE
    LEAPS ACROSS A LIFE'S RAVINE
TO AN OTHER, OTHER-WORLDLY RIDGE
    WHERE RITA'S SEEN.

———————

Act II

When Act II opens TOBY, *standing on his chair, begins to sing to a Country semi-sacred sound.* STELLA, DELLA, *and* RAY *are back upstage with* ROMEO, *tying him to the chair. In their midst and helping them to tie up* ROMEO *is* ACE, *a personable young man with a typewriter strapped to his back.* MAY *is in the* CROWD *watching the whole procedure with great fascination. Several* MUSICIANS *are on stage.*

TOBY:

> I AM DEATH IN LIFE,
> I AM DEATH, SO GRIM!
> WHEN I TAKE A WIFE
> HER CHANCES ARE THIN!
>
> WHEN I CHOOSE A GAL IN THE GRAVE TO BURY,
> AFTER LEARNING MY CHOICE SHE BECOMES QUITE MERRY!
> YES, I AM THE KILLER OF EVERY GIRL DEAD —
> WANNA COUNT THE NUMBER OF DAUGHTERS YA BRED?

ALL:

> TOBY'S DEATH IN LIFE,
> TOBY'S DEATH, SO GRIM!
> WHEN HE PICKS A WIFE
> HER CHANCES ARE SLIM!

TOBY:

> BUT I AM THE GOOD, AND THE PARENTS THE BAD
> SINCE CHILDREN BROUGHT UP HAVE REALLY BEEN HAD: —
> HENCE I'M SALVATION WHEN EVERY GIRL'S DEAD —
> WANNA STILL HAVE CHILDREN AMID SUCH DREAD?

ACE: (*Almost pontificating.*) Who slurs his song slurs trash. It's a sometime thing, nothing. But he who slurs his act's intent slurs what intends to make this town a unity — and cannot quit until it does.

STELLA: (*To* ACE.) Lemme have that rope, will ya?

ACE: Oh, er, certainly.

RAY: Ain't a one a these brats is up to behavin' like the good St. Theresa Genoacheese instructs. I tell ya, ain't a one a them's different!

ROMEO: But yer wrong, you ladies got me all wrong. I am different. I tell ya, I am different!

TOBY: No, no, *I'm* different!

MAY: I'm sensitive.

RAY: What does it matter? — They's all the same when their pants is hot.

ACE: She speaks fer the house.

STRIPPER: What house? Never worked in a house. Never even had a house.

STELLA: Ladies, ya wanna clean up them Vegas strippers around here.

ACE: Could go harder on yer beds if ya do.

RAY: Don't get cute. We'll attend to the morals problem in good time.

DELLA: Yes, we shall look into these strippers.

TOBY: 'N have a good time doin' i —

ROMEO: Please, hear me out! May is in danger! Grave danger!

STELLA: Not any more now that yer tied up!

ROMEO: Yer mistook! I love her: why should *I* hurt her?

RAY: A course you love her: that's why you attacked her: you love her and you wanted to make love to her! It's love we gotta watch out fer, girls, love that waylays our daughters 'n drags them off inta clumps a sage 'n tumbleweed fer a tumble!

DELLA: The lie of the land.

ACE: How powerfully she grasps that pithy substitute of land for lingo.

STELLA: Della's learned.

RAY: Was brung up in a convent, oughta be.

DELLA: Yeah, I oughta be.

TOBY: Oughta be run outta town with the rest a you guardians a public decency.

STELLA: We done our duty re Romeo as we seen it, right, Ray?

RAY: We are always right, Stella. What do you think, Della?

STRIPPER: Stella, Della, Ray.

DELLA: Let's notify the Department of Health, Education and Welfare, Stella.

RAY: Let's notify a nationally syndicated newspaper, Della. Pleasure or Kiss — or one a them.

STELLA: Let's notify the community bulletin board, Ray. Put it on the air, wake the town and scare the people.

RAY: Yeah, we'll spread it around. We'll spread it around.

TOBY: Mary, May, Maude. Stella, Della, Rayburn.

STRIPPER: And the thirty-second fact of life is that strippers get looked into . . .

ACE: Better beat it fer now, Miss.

RAY: We'll look inta this matter a the strippas 'n she don't!

TOBY: Wait, ma, when'll I see ya?

STRIPPER: Soon, sonny, soon. I'm booked fer a night in our town. (*To* ACE.)
Be worth yer while to be here then. Ya come around here often?
ACE: Well, probably more often from now on.
STRIPPER: (*To* MUSICIANS.) See you boys over in Vegas. Gotta attend to dates
in that vicinity. Bye, Toby, my boy. Nothin' comes easy.
TOBY: That it does.

(STELLA, DELLA, RAY, *and* MAY *take their seats as the* STRIPPER *exits.* ACE
*takes a seat right in the middle of the women, removes his typewriter from
his back, places it on his lap, puts paper into it, and prepares to type.* RAY
hangs onto her rifle and DELLA *takes up her knitting.* STELLA *is restless, she
can't seem to sleep.* MAY *reads Playboy, Screw, Kiss, etc.*)

DELLA: Wonder if Lana's in bed now. Poor Lana, had some kinda paralysis
when she was little.
ACE: Poor Rita.
DELLA: Wonder if Rita's in bed now . . .
STELLA: Had some kinda paralysis when she was little, didn't she, Dell?
MAY: What did ya tie Romeo up that way for, ma?
ACE: Why, May, child, we done it fer Romeo's own good. You know Romeo
can't sleep unless he's tied up spread-eagle to his bed on account a he is
conditioned that way since he was a child and had leprosy and had to be
tied up and restrained from scratchin' hisself durin' the bydee-by hours a
the night, scratchin' all them awful sores, unsightly sores, and we did
want him to catch a bit a bydee-by, he's had a long preventful day,
Romeo has.
RAY: (*To* ACE) Who the hell are you?
ACE: Who the hell am I? Ain't no mere morbid curiosity seeker, I kin tell ya
that much, madam!
DELLA: (*Automatically, without loking at* ACE) He's my son-in-law . . . or fu-
ture son-in-law?
ACE: Future son-in-law.
STELLA: Elaborate.
MAY: (*Bored to the point of suicide.*) Oooooooooo. . .!
ACE: Name's Andrew Ace, reporter, came out here to do a story on that le-
thal gas leak in the stock piles. Six thousand sheep croaked, notice they
never say nothin' 'bout how many people? That was to be my job.
RAY: How absorbing.
ACE: Anyhow, met Rita when I come out here, fell quickly in love, and I will
marry her.
STELLA: Ya really a reporter?
ACE: Is the pope Catlick?
RAY: That's anough about him, now me.
DELLA: Whatcha bag today, Ray?
RAY: (*Standing and lifting up a heavy burlap sack.*) Side from Romeo, git
me this real big she-lion. Right between the—but, ssh, I don't want May
to hear.

TOBY: Hear that, May, yer ol' bag bagged a big cat today. Didja drag it across to the viaduct—(*Pointing to the diagonal girder.*)

RAY: Yup, 'n tossed it on over inta the Red River right side a Romeo—(*She heaves the burlap sack over the girder; it clears the height and comes crashing down on* ROMEO.) *Wake the hell up!* Look at that—a-sleepin' on the job!!

ROMEO: (*Bombarded into wakefulness.*) "Maytime, Maytime, Maytime . . ."

MAY: (*Pulling on* RAY's *sleeve, almost fighting to bring* RAY *back to her chair, fighting to ensure the immobility that will allow the murders to proceed.*) Sssssssh, set ye down, mine lover earned his sleep! Sleep did come on him a just reward much as the Maytime thaw pours on the penitent wintry scrub in patient wait within the plain below.

TOBY: Bellow. Listen to him bellow.

DELLA: Romeo bellows in his sleep for his lady love.

RAY: (*Giving up, sitting down.*) And quiet steals upon the town . . . (*Mumbling to herself.*) need some action around here . . .

STELLA: Toby steals, too. Or so I heard tell. Steals his opportunities from the jaws of stiff competition . . .

RAY: Steals personal keepsakes, tips from barroom counters . . .

MAY: Steals girls' hearts with his deep, meaningful eyes . . .

RAY: Hush, child, do not speak of amorous matter.

TOBY: (*Toying with the hair curler and paper clamp that he has been using to pinch his anger vein.*) Stella, Della, Ray. Mary, May, Maude. Oh, "M 'n M" over "M," I know how to make love a hundred different ways. Mom, I *have* made love a hundred different ways. Everything I do is an act of love, each inch I grow a testimony to my arch triumph. Look, this blackish beauty: —it is huge this purpleblack and beautiful anger vein, isn't it? Why would a man raise such a vein upon his pisser if not for love, in the libel of love, as the label of love, because of it, his wanting it, and this black vein of anger is it, is *love*, furious, unicorn and phallic. The people know it, too. Ah, yes, everyone in and on the edge of town knows it. People on the edge of a town. Verging. Precisely why they claim I'm too short, ill-founded claim, unripe, still verging, that claims I can't tip-toe up enough to bend me down a bunch of grapes of grafted love. Sweet grapes of grafted love. Because the labor in matching my reach, in reaching up to reach my reach is not a labor of love for them. Everything seems easier to them—the jump to conclusions, the sealing of the holy books, manhunts, murder trials, death in a family . . . But I shan't be caught by that, caught short by that, hunted, murdered, tried to a man and put to death. Were I caught short by such as that I had not ever have reached the height I have. And I have reached a height above the groveling mass, the black beauty mass of which I am the solitary priest. So say I my said say and, having said, know everybody knows it.

MAY: Knows what?

TOBY: Knows how a self-made man thru painful thought knows how love may be made in a hundred different ways. Slaying, fer inst —

MAY: The hell! Yer the original Mormon monk. You probably levitate in yer cell you've got so much repressed.

TOBY: Ain't you sweet.

ACE: Sweets to the sweeties, farewell.

STELLA: Farewell, my Mary, farewell.

MAY: He said to the *sweeties* — call Mary a sweetie?

STELLA: Oh, you stir my blood!

ACE: As spring stirs frozen lakes. What an Easter downpour penetrates our unprepared young prairie. Stella, Della, Ray.

MAY: But I get bored even at Toby's pad —

ACE: (*Typing.*) True. She's sick a all that sweet talk —

DELLA: 'n flippin' thru *Playboy* — they call it adolescent melancholia —

MAY: sick a flippin', sick a the flip sides those same ol' Enis Penis records, sick a sippin' beer, beer brewed with clear mountain valley water.

RAY: She oughta be sick considerin' all that sick litracha she devours like it was candy or somethin'. Readin' rots the brain. Specially that chamber-maid crap.

MAY: Oh, ma.

TOBY: I read this novel once, "Hair Today, Gone to Merkin."

ACE: (*Typing.*) 'Bout a chick gets a bright idea 'n commits suicide over this guy.

TOBY: I always dreampt a havin' a chick git the idea 'n commit suicide over me — that would be absolute, that would be proof!

DELLA: Well, gals are slow to that kinda romanticism these days, Toby, sometimes they have to be helped along.

TOBY: I'll help them along. Specially blondes like Maude the frump. That fat frump's my trump card.

MAY: (*Vicious.*) Toby *dyed* Maude's hair blonde. Also dyed Maude's kid sister, Lynn's, hair blonde. Went out 'n got engaged to both a them on the same day.

TOBY: I bought them both diamond engagement rings, fer five bucks each. 'N courted 'em with songs would break any gal's heart. (*Taking the mike, singing to Country sacred music:*)

IF I FOUND A GAL I COULD CALL A REAL GAL,

COULD BE MY DISCIPLE, MY WIFE, 'N MY PAL,

I'D GO OUT IN THE DESERT ON BARE BLISTERED FEET

AND THERE GATHER MANNA FER MY GAL TO EAT.

   I'D RAIN HOLY BREAD FROM THE HEAVENS FOR HER

   LIGHT AS THE HOAR FROST UNDER THE FIR,

   RARE AS THE CORIAND, PRICE BEYOND MONEY,

   WITH A TASTE LIKE WAFERS, MEAD, 'N BEES' HONEY.

IF I KNEW A GAL, JIST ONE PERFECT GAL,

COULD MATCH WHAT I FEEL, 'N LOVE WHAT I SHALL,

I'D GO OUT IN THE DESERT ON TORN, BLEEDING FEET

AND THERE GATHER MANNA FER MY GAL TO EAT.

I'D RAIN HOLY BREAD FROM THE HEAVENS FOR HER
LIGHT AS THE HOAR FROST UNDER THE FIR,
RARE AS THE CORIAND, PRICE BEYOND MONEY,
WITH A TASTE LIKE WAFERS, MEAD, 'N BEES' HONEY.

IF I HAD A GAL, A MADONNA-LIKE GAL,
COULD DRESS IN MY CLOTHES 'N NURSE MY MORALE,
I'D FILL UP AN OMER OF MANNA FOR HER
AND GENERATIONS THAT IN HER STOMACH SHALL STIR.

(MAUDE, *a high school tramp, enters, followed by* LYNN, *her pre-adolescent sister. Both have badly dyed blonde hair.*)

MAUDE: (*Flaunting her ring.*) I think girls are dumb fools who go out with fellas 'n don't git paid for it.

TOBY: Hi ya, Maude. That there's Maude. I'd like to kill her.

LYNN: (*As everyone laughs.*) My big sister Maude once showed at a formal with a bunch a guys all dressed up like beatniks. That's guts. Maude's dreamy. She cuts classes 'n got recommended fer Psychiatric help.

TOBY: Hi ya, Lynn.

LYNN: Hello up there, fiancé. Didja set the date yet?

TOBY: Today, little Lynn, today I think. — I'd dig killin' her, too. Her youth 'n all, it'd have shock value. But I need help, the same in the beginning was with God, the *Word* was with God, and *I*, also, need a particeps criminis: I can't reach them sistas from a Way up here.

MAUDE: You still dribblin' off at the mouth, shrimpo?

TOBY: Are you my gal, Maude?

MAUDE: Natch, Toby, we're engaged, ain't we?

TOBY: Who ya goin' with now, Maude?

MAUDE: Bad Butch.

(BAD BUTCH, *a huge hell's angel type with a lion's head sewn to the back of his jacket, comes bounding in.*)

BUTCH: Mah label's Bad Butch, Big Bad Butch, very big on the strip 'n with the babes. It's mah get-up gets 'em. They's impressed with the motif — this here fierce a face King a the Beasts. Grrroooowwwlllll!!! Heh, heh, heh, heh! Ah am more than a small town figger 'n figger that makes this more 'n a small town. Ah am a symptom a what this country's comin' to. 'N ah think it's comin' to this small town.

ACE: (*Getting up and going to* BUTCH *with a pencil and writing pad in hand.*) Lo, there, son. I really dig yer bikecap 'n maltese cross 'n them holsters with knives stead a pistols.

DELLA: I'm really crazy 'bout them jab-em-in-the-flanks hundred per cent silva spurs on his loafers, m'self.

ACE: Son, I'm tryin' to locate Toby Short. Think ya kin help me out?

BUTCH: Why, Ah'm surprised at you, buckeroo! Would *Ah* know the lo-ca-shun a a unsavory type like Toby Short?

RAY: Would *he* know the lo-ca-shun a a unsavory type like Toby Short?

ACE: Well, would you?

BUTCH: Is a matter a fact Ah would, Ah sure would, Sir Dick.

ACE: Yes?

BUTCH: Folla that there girder what counteth the steps a the sun, git off afore the vortex 'n then carry ya inquisitive self right round under it. After that, he's straight ahead, ya can't miss him.

ACE: (*Exiting*.) Thanks, fella.

TOBY: Thanks, Butch.

RAY: Hey, that there's the way to the dressin' rooms. Toby's out here!

BUTCH: No kiddin'? Ya'd never believe it from the way you ladies behave. Ah coulda sworn he was down in them dressin' rooms. (*Dropping a coin in a wall phone on the girder*.) Hello, operator? Put me in to the Attorney General.

TOBY: What fer?

BUTCH: What fer? Ah got some dope on a creep round here been doin' gals in. Figger thar's quite a *re*ward. No sense lettin' some outsider git it. (*As* TOBY, *with minimum effort, cuts the phone wires*.) Name's — hello, operator? operator??

TOBY: So ya goin' with Bad Butch, eh Maude? Now he could be a help steada a —

MAUDE: Whatcha mean a help? Ain'tcha jealous? Listen here, I don't want ya allowin' me to go out with other goons before or after we're married neither, I want ya to ring me up 'n bring me up records 'n chocolates stuffed with stale jam. I can't stand it when ya ferget 'n I don't take after yer always bein' busy neither. I'm suspicious of you.

TOBY: (*Calculating, both staring at* BUTCH *wrestling with the phone*.) That's groovey, Maude . . . Seen yer shrink lately?

MAUDE: Ain't nobody kin shrink me down to yer size.

STELLA: Toby and Maude were made fer each other.

MAY: He'd have made that maid if maid there was to have made.

MAUDE: Hi, May. Where's Romeo?

MAY: He's tied up at the moment.

DELLA: Is that supposed to be clever?

MAY: Oh, why don't you go back to county-fair chorus lines — or can't you kick anymore?

MAUDE: That there's May. I'd as soon see her dead as anything. Why not?

ROMEO: (*Groaning in his sleep*.) May! May! May's in bad trouble, she's . . . girls gits into . . . trouble . . .

TOBY: True. Maude's a harlot. I suspect she got venereal disease.

STELLA: (*Shocked*.) Why, Toby, I'm shocked! — What makes you think so?

TOBY: Well, is it cancer makes yer zippo look like a Grunewald? Anyhow, I wrote a letter to the Department a Health 'n informed them that Maude was contaminated 'n spreadin' it all around town.

DELLA: Ya done yer duty, son, above 'n beyond the call a a fascist state.

RAY: In his way, Toby *does* set an example.

STELLA: Sure, there *is* some kinda contamination in this town even if it's only syph 'n someone must be a-spreadin' it.

MAUDE: I'd give him syph. I'd give him anything. Why not? He's my man.

TOBY: Maude, kin ya reach Big Butch fer me?

MAUDE: I ain't no messenger service. Reach fer him yerself. Why don'tcha git off that there chair so ya kin reach him yerself?

TOBY: (*Deeply hurt.*) Thanks, Maude. Hey, Lynn —

ROMEO: (*In his sleep.*) May, poor May, look out!

TOBY: Wanna help me out?

LYNN: (*Sympathetic.*) Awww, right a way, romantic Toby. I'll reach Butchy-boy for you. Stay put.

TOBY: Mercies, Lynn, yer a real trooper. And I shall reward you for this.

(LYNN *skips over to* BAD BUTCH, *completely entangled in the phone.*)

BUTCH: (*Lecherous.*) Ya old enough to date now, Lynn?

LYNN: Sure, but I'm a-spoke fer by Toby. 'N he's a-waitin' on ya.

BUTCH: Kin Ah gitcha somethin', Sir Tob?

TOBY: A rope'd go good.

ROMEO: Wanna git me a glass a water, May? Like Esmeralda? 'N while yer at it some suave fer me sores?

BUTCH: (*Attracted by* ROMEO's *moans.*) One rope a-comin' up!

LYNN: (*As* BUTCH *unties a rope binding* ROMEO's *hand.*) It's a goof to go out with other guys while yer engaged. Specially if they're older. 'N big!

BUTCH: Is this hemp to order, Tob? If in knot, I'll —

TOBY: Great, Butch, that'll more'n do. Give it here, will ya?

BUTCH: (*Withholding the rope.*) Straightaway. Whatcha got in mind?

TOBY: I'll ask the questions, babe. Yer ma inferior 'n while ya are I'm still runnin' this outfit 'n this here town, too. Git it?

BUTCH: Little bit too well; but you don't; not the rope at any rate. Ah don't take no stiff uppa lip offa anyone, Tob, not even stiff-on-the-brain you, Tob. Here, Lynn, Ah'm givin' ya 'nougha the rope to — (*Giving the rope to* LYNN.)

TOBY: You don't seem to git the hang of i —

STELLA: (*Agitated, getting up and coming down to the edge of the stage.*) I hired private dicks on this case. No one lays much by it, but the way I've got it figgered out ma little girl has come to foul play, even as you have — come to a foul play. Strickly Inge-fringe. Foul because it breaks your trust, bigots your openness, and on point after point loses its patience with you; is seldom humble and almost never willing to accept its position as the most humiliating feat a group of people could be part of and hope to profit from: placing themselves before an unsuspecting public that is right to have every right not to be lectured to. The implicit assumption in pieces like this is that "our town" is always and necessarily wrong. Well, it jist ain't necessarily so. There's a rightness to things as all things go, and only the small of heart, like certain immature and impotent plays say no.

RAY: Some crust, huh? Anyhow, Stella's privately-hired dicks've been hangin' out around Toby's Hollywood-style furnished pad a-lookin' fer a lead. Once a beer can come flyin' out the window 'n hit one a them in the head. That made 'em suspicious.

BUTCH: While Ah don't know much on it, yer a bit a boilin' oil, Sir Tob, some powerful strange tough guys been upta yer place. They seems to be suspicious.

TOBY: They *are* suspicious. But then why hang out around my place? I'm here.

STELLA: Them dicks'll find somethin', I know they will, they'll find out what happened to ma little girl 'n if she was assaulted first afore it happened. Sheriff claims she jist run away, but I know fer sure that's not sure. The truth lays somewhere else. I have a premonition. I have supper on now. (*Taking her seat.*)

DELLA: Stell's got a premonition 'n she's got every right to it: — makes it more proper to claim her high school aged daughter come by foul play than to admit she jist up 'n run away. And we women in this here town is nothin' if we ain't respectable.

RAY: Well we other women ain't so sure about you. Y'all hallucinate a lot, ya know?

TOBY: Wanna do me a favor, Butch, 'n —

BUTCH: Not if Ah kin do ya dirt with as little Hell's Angel effort!

TOBY: Son of a butch! ya couldn't. Hold old Lynn upta me. That's the minimum effort I kin imagine ya makin'.

BUTCH: Well, why didn't ya behest such request before? Nothin' could give more a a cheap thrill — her tiny jist-breakin' nubile bubs in the champagne cups a mah callused palms —

LYNN: Except hold me lower. My knees!

(BUTCH *sweeps* LYNN *off her feet and, holding her high, offers her to* TOBY. LYNN *has the rope in her hand. The* WOMEN *watch the scene with approval.* MAY *is drinking beer.*)

LYNN: Weeeeee . . . what a ride! I kin fly like a angel.

TOBY: Hello, angel.

LYNN: Hi ya, Toby, didn't know you was a angel, too. I always wondered what the air was like up in the clouds around you'short fellas.

TOBY: And what, Angelica, do you discover it to be analogous to now that you've finally made the flight?

LYNN: Oh, it ain't much different from the air everybody else down in town breathes.

TOBY: (*Reaching, unsuccessfully, for her,* BUTCH *pulling slightly away.*) That's what I want to hear.

LYNN: Ya know, Toby, you ain't so special, even if I did accept yer proposal . . .

TOBY: (*Taking the rope from her hand.*) I know that, Lynn-chin.

RAY: Will ya look at that: — the creep's got a heart a gold.

DELLA: Takes time out to play rope with the little girl from down the street.

STELLA: Plays real nice he does, has a real way with the ladies don't matter what their age.

RAY: Has a good heart that creep. Little girl's no bigger'n he is.

BUTCH: Ah tried to contact the Attorney General 'bout yer idiomsyncratic activities, Tob.

TOBY: (*Fixing the rope around* LYNN's *neck.*) You would, Butch, it's jist like you, babe.

BUTCH: They hung up the phone on me though, Tob.

TOBY: They would, Butch, it's jist like them, babe.

ROMEO: (*Tossing wildly.*) May! Beat it! Beat it outta town! Make yer getaway good!

BUTCH: (*Frightened.*) Ol' Rom! him 'n his idiomsyncratic sleepin' habits: he don't let no one turn in once he's been turned in.

TOBY: (*Garrotting* LYNN.) Lynn-chin gonna have a hung chin.

RAY: (*Still watching.*) There'll be a hung jury over this.

MAY: (*Getting high.*) How's the family, Maude?

MAUDE: (*Eating chocolates.*) Home hangs me up, ya know that, Maude.

MAY: I'm hip, May.

TOBY: (*Conjugating, funereally.*) Mary, May, Maudlin. Stella, Della, Rayburn. From cloud to clod in half the time; no grease, no grime . . . (TOBY *slowly releases* LYNN, *letting her limp body lie in* BUTCH's *arms. The suddenness of her death leaves* BUTCH *incredulous.*)

MAY: I'd look back in hanger if I was you, Maude. I'd turn around 'n look back after my fiancé if I was you. Never could tell but when he'd be flyin' high with other birds. Birds baby-faced, younger, not yet broke in, not yet broke down. Down. Down . . .

MAUDE: Don't need all a yer experience, sista, jist to know howda hang onta a guy.

(ACE, *wearing a reporter's fedora and scratching his head with incomprehension, comes wandering back around the vortex.*)

ACE: Hey, hang on there, you kids — mind if I shoot some questions at ya?

MAUDE: Who're you?

ACE: Andrew Ace, reporter, a outta space reporter, from —

MAUDE: Why don'tcha fly back to outta space! We git any cash fer gittin' grilled?

ACE: It's worth more'n one pizza to ya. Know anythin' about a kid named Toby said to have a black anger vein he developed by standin' on his hands till it showed, then pinchin' it fer several hours a day with a tin curler or clipboard clamp?

RAY: Sure. Toby's anger vein's plain as the fed fedora on yer head. Why, even Toby kin probably spot that there fed fedora ya sport. — Stell, lay ya five to ten Toby can.

STELLA: I ain't the sportin' type.

TOBY: But *I* am: — listen here: (*Singing a hill-billy tune.*)

I'M GONNA PAY FER CRIMES I OUGHT'VE DONE,
GONNA FRY FER WHAT I DIDN'T DO!
   YOU FORCE ME,
   YOU FOLKS ALL FORCE ME!
IF I STOP NOW YOU FOLKS KIN SHUN
ALL THE WORK THAT I'VE BEGUN –
   I'VE JIST BEGUN,
   I'M A DREAMER TOO.

ALL:

   OL' SALT A SALT LAKE CITY
   HE GITS DOWN TO THE NITTY-GRITTY
   HE DON'T WASTE A TEAR A PITY
   EVEN IF THE GAL IS PRETTY:
      NO SALTY TEAR –
      SALT A SALT LAKE CITY!

TOBY:

I'M GONNA PAY FER CRIMES I OUGHT'VE DONE,
GONNA FRY DON'T MATTER WHAT I DO:
   YOU'LL FRY ME,
   O YES, YOU'LL FRY ME!
IF WHAT I WANT'S NOT EASY WON,
ALL THE MORE IT'S GONNA STUN –
   I'VE JIST BEGUN,
   I'M A DREAMER TOO.

ALL:

   OL' SALT A SALT LAKE CITY
   HE GITS DOWN TO THE NITTY-GRITTY
   HE DON'T WASTE A TEAR A PITY
   EVEN IF THE GAL IS PRETTY:
      NO SALTY TEAR –
      SALT A SALT LAKE CITY!

BUTCH: Greetin's, Sir Andrew *Re*port-tage, you has the look a the Inevitable on yer newspaper puss. How goes it with that mass medium up in Big Town, U.S.A.?

ACE: Takes all of a mass medium to deal with a mass murderer, a murderer fer the masses, a chocolate fer their sweet tooth.

MAY: (*Quite high.*) Toby's gonna turn *our* town into Big Town!

STELLA: Turn the eyes 'n ears a the nation on us.

ACE: All you folks is knee-deep in hot water lemme tell ya that right now! Willful withholdin' is called criminal neglect, ya know.

BUTCH: We know, 'n it's yer yella-daily what puts us there.

ACE: I know, 'n it's yer blatant confessional no-holes-barred song what's put me *here*.

TOBY: Put Lynn down.

BUTCH: We're trapped by the Word! Done in afore we even gits a start by a lotta language, Tob!

TOBY: I'm hip.

BUTCH: (*Threatening.*) So don't write nothin' ya hear? Not if ya wanna git outta Utah with yer fed fedora on whatcha'd still wanna call a head!

ACE: Such a thing as freedom a the press, bully, I'll exploit what I want when —

BUTCH: Ah'll folla ya, Ah'll smoke ya out wherever ya go, Sir Andrew, 'n Ah'll cripple yer scribblin' hand sure as Ah'm wearin' Luftwaffe wings!

ACE: Relax! take it easy, no harm intended.

STELLA: Graveyard's cluttered with corpses come there no harm intended.

DELLA: (*Deeply distressed.*) My poor brother, his last letter afore he was shot —

RAY: (*Fed up.*) She gonna start up agin!

ACE: (*To* MAUDE.) Kin I stand ya to a pizza, girlie?

RAY: You been standin' enough! (*Removing* ACE's *fedora and slamming him on the head with her rifle; he falls into a chair.*) Try sittin' a little. Got a rope, Stell?

STELLA: (*Pulling the rope off* LYNN's *neck and helping* RAY *to tie* ACE *to the chair.*) This one a them outside agitaters, eh, Ray?

RAY: Yup! Sheriff'll run him outta town in the mornin'. Upta us to keep him static as the resta us till then.

BUTCH: (*Looking with amazement at the devastation the townswomen are capable of bringing so quickly about.*) Poor agitaters, they really don't do nothin' except use a lotta language.

TOBY: Ya wanna live up to a lotta language used in your behalf . . . somehow ya do . . .

DELLA: Or half of it. And the changes it makes in you. I feel blue.

(*As they all retake their seats the focus comes to rest for a strange moment on* BUTCH *with the body of* LYNN *still in his large arms. After a while he mutters to himself.*)

BUTCH: Ya was such a wee li'l new 'n nubile thing. Nobody'd even laid ya yet.

TOBY: Put her on the floor, Bleedin' Heart. Right here.

BUTCH: (*Placing the body at the foot of* TOBY's *chair*) Whatcha gonna do with her?

TOBY: Nothin'. Jist leave her here, will ya. It looks like she's sleepin'.

BUTCH: Seems like somethin' oughta be done. So young.

TOBY: What fer? Lotta wasted initiative. Got better things to do.

BUTCH: Yeah?

TOBY: Walk her sister over here.

BUTCH: Oh, no, not me! Not me again! Ya can't fool me twice!

TOBY: I'm *squarin'* with ya same as I am with everyone else! Now take that , fat frump —

BUTCH: Never!

TOBY: I really don't need ya that much, Butch. She'll come by herself if it comes to that.

MAUDE: I kin come by myself if it comes to that . . .

TOBY: So ya might as well bring her. It'll give ya a sense a accomplishment.

BUTCH: Watcha mean ya don't need me? I'm yer sidekick, yer side-line in life, yer by-line in the papers, yer doin' all this jist to impress me counta Ah'm the only one kin be aware a it. Then ya kin read yer own sense a accomplishment in Hell's mirror!

TOBY: It is in the nature a the sense a accomplishment to have to read it somewhere. Please, take Maude's hand 'n strollin' her arm 'n arm —

BUTCH: Ah ain't no gigolo!

TOBY: I didn't think ya were. You shouldn't think ya are, either. Ya oughta think a yerself as a escort or a companion a destiny.

DELLA: You oughta think of yourself.

MAY: I think I'd attend to my fiancé if I was —

MAUDE: But you ain't! — Er, think I'll see what my Toby's up to.

RAY: Everybody's thinkin.

BUTCH: (As MAUDE crosses by him.) Hey, Maude, fancy runnin' inta you!

DELLA: Huh! He was expectin' ya.

MAUDE: What fer?

TOBY: Kinda hard to explain.

BUTCH: (Taking her arm in arm.) Yeah, ya wouldn't undastand.

TOBY: Oh, she'll under-stand. Jist might not appreciate it, that's all. Too un-sohphisticated. Takes some body really on top of it to appreciate the senseless.

DELLA: Oh, I think it makes a lotta sense.

MAUDE: Who ya callin' senseless?

TOBY: Nobody whose thickness I couldn't knock a little sense inta. Come on, I'll knock ya up here.

MAUDE: (Stepping over her sister's corpse, TOBY pulling her up on his chair with a single jolt.) What wit.

(ROMEO snaps out of his sleep and discovers his unbound hand. He begins to unite the remaining ropes in wild agitation.)

ROMEO: May, blonde May! Toby's stranglin' her!! Hey, look, the ropes is loose, jist like in a serial.

TOBY: How are ya, sweetie? Yer my favorite, know that don't ya?

MAUDE: Feel kinda even, Toby, even with ya, with a lotta names flashin' thru my head, names you know, a series of names like during a orgasm.

TOBY: I know. A series of names. A string of words. Jist a string of — now, easy, Maude, take it easy 'n this won't take long — (He presses his thumb on her windpipe.)

MAUDE: Take yer time; I got all my life nothin' much else to do in this here town anyway . . .

MAY: I'll say — lessen ya wanna jist keep makin' out.

RAY: Y'all mean like them two? Ya oughta know better'n that, May.

STELLA: Thank heavens I didn't bring up my Mary so's she'd carry on like that there proxide blonde.

DELLA: They sure go at it kinda rough, don't they? Kids!

MAY: Oh, you parents talk the dullest tripe! Yer conversation really smells.

BUTCH: (*Sniffing.*) Lynn's stiff is beginnin' to stink.

TOBY: It is human to smell; when we're dead we smell more; that means that when we're dead we're more human; that's why I don't have no compunctions about killin' people: that's why I'd like to be dead myself.

BUTCH: That's jist great but what are ya goin' to do with Lynn's stiff? Ah'm tellin' ya, it really stinks.

TOBY: We'll dump it in the trunk a my car. My *groovey* car. We'll dump Maude's stiff in there too soon as I'm finished stranglin' her. That's the most obvious cache I kin think of 'n I want them in the most obvious cache of all cause I jist don't care any more. I kin always ditch the car, groovey though it is, 'n wipe the chrome clean.

MAY: Ditch the bitches.

TOBY: O moment that exquisites!

(MAUDE *screams — a blood-curdling shriek that shakes the stage.* ROMEO *breaks into the semi-circle of chairs. He flies from one confused person to the next. Each is weakly wavering between ignoring the crime and turning slightly toward it.*)

ROMEO: Help police! posie! sheriff! help! Toby's — Tob — Roby's murderin' May!

RAY: (*Taut.*) Don't be silly, Bad Butch, May's a-settin' here.

ROMEO: It's me — Romeo!

MAY: It's me, May!

RAY: It's thee, Romeo: — wherefor wert thou?

ROMEO: Asleep! 'N tied up to ma sleep like all the citizens in our town.

STELLA: Don't you be a-goin' around makin' them trashy irresponsible accusations. We's all quite awake 'n tryin' to do our duty as citizens, do the most dutiful accordin' to our duty accordin' to how we sees it.

ROMEO: Well, see it! See it! Yer duty's to open yer eyes 'n hearin' ears 'n discriminate what's a-happenin'!

RAY: Discriminate?

ROMEO: Oh, look! Look up there!

DELLA: Look at what? At _____ (*Using the* ACTOR's *real name.*) We seen him before, seen him at damn near every rehearsal.

ROMEO: Look what he's doing!!

STELLA: What's he doing? Does that damn near every night 'bout this point.

RAY: Yeah, why should we look? What's in it fer us 'cept concedin' the scene to him?

MAY: (*Her sense of stage-hogging reignited.*) Ma's right. What's the profit?

ROMEO: Toby's killin' a girl!!!

STELLA: Maybe.

ROMEO: (*Shrieking.*) BUT HE'S KILLING HER!!!

(MAUDE *is dead.* TOBY *begins to calmly lower her corpse. The crowd freezes completely, stares dead ahead into the audience.*)

STELLA: Feel frozen here. How very much a working day of life this is to sit so
still while rodeos of America Hysterica ben-hur around our head.

DELLA: Stiff-heck, *that's* what it is . . . never had such a bad 'n stiff stiff-neck
like this afore . . . must've caught a cross-ventilation draft in the drive-in
the-a-ter the other nigh . . .

MAY: Downed a draught in the beer parlor the other night. Was hard to bal-
ance on the chair once the beer got hold a my brain. Was jist the other
night . . . Last night, maybe it was. :The thirty-first of May.

TOBY: That was your last night, May. *Your* month's run out. Goodbye.

MAY: (*In a trance.*) Goodbye, Toby. Goodbye, ma. Goodbye, Romeo. It's
June now.

ROMEO: (*Frantic.*) But May —

MAY: (*Emphatic.*) I said, It is June now.

(*As in a sudden dispersal of clouds, the lights go up on the top of the girder
that rises from* TOBY's *chair and bends over the circumference of the vortex.
There, at the pinnacle, stands* RITA. *She has an absolutely other-wordly appearance.* DELLA *is brushed by the strange light and turns her face slowly
toward* RITA, *reaching for the blue cloak as she does so.*)

DELLA: Wanna get over one day soon 'n see that there monument they erected for . . . my brother . . .

RAY: Erected, huh?

DELLA: (*Standing and moving toward* RITA *as* RITA *begins to descend the
girder.*) 'N I'll take Rita along with me I will. Hello Rita. I've got yer
cloak.

RAY: Her brain's decayed. I'm tellin' ya, her brain's really decayed.

ROMEO: (*Weeping with rage.*) What's goin' on around here? Don'tcha all
hear me? Do something for God's sake!!!

TOBY: Is there something for God's sake, or will God punish me no matter?

DELLA: (*Fixing the long cloak around* RITA's *shoulders.*) God punishes you,
Toby, when ya try to hide from Him like Cain. Gotta stand up 'n out in
the light where He kin see ya 'n judge ya at yer doin's 'n at the intent of yer
supplications. Oughta supplicate to Him all the time: — Now I lay me —

RITA: Down to doom, down to drown in the salt lake.
     With sea salt and tears are mine eyes crusted o'er.
     Closed as the muscles that barnacle the shore.

TOBY and RITA: (*Together.*)
     Down from the straight-back chair on the stairway to God,
     My heart is in the Heavens but my sandals are in the sod.
     Mighty Moses might mount high, there listen and call,
     Yet could write nothing but his own word, then turn round and fall.

STELLA: (*Seeing* RITA.) An angel caught round with sashes of gilt drops from
the sky, descends our only steeple needle, comes down directly counter-
point to our steeple's ever narrowin' point.

DELLA: We're a-narrowin' down to the point.

ROMEO: (*Seeing* RITA; *transfixed.*) Look, look at her above that Dali chair that on the desert thrives. She is the angel he makes of all thy daughters' lives!

RAY: (*Seeing nothing.*) His infatuation for my daughter hath caused him wax poetic. License like that, Romeo, malicious speculation, kin ruin innocent people's lives.

RITA: Yet we are all, all of us innocent, the guilty along with the mad.

TOBY: For we know not what we do, neither her selves nor my self.

RITA: Neither for our names' sake, our mothers', nor the Lord's.

BUTCH: (*Fastidiously arranging the bodies of the sisters at the base of* TOBY's *chair.*) Sorta hard to git 'em really even-steven, Sir Tob, seein' as how one is so much shorter in measure from the other. The virgin's not nearly as long as the frump.

(*This scene of tensely confused attentions is suddenly splintered by the appearance of the* STRIPPER, *dressed in modest street clothes. She bursts into shattering song*:)

STRIPPER:
I'M GONNA TAKE IT OFF,
I'M GONNA DOFF
MY GARB,
I'M GONNA SHOW YIS WHAT I GOT
LIKE IT OR NOT!
   HEY! HEY! HEY!
   LOOK, IF YIS CAN —
   LOOK! LOOK! LOOK!
   LOOK! IF YER A MAN!

(*Standing above, and pointing to, the bodies of the sisters. The crowd pulls away from her.*)

I'M GONNA PULL OFF THE MASK —
THAT'S MY TASK,
THEN I'M DONE.
I'M GONNA SHOW YA TWO BODIES:
MY OWN 'N MY SON'S!
   HEY! HEY! HEY!
   LOOK, IF YIS CAN —
   LOOK! LOOK! LOOK!
   LOOK, IF YER A MAN!

STELLA: Oh, how disgusting — I can't look!

(*The stripping music suddenly aborts.* RITA *has reascended the girder above* TOBY's *chair and is standing on the platform that joins the two girders. She begins to sing a sad and melodic Country ballad. The* MUSICIANS *accompany her, very softly at first. As she sings,* RITA *slowly strides the diagonal girder, reaching its end downstage right as she finishes her song. The movement of the blue cloak over her arms gives the uncanny impression of the wings of an angel wounded by man. The crowd is transfixed in holy awe.)*

RITA:

    THERE'S A LAND OF NO ONE DYING,
       A LAND THAT DEATH FORGOT,
    THOUGH SO MANY THERE ARE LYING
       IN A SPACE WHERE BREATH IS NOT.

    THOUGH THE ELDER BRANCH IS GROWING
       AND THE ELM ON ELM ROW SPREADS
    TOP OF EVERGREEN O'ERFLOWING
       FROM THEIR CEMETERY BEDS

    AND A MAN'S NOT SPOKE FOR SURELY
       VERY LONG UPON THIS EARTH
    WHETHER HE'S THE FIEND'S WORK PURELY
       OR A PERFECT SAINT IN WORTH,

    STILL A LAND ALL DEATH DENYING
       ON THIS CONTINENT I KNOW:
    IT'S A PLACE OF NO ONE DYING
       THOUGH THE LORD LAYS ALL MEN LOW.

    THER'S A LAND OF NO ONE DYING,
       A LAND THAT DEATH FORGOT,
    THOUGH SO MANY THERE ARE LYING
       IN A SPACE WHERE BREATH IS NOT.

    WELL, IT'S PRETTY MYSTIFYING
       HOW THE DEAD ARE MADE TO LIE
    IN A GRAVE WITHOUT FIRST DYING
       UNDER SIGHT OF HIM ON HIGH.

    CAN IT BE THEY'RE JUSTIFYING
       WHAT THE PREACHER-MAN HAS SAID:
    THAT ALL HARDSHIP AND ALL CRYING
       IS REVERSED WHEN YOU SEEM DEAD?

(Speaking this stanza.)

    OR HAS SOME TRUTH COME O'ER THIS NATION
       WHERE THE FOLKS CAN NEVER DIE,
    HOLDS THEM TO THE SEPARATION
       THAT MAKES THEIR LIVES A LIE?

    STILL I FIND IT TERRIFYING
       TO HAVE SEVERED EVERY BOND
    IN A LAND WHERE NO ONE'S DYING
       WHO IS TRYING TO RESPOND.

OTHER LANDS MAY BE PRETENDING
   THAT THE TEAR-STAINED STONE IS BAD,
THAT A MAN'S APPROACHED HIS ENDING
   SHOULD BE SOLEMN, SHOULD BE SAD.

BUT I SENSE SOME MODIFYING
   TO OUR LIVES AND TO OUR NEEDS:
FOR A LAND WHERE NO ONE'S DYING,
   SAMEWISE NO ONE'S SOWING SEEDS.

YES, IT'S TRULY TERRIFYING
   LOVING EYES THAT HIDE NO TEARS,
HOLDING HANDS WITHOUT ALLYING –
   HANDS HAVE FEELING, HANDS HAVE FEARS.

GOD! OH GOD! IT'S TERRIFYING
   HAVING HITCHED FROM COAST TO COAST
IN A LAND OF NO ONE DYING,
   NOT A LIVING SOUL TO BOAST.

(*The* STRIPPER *confronts the crowd as the ballad ends, wildly tearing off her street clothes to savage stripping drums and throwing the various articles directly into the faces of* STELLA, DELLA, *and* RAY. *Darkness clouds over* RITA *and she seems to etherealize in her position high on the girder. An article of the* STRIPPER'*s clothing hits* ACE *in the head and he wakes up.*)

STELLA: That Vegas woman — oh, she's jist too obscene for American words! I can't look her in the eye.

RAY: She's the queen of the obscene. Really revoltin'. We must protect our children from such a fright, a, sight!

ROMEO: Strippas do make a guy uneasy: it's you'n breasts all alone together. The three a ya.

BUTCH: So vulga. Oh, my, soooooo vulga.

MAY: What a debased unabashed ol' bag. Why, she's all beat up. Completely over the hill. Couldn't hook near a mile from Main in that condition.

DELLA: Common, pronographic, appealin' to libidinous interests, the vested interests, illicit, prurient, salacious, delicious, spaghetti sauce, what cheek, what sauce —

STELLA: Not up to community standards.

RAY: Tart, smart tart, hussey, ruth, rue the day we ev —

(*The crowd, unable to withstand the* STRIPPER'*s attack, is forced to turn their faces from her: in doing so they are all confronted with the bodies of* MAUDE *and* LYNN. *The dummies rise* en masse, *bloated with air, to stare down at the corpses. The music ends abruptly.* BUTCH, *hands clasped, is smiling wryly.* TOBY *sits on his chair.*)

STELLA: Will ya look at that: laid out. The two of 'em!

RAY: What a sight — makes yer stomach do slow turns . . .

BUTCH: Y'all makin' a reference to me, Madame Mixer?

RAY: Don't get smart, Nazi.

DELLA: Never a dull moment in our town, eh?

MAY: My school mates — dead! DEAD! Gee . . .

BUTCH: Wonder if they notices anythin' unusual . . .

ROMEO: See there, now you see — both sistas murdered!

RAY: But you said Toby was out to do in mah May.

ROMEO: Well, it's jist another crevice, jist another burrow.

DELLA: Matter a fact, two crevices, two burrows.

ROMEO: No matter, mah point is made. There they be plain as the pose on yer face. Both of 'em, homicides.

RAY: They're dead fer certain — deader'n a skunk run down on route 30. 'N stink as much. But that they is homicides is jumpin' to conclusions.

ROMEO: Sure they's homicides — girls don't git to look like that from adolescent heart-attacks. They was real done in 'n Toby's what done the doin' in.

TOBY: (*Pulling the clipboard clamp off his anger vein.*) Thanks, Romeo.

STELLA: Now listen here, Butch, don't —

ROMEO: But *I* ain't Butch —

STELLA: Don't start in if ya jist tryin' to even up a score with Toby count of a gal or other he beat ya out of.

DELLA: (*Pensive.*) Murder's a pretty serious accusal.

BUTCH: They's laid out sorta pretty. Like in a funeral home.

MAY: Gosh, don't they look *ugly.*

BUTCH: Well . . . on such short notice . . .

MAY: Dirty 'n mangled 'n all. The frump looks worst.

ROMEO: What? — Are yis all crazy? I don't think I'm hearin' right!

STELLA: Now don't hear us wrong: — a course, Toby mighta killed 'em. But so might any a us here. Or somebody not here. After all, there's a lotta strange dicks in town.

ACE: What crust!

RAY: Maybe you done it, Romeo. Ya know a awful lot about it.

STELLA: Yeah . . . maybe you done it, Romeo, 'n yer jist tryin' to throw us off the track.

MAY: (*Aggressive, rushing down to tell the audience.*) Sure: after all, Toby's a righteous fella, his fingers feel out situations with infallable sensitivity. And nativity. Yes, that's the word, that's finally the right word. He may practice a kinda Byronic barbarism,

TOBY: — jist ouside a town, where haybelly cows graze God's grass while a whole lost language rots around yer tongue like so much mulch 'n peat,

MAY: — but that alone's no reason to be prejudiced for him. People who are jist a little more glamorous than the vast majority of folks are always made the scapegoat.

TOBY: Could ya come a little closer when ya express such so solid principals, May?

ACE: You folks oughta proceed with the order a the day. Ray?

RAY: Ace's right. Why don't we *ask* Toby if he done it?

ROMEO: Yeah, why don't ya? I will. — Toby, you killed these young girls, didn't you?

TOBY: Hi ya, Rom, how ya doin? Have a restful sleep? Or was it fraught with fearful trailers of a nightmare yet to come? Sorry, Romeo, but I ain't sayin' nothin' till I see my lawyer.

STELLA: Good! that's a good boy. Toby knows his rights.

MAY: You could be arrested fer slander, Romeo, ya know that? Willful slander of a poet 'n prophet. A man who draws more'n draws offa girls. You could go to jail fer that. I hope you do.

ROMEO: I don't care, May, I don't care what you say jist as long as yer safe.

MAY: Bull — pure Taurus bull. What a snow job.

ROMEO: Ain't no snow job! I'll fight this thing. I'll fight it all the way up to the Supreme Court of America!

MAY: Stop pawing me! First you scratch yer sores and then you put yer hands all over —

DELLA: (*Taking the initiative.*) Why *are* you so keen on seein' to Toby's bein' tossed in the clink?

ROMEO: Cause in the clink he can't git at May. He's countin' on murderin' May next, jist give him half the chance. I saved her once already when y'all hadda go 'n tie me up!

STELLA: That's as fulla holes as everythin' else you've annotated.

MAY: Holes ya dug with yer nails ya scratch yerself so muc —

ACE: True, but apparently there *has* been a crime around her, and until you're certain there wasn't, it's your duty to make arrests.

STELLA: Very true. But then, who should we arrest?

DELLA: (*Taking over.*) Considerin' the ambiguous climate a the case, we should arrest *two* suspects — Romeo *and* Toby — 'n proceed to thoroughly investigate both a them. 'N we could search 'em too.

RAY: We'd have every right to.

DELLA: (*Untying* ACE.) Mind doin' yer prospective ma-in-law a favor, Ace? I'm a settin' ya free so's ya kin make the arrests. Kin I trust ya?

ACE: Sooner or later ya gotta trust someone.

DELLA: I entrust my daughter to ya.

STRIPPER: And I my son.

ACE: (*Rubbing his stiff wrists.*) Thanks, madame.

BUTCH: (*Situated near the* STRIPPER.) Hey, madame, wanna keep time with somethin' sizeable? Ah'm real *good*.

STRIPPER: How much ya good fer?

BUTCH: Fer nothin'! Ya oughta pay me yer so damn old.

STRIPPER: I don't take care a no one fer nothin'.

TOBY: She don't take care a no one.

ACE: (*Jealous.*) Hey, what about Bad Butch? Maybe he had somethin' to do with this — ummm — affair.

STELLA: Nah, Bad Butch couldn't a had nothin' to do with it. He ain't the type. Them what got the reputation fer bein' bad like Bad Butch, never does nothin' bad actually.

MAY: (*To the audience, unable to bear the attention now focusing on* TOBY.) I'm glad they're arrestin' him. It'll gimme a chance to see exactly jist how short the poet is.

ACE: (*Helping* TOBY *up out of his sitting position.*) Now come along calm 'n ain't nobody gonna git hurt.

TOBY: May you always believe that.

MAY: Ha! Why, he's no higher'n my bubbies!

TOBY: Grounded at last. On an equal level with everybody else. What more could a fella ask for?

ACE: (*Taking* ROMEO.) Let's hustle, you two.

ROMEO: What a fix, what a goddamn fix to be in! . . .

TOBY: Now you 'n me's on equal footin'. Feels great, don't it?

ROMEO: Don't see why. Feels 'bout the same as every other day.

TOBY: Alas! It *is* about the same as every other day.

ACE: 'N after all you done!

TOBY: Yeah. But I kin change that, Ace.

ACE: Yeah?

TOBY: Did ya know the other day old Rom got inta some upstage business could set ya right straight who the criminal is?

ROMEO: It's a frame! A shame 'n a frame! — What kinda business?

TOBY: Ya wanna all look behind ma chair to uncover the answer to that query. Ya see that mounda dirt behind ma chair? Ya wanna dig in 'n uncover that dirt!

ROMEO: Oh, boy, I plumb fergot all about that . . .

(*The crowd, except for* TOBY *and* ROMEO, *rushes up to the mound behind* TOBY's *chair.* TOBY *crosses to* BUTCH *who is now trying to carry the* STRIPPER *off into the wings.*)

TOBY: Break fer it now, Romeo, while they's up there practicin' a bit a amateur archeology! — 'N as fer you, Butch, lay off my ma!

BUTCH: Ah was jist gonna lay yer m —

STRIPPER: Oh! . . .

TOBY: (*Pulling two knives out from the gun holsters on* BUTCH's *hips, and holding their edges outward in his trembling fists.*) Yer too slow, Nazi, to lay anythin' got ma tag on it! Now: — step lively!!

ROMEO: I better step lively 'n beat it while they's all on that desert experdition. (*He turns about frantically and rushes up the vortex girder and onto the diagonal girder.*)

BUTCH: Now, Tob, ya make everythin' too serious —

DELLA: Why, look at that: it's a corpis delectis!

STRIPPER: Son, please —

STELLA: No it ain't. It's a gal's corpse. A young gal.

RAY: Ever see a town so big on gals' corpses?

MAY: Look! Look, everybody! Romeo the pocked-marked murderer is escaping over the viaduct!

ALL: Git him! Git him! Don't let him excape! Lynch him! Swing him high!

etc., etc., etc.

(The crowd, with murder on its mind, tears across the stage. Some pick up the discarded ropes, others the tangled telephone wires, and they scamper up the girders after the distraught ROMEO. *The second he is captured, the noose is put around his neck.* MAY *rushes down centerstage, cheering the mob on and urging them to hang* ROMEO *from the girder.* TOBY, *having thoroughly cowed* BUTCH *and the* STRIPPER, *turns the knives toward* MAY. *Having secured the noose, the mob kicks* ROMEO *to his death. There is more than madness in* MAY's *eyes. She draws* TOBY *to her.)*

MAY: Swing the Grunewald from the viaduct! Let him blow in the breeze! This shall make a epic! A epic for all time! It inspires me to the very heights!! Heaven its —
TOBY: Let my work be forever finished!

*(*TOBY *faces* MAY *directly and thrusts both knives into her diaphragm. Her shreik carries over the cries of the crowd. They all stop short and turn to look down at her. She staggers for a moment with her blood-drenched hands over her wounds and then falls dead. The mob is stunned for several long moments. Then it gathers silently together and moves* en masse *down onto the stage.* RITA, *draped in the long blue cloak, appears on the platform above the vortex girder and begins silently to descend.* TOBY *walks at the head of the crowd and leads it to the semi-circle of chairs. As* TOBY *sits in his chair,* RITA *raises her arms like wings above him and places a steel head-cap, encrusted with jewels like a crown, over his black hair. Except for the* STRIPPER, *all the others file along quietly and take seats within the semi-circle. They sit without motion for some time; the swaying body grows motionless. All stare directly ahead into the audience. Finally,* TOBY *speaks, stretching out his arms to either flank of chairs; as he does so, the townspeople turn and fix their gaze on him.* RITA *is behind his chair, raised a step or two on the girder, with her face and hands lifted upward.)*

TOBY and RITA: *(Together, slowly.)* Let us close this circle of chairs. Rest your eyes on me.

(The lights grow imperceptibly dimmer except for a reddish glow about TOBY *which suggests his electric execution. The* STRIPPER *wanders in a soft spot downstage, tottering wearily and bewildered. She sings a Country ballad and makes a half-hearted attempt at a simple dance. Her spotlight gradually dims.)*

STRIPPER:
WELL MAH DADDY KEPT HIS CHAIR, CHAIR, WARM FOR ME,
WELL MAH LONESOME DADDY WAITED AND HE HAD TO BE
MAH DADDY CAUSE HE KEPT HIS CHAIR WARM FOR ME,
SO WARM THRU THE CHILLY THAW, THE MAYTIME PLEA.

AND I'D LOVE TO BE COZY ON THAT CHAIR WITH HIM
STEAD A SITTIN' ALL ALONE ON THE EDGE OF THE RIM

WHERE A LONELINESS PREVAILS NOT ASSAILED BY A HYMN:
WELL AT LEAST HE KEPT THAT CHAIR, WARM, WARM,
   I'M GONNA SING AND DANCE ME UP A STORM!
   I'M GONNA SING AND DANCE ME UP A STORM!

WELL MAH DADDY KEPT HIS CHAIR, CHAIR, WARM FOR ME,
WELL MAH LONESOME DADDY WAITED AND HE HAD TO BE
MAH DADDY CAUSE HE KEPT HIS CHAIR WARM FOR ME,
SO WARM THRU THE CHILLY THAW, THE MAYTIME PLEA.

O HOW LONG I MUST WONDER WILL THIS EARTH STILL SPIN
WHERE MY BODY SEEMS TO FEEL THAT IT NEVER HAS BEEN
AND MY HEART'S NO ANSWER, DAD, FOR A KIND HEART AKIN:
WELL AT LEAST HE KEPT THAT CHAIR, WARM, WARM,
   I'M GONNA SING AND DANCE ME UP A STORM!
   I'M GONNA SING AND DANCE ME UP A STORM!

Naropa

Jean-Claude van Itallie

[being the Incredibly Frustrating Adventures
of a Middle-aged University Professor on
His Way to Perfect Enlightenment]

a play for puppets and people

adapted from the translation by
Herbert V. Guenther of Tibetan texts

©1979, 1980 Copyright by Jean-Claude van Itallie.
CAUTION: No performances or readings of this work may be given without the ex-
press authorization of the author's agent. For production rights contact: Lynn
Davis, Davis-Cohen, 513 Sixth Avenue, New York, N.Y. 10011.

People and Puppets in the Play

People in the play

Naropa
monk-musician-chanters
    (also local king, people
    on the plain)
first puppeteer
    (also man with his parents
second puppeteer
Tilopa
    (also beggar)
butcher
surgeon
man with a burden
leper lady
hunter
old man
    (some of the above may be
    double cast but Tilopa
    must never look as he does as
    the beggar and in the
    last scene)

Puppets in the play

Naropa
cleaning woman
sick dog
man's mother (also old woman)
man's father (also old man)
King
Princess Maya
first guard
second guard
dancers at the festival
    (although these may be
    silhouettes)
fish, frogs, worms

Characters in the play, puppets and people are costumed in the style of India circa 1000. The musician-monks, however, may be Tibetan monks, or dressed in the style thereof, playing Tibetan instruments as the story of Naropa is told as part of their lineage. The puppets are manipulated by puppeteers dressed in black and black-hooded (as in the Japanese Bunraku). The music is basically Tibetan Buddhist ritual music (low chanting, long horn, cymbal, drum, drones, flute, bells, etc.); it is enthusiastic. The musicians and chanters sit on a specially provided platform, visible throughout the play, on one side (as on Bunraku and Kabuki stages).

NAROPA, *a man of about forty, sits reading from texts in his study. He wears monk's robes—he is the Buddhist abbot of Nalanda University, the Harvard-Oxford of its time. he sits cross-legged on a sitting cushion. In front of him on a low table is a handwritten sacred text, pages of which he is reading one by one. Other texts, wrapped in cloths, are piled around him. The countryside of Northern India is visible through a small window. The music is peaceful—perhaps a raga of the early afternoon.* NAROPA *is bothered by an occasional fly which he swats unthinkingly with his hand. A* CLEANING WOMAN *of the untouchable caste enters, her twig broom in her hand; she starts to clean.* NAROPA *pays her no mind.*

MONK: (*Chanting low from the side musicians' platform.*) Once upon a time in the year 1000 in India it happened that the great abbot of Nalanda sat reading from the sacred texts. When the cleaning woman of the untouchable caste entered his study the great Naropa paid her no mind. Her eyes were red, they say, and her hair dishevelled, and her face was shrivelled, and her complexion darkish blue. Her ears were long and lumpy, they say, and her nose enflamed and twisted, and her mouth gaped, and her teeth were rotting and she made sucking noises with her tongue.

(*The* CLEANING WOMAN *is played by a puppet who is manipulated by one or two black-hooded and black-dressed* PUPPETEERS. *Sucking noises are made for the* CLEANING WOMAN, *and her voice will come from the narrator's platform. She is humpbacked and bent over her broom. She seems to be trying to catch* NAROPA's *attention. She cleans very close to his legs. She actually sweeps his feet. He merely twitches, reacting as if to a fly. Nothing else availing, she jumps onto the text on his table.*)

CLEANING WOMAN: Hah!

NAROPA: (*Startled at last.*) What? What is it?

CLEANING WOMAN: What is it with you, Ugly?

NAROPA: What do you want?

CLEANING WOMAN: I'm cleaning. What do you want, Ugly?

NAROPA: I'm reading, if you don't mind.

(*He attempts to go back to his text.*)

CLEANING WOMAN: Reading? And what is it you're reading, Sir, if you don't mind?

NAROPA: (*Speaking as if to an idiot.*) Words. I am reading words. They are written here on this page.

CLEANING WOMAN: (*Jumping up and down on the texts with glee.*) That's wonderful, just wonderful. (*She stops jumping.*) What words are these? (*She points.*)

NAROPA: (*Reading to her from the title page.*) A Critique of The Divine Doctrine of Infinitely Divisible Universes Arbitrarily Partitioned Into the Air, Earth, Fire and Water Worlds by the Astrologer Nawa in the Days Before Anything was as it is Now, or How The Ancients May or May not Have Changed Lead into Gold Sometimes.

CLEANING WOMAN: (*Seemingly impressed.*) Oh, I see. You can actually read. Your mother must be very proud of you, Sir. And do you also understand what the words mean?

NAROPA: (*Impatient.*) Of course.

(*Now the* CLEANING WOMAN *jumps up and down and around in a fit of prolonged grief. She shrieks with dismay.*)

CLEANING WOMAN: (*Wailing.*) Ohhhh, I was so proud of you. But now I see you're just another silly professor hunched over his words. You're a hunchback, Naropa, a liar. And you look so old, Naropa ... You're getting fat. Your nose is twisted and inflamed. You digest nothing. You'll soon explode, Naropa. Your eyes are red. Your teeth are rotting. Your face is blue. Want a mirror? Look at me! You read all those books but you don't understand anything!

(*He is thunderstruck. She stands a moment longer on his texts, then wipes her face off — it was a mask. Under it the* CLEANING-WOMAN *puppet is beautiful, young-looking. Amazed, he slowly reaches out his hand to touch her, to see if she's real. She lightly leaps off his desk.*)

CLEANING WOMAN: Don't touch me, Naropa, I'm untouchable.

NAROPA: Excuse me, I'm sorry. I lied. I am getting fat. I don't understand anything, it's true. Help me.

CLEANING WOMAN: Don't be silly, little Naropa. Your books tell you 'help yourself.'

NAROPA: Tell me how.

CLEANING WOMAN: Well, look at you. What are you doing in here? You're going blind. You couldn't even see me when I was sweeping your feet.

NAROPA: Be my teacher.

CLEANING WOMAN: That would be too easy, wouldn't it, Sweetheart? But . . . perhaps, if my brother were willing . . . he deals with the hardest cases, like yours, sometimes, if he wants to . . .

NAROPA: What't his name?

CLEANING WOMAN: Tilopa.

(NAROPA *falls on the floor, prostrating — traditional upon hearing for the first time the name of one's teacher.*)

NAROPA: Tilopa! Where does he teach? I'll enroll. I'll take a leave of absence.

CLEANING WOMAN: Naro, my sweet little Naro, you're so funny. There's nowhere to enroll. My brother hates universities. He's not like you. You have to abandon this place completely, forget it, leave this cozy room, develop callouses.

NAROPA: Is he in a village? Is he a king? Does he teach in cities?

CLEANING WOMAN: No hints. Ask around, my dear. Try the East; it's traditional. And put your notebook away. You're so serious, Naropa. Really.

(*The scene changes. This is* NAROPA'*s formal leave-taking. Everyone at the university is disturbed that he is leaving. He stands in the middle of the stage on a little platform, the abbot. The important* TEACHER-MONKS *and the* LOCAL KING *stand formally around him in a mandala: the* TEACHERS *are in front, behind, and to his right; the* LOCAL KING *is to his left. Younger* STUDENT-MONKS *are around less formally. As people chant in this scene they are lightly accompanied by music. All are dressed appropriately, saffron robes for the monks, etc.*)

MONK: (*Chanting in front of* NAROPA, *which is traditionally the Eastern direction, and this monk the 'Teacher of the Eastern Gate.'*) Glorious abbot, our noble Naropa: community, as you have often told us, is the base of the teachings. To leave your community is to go against the teachings. Stay with us — for our sake.

STUDENT MONK: (*Pleading in a whiney tone.*) Sir, you're our best professor, our most famous professor. Stay, Sir, please.

MONK: (*Chanting to* NAROPA'*s right, traditionally the South, and this the 'Teacher of the Southern Gate.'*) Dear Naropa, it is known that friendship is the root of the teachings. Don't abandon us, your colleagues, your students, your friends. Stay with us, for our sake.

STUDENT MONK: (*Speaking very rapidly, avidly.*) I can only understand the texts when you explain them, Naropa. Grammar and logic make no sense to me except when you talk about them.

MONK: (*Chanting in back of* NAROPA, *traditionally the West, and this monk the 'Teacher of the Western Gate.'*) Glorious abbot: you are this university's and this country's greatest scholar. To explicate the doctrine is the proper calling for such a one. Stay for our sake, if not for your own.

YOUNG MONK: (*Speaking.*) When you give meditation instruction you explain everything so clearly. You tell me what all my sitting experiences mean. If you leave, I'll be like a fish out of water.

LOCAL KING: (*Chanting, he is on* NAROPA's *left, traditionally the North.*) Wise abbot, if you leave this place there will be no doctor for the spiritual ills of the people. To us you are the embodiment of the teachings. You cure our diseases of blindness and ignorance. You are our teacher. We the king beg you to remain with us, to continue to teach us.

(NAROPA *addresses the audience as if it were the congregation of Nalanda University. At this point* NAROPA-*the-puppet, a puppet playing the same role as the actor, is introduced. This puppet too is manipulated by black-hooded and black-dressed* PUPPETEER(s) *but its voice is spoken by* NAROPA *the actor, and of course they are dressed identically.*)

NAROPA: (*He starts a little too composedly.*) Friends, fellow scholars and monks, respected colleagues of the Eastern, Southern and Western Gates, Gracious King, and dear Nalanda students: Thank you for the honor you have shown us. We are touched that you desire us to remain with you. But, we remind you, nothing is permanent. Sooner or later we would have parted ways. Death breaks all ties. No doubt our decision to leave Nalanda appears selfish to you, and perhaps it is. You may judge us unfriendly to leave such devoted friends, such needy students. But we have come to realize — just recently — that in our position as abbot, and as doctor, too, of the five great branches of learning, and of grammar, and of epistemology, that we, that I —

(*The puppet cannot perform a gesture that the actor performs.*)

am stuck.

(*There is murmuring at* NAROPA's *using the word 'stuck' but* NAROPA — *puppet and actor — holds up his hand for silence.*)

Some of you may think that the teachings can be absorbed into your systems just by hearing. But, if you have no idea of the personal experience, of the really real experience...

(*Once more the puppet is unable to follow a gesture of the actor.* NAROPA *plunges on, more anxiously.*)

'Without an inspired teacher,' the texts say, 'You can't stamp out your own desires. And if I continue here — I'll never know anything. I'll never get beyond — this. (*Puppet and actor gesture to their heads.*)

(*Murmuring as* NAROPA *seems to be getting a little irrational.*)

I'll never see in this lifetime if I don't ... Don't hold me back, please ... that would be unfair. 'To be a state of grace: go and seek an inspired teacher.' How many times have I told you that? Now I say it to myself.

(*The puppet takes a bowl and staff and begins to travel ceremoniously away through a file of* MONKS *who bow and wave. The* MONKS *and* LOCAL KING *now go to the* MUSICIANS' *platform on which they will sit, visible, for most of the rest of the play. As* NAROPA *the puppet travels slowly,* NAROPA *the actor sings or chants the 'Song of Samsara' along with the* MUSICIANS. *Because the* MONKS — *who traditionally play these musical instruments in Tibet and Northern India* — *are constantly visible on the side chanting and accompanying with music, it is in one sense as if it is they who are telling the traditional story of 'Naropa.'*)

NAROPA: (*Singing.*)
I live in a bowl of fire, in a dungeon,
In a poisonous swamp.

I find fault with others; I'm caught in a web;
Entangled in my own desires,
I'm bound hand and neck.

I'm drowning in my own excretions.

Like a deer chasing a mirage
I'm enthralled by illusion;
Chased by Death's rough-coated dogs,
The hunter knowing no mercy,
The path unsafe,

I'm trapped in a snare.
I'm caught in the net of my own thoughts,
In bondage to lies.

Thoughtlessly I milk the cow of life.

In the meadow of illusion
I ride a hesitant horse.

A pointed spear marks time in my heart.

I laugh with sharpened fangs.

I'm a fragile water plant.
In the mist the moon sits on the rippling pond:
Bubble of enchantment, I cannot touch it.

Climbing trees with poisonous leaves
I move through the world like a snake,
Inspiring fear.

I lick honey from a razor blade.

Confused, I shoot an arrow of disturbed emotions,
Only to pierce the already wounded.

Knowing that I am growing old and will die soon,

My life flickers on like a flame in the wind,
Full of half-truths.
A dream,
A bewilderment within a bewidlerment.
Living from emotion to emotion
I constantly deceive myself.

I must, I must find a teacher.

(*The puppet still travelling, a white screen is placed in front of the actor*
NAROPA. *The Song of Samsara continues immediately into the vigorous
travelling chant, chanted by the* MUSICIANS.)

MUSICIANS: (*As the puppet travels.*) Om hri, ha ha hum hum phat; on hri,
ha ha hum hum phat; om hri, ha ha hum hum phat . . . etc — — —

MONK: (*Speaking.*) An then, after a month of travelling, Naropa came to a
graveyard, where he rested in front of a grass hut.

(NAROPA *(the puppet) comes to and sits in front of a grass hut in a
graveyard (all puppet-size). The puppet (with the actor's voice) addresses
the audience directly.*)

NAROPA: No teacher, Nothing.
MUSICIANS: (*Continuing softly under.*) Om hri, ha ha hum hum phat . . .
NAROPA: (*Putting his face in his hands.*) What am I doing here?
MUSICIANS: Om hri, ha ha hum hum phat . . . .
NAROPA: (*Getting up and starting to walk again with his staff and bowl.*)
Or . . . I'm just not trying hard enough. Try harder, Naropa.
MUSICIANS and NAROPA: Om hri, ha ha hum hum phat . . . etc . . . .

MONK: (*Chanting.*) As Naropa was walking along a narrow mountain
path, high rocks on one side, a river far below, he came upon a lady
with no hands and no feet.

(*In blueish light* NAROPA *(the puppet) is stopped short by the bulk of
human-sized elderly* LADY, *not inelegantly dressed, seated in a sort of
wooden wheel-chair. The chanting stops as* NAROPA *stops. His path is
blocked. He stares at her. She looks back. He nods. She nods.*)

NAROPA: Excuse me, I'm sorry . . . but you're blocking the path.
LADY: Excuse me, I'm very sorry but I can't help it. You see I haven't the
use of my hands or feet.
NAROPA: I'm sorry. Excuse me, but the path is too narrow. Allow me to
push you out of the way.

(*He prepares to do so but she stops him.*)

LADY: I'm sorry. Excuse me, but I wouldn't do that.
NAROPA: Excuse me, but why not?
LADY: I'm sorry but, you see, I'm a leper.
NAROPA: Oh.

(He is stopped in mid-movement before touching her or her chair.)

NAROPA: Excuse me. I'm sorry.

(Not certain what to do at first, he tries to see if he can squeeze by without touching her, but he can't.)

NAROPA: I'm sorry. Excuse me, but the path — I'm sorry, but I can't go by . . . without touching you. What do you suggest?

LADY: Excuse me, I'm sorry, but perhaps you'd better turn back and go another way.

NAROPA: I'm sorry but, you see, I can't. I'm a pilgrim. I'm on a quest. I can't turn back. Excuse me but you see I have to journey East to find my teacher.

LADY: I'm sorry then, but if you're in such a hurry, excuse me, but you'll have to jump over me.

NAROPA: Oh. I'm sorry. Please excuse me. I'm sorry.

(Moving back, his robe, staff and bowl all gathered in one hand, holding his nose with the other, NAROPA *leaps over her and lands behind the screen on the other side, which is moved away and* NAROPA *(the actor), robe, bowl, etc., lie all in a heap, as if he too has just leaped. Also, as soon as he has jumped, the* LADY *is seen in dark blue light, laughing gently, and we recognize her voice as that of the* CLEANING WOMAN *in the first scene after her transformation.)*

LADY: Poor, poor little Naro. Tilopa, whom you're so eager to find, unlike you, is quite free of preconceptions. So, my sweetheart, if you refuse to use your very own critical mind to cut through those polite habits of thought, you'll never find your Tilopa.

(A white screen is placed over the LADY *in the wheel-chair and* NAROPA *(the actor) is lying, stunned and furious with himself.)*

NAROPA: *(In a rage.)* Nuts!

MUSICIANS: *(Continuing softly.)* Om hri, ha ha hum hum phat . . . .

NAROPA: From now everyone I meet I ask for instruction.

MUSICIANS: *(Joined by* NAROPA *who starts to travel again in exactly the same manner the puppet* NAROPA *traveled.)* Om hri, ha ha hum hum phat . . . .

MONK: *(Chanting.)* And then the former abbot Naropa came upon a smelly dog, sick and crawling with worms and insects. Immediately, and without any hesitation, he gathered his robe about him, held his nose, and jumped.

*(*NAROPA *does just that, the actor moving in the identical manner that the puppet jumped over the leper* LADY. *The* DOG *is then seen in dark blue strobe light.* NAROPA *has landed behind the screen again.)*

DOG: *(Spoken in a gravelly dog voice.)* If you jump over me, what makes you think your teacher will accept you, you smelly dog?

(*The white screen is placed over the* DOG; *as it is moved it reveals* NAROPA *the puppet.*)

NAROPA: (*Once more having fallen on the ground in the same spot.*) Nuts, nuts, nuts! From now on I ask *everyone* to teach me.
MUSICIANS: (*Softly.*) Om hri, ha ha hum hum phat....

(*Immediately* NAROPA *has spoken his last line, and as he is still on the ground, a* MAN (*an actor, not a puppet*) *enters carrying a heavy burden, a huge burlap sack. The sack is so huge in fact—as high and wide as the dimensions of the stage will allow, completely out of scale—that the struggling* MAN *is barely visible under it; his face can't be seen. He weaves from side to side under his vast burden.* NAROPA *hesitates to annoy such a one but nonetheless, firmly resolved now to ask anyone he meets, he finally speaks.*)

NAROPA: Excuse me ...

(*The* MAN *continues weaving around, trying to go forward.* NAROPA *has to shout to make himself heard.*)

NAROPA: Hello! Hello!

(*The* MAN *stops weaving quite so much. He has heard faintly that someone is trying to reach him.*)

NAROPA: Hello ... Excuse me, but—

(*With tremendous difficulty and very very slowly the* MAN *extricates himself from his burden; he manages at last to look at* NAROPA—*he is a strong red-faced man, exhausted and angry. He glares.*)

NAROPA: (*Hesitantly, afraid of angering the* MAN *further.*) Have you seen my teacher?
MAN: (*Hardly believing his ears that he has been disturbed by this person.*) What?
NAROPA: I'm sorry to ... but—I'm looking for my teacher, Tilopa. Have you seen him?
MAN: *What* did you say?
NAROPA: I'm looking for—
MAN: (*Interrupting him, livid.*) Grrrrrr. Listen, you stupid—(*He wants to hit* NAROPA *but decides it's not worth the energy.*) Oh, shit ... (*He starts shouldering his burden again.*) Listen, you stupid—there's another asshole on the other side of this mountain. Go fuck each other. Pair of assholes. And leave me alone!

(*The* MAN *with the burden weaves off.* NAROPA (*the puppet*) *gathers his staff and bowl and starts to walk in the other direction from which the* MAN *with the burden came.* NAROPA *the puppet is joined by* NAROPA *the actor and they both, one behind the other, circle the stage in a way that would indicate climbing up a weaving mountain road and climbing down it; the puppet and the actor move identically.*)

MUSICIANS: Om hri, ha ha hum hum phat . . . om hri, ha ha hum hum phat . . . The bear went over the mountain . . . The bear went over the mountain . . . om hri, ha ha hum hum phat . . . the bear went over the mountain . . . om hri, ha ha hum hum phat. . . . (*Here, as at other points, the travel chant is varied in volume and rapidity, and accompanied or not by various instruments.*)

(*The white screen is removed to reveal a* MAN *who stands between two gagged and bound people, his* PARENTS. *The* MAN *is played by a* PUPPETEER, *this time not hooded. The* PARENTS *are played by puppets, as is* NAROPA, *while the actor* NAROPA *stands back but is visible, speaking for the character. The* MAN *is tying up his* PARENTS — *he is busy torturing them.*)

MAN: I could use some help.
NAROPA: What?
MAN: I said I could use some help with these people.
NAROPA: Who are they?
MAN: My parents.
NAROPA: Well . . . what have they done?
MAN: (*As if this explanation were quite obvious.*) I just told you: they're my parents.
NAROPA: But — why that?
MAN (*Exasperated.*): They're my *parents!* (*He hits his* FATHER *with a stick.*) Hold his hands for me. (NAROPA *doesn't. The* MAN *strokes his* MOTHER's *breasts.*) Nice little mama, nice . . . (*Then he hits her.*)
NAROPA: Stop it!
MAN: Shove her head against this tree.
NAROPA: I will not!
MAN: You mean you've never done this to yours?
NAROPA: I love my parents.
MAN: Pass me that rope. (NAROPA *doesn't. The* MAN *reaches the rope himself and uses it to tie up his* PARENTS *more tightly.*)
NAROPA: I'm a monk. I don't perform violence.
MAN: (*Beating his* FATHER *hard with a stick.*) And you haven't killed your parents yet?
NAROPA: You're crazy.

(NAROPA *the puppet starts to leave. During the scene* NAROPA *the actor has come slowly closer to the* MAN *with his* PARENTS. *Now, unexpectedly, the* MAN *with the* PARENTS *turns to* NAROPA *the actor, holding his head in his hands, speaking to him as a kindly doctor. The light has turned a dark blue-green on them.*)

MAN: Naropa, how are you ever going to know anything if you won't recog-

nize your own feelings? Try to break open your own hard head. You're
so uptight. You're such a numbskull.

(*Both* NAROPA *the actor and* NAROPA *the puppet swoon. The white screen
covers the* MAN *with his* PARENTS. *A little uncertainly the puppet* NAROPA
gets up and continues to travel. NAROPA *the actor remains lying on the
ground.*)

MUSICIANS: Om hri, ha ha hum hum phat ... the bear went over the
mountain....

MONK: (*Speaking.*) It was nearly sunset when Naropa came upon the
butcher.

(*In the late afternoon light the* MUSICIANS *play something like a raga of the
late afternoon—exciting and soothing at once, as* NAROPA *the puppet is
travelling, and beginning to enjoy it more. Suddenly the white screen is
pulled away to reveal a* BUTCHER *pulling the intestines out of a dead
animal. The* BUTCHER *is human, and the dead animal looks as much as
possible like a real gory dead animal, perhaps a deer.* NAROPA *the puppet
steps back in revulsion; he watches as the* BUTCHER *pulls the intestines out
of the dead animal (the intestines should be wet and as lifelike as possible).
Finally he gathers enough courage to step forward and speak.*)

NAROPA: (*The actor, his voice coming timidly from his prone body, as if he
were dreaming.*) Excuse me ... I'm looking for my teacher, Tilopa.
Have you seen him?

(*The* BUTCHER *doesn't answer but pulls up a long length of intestines toward*
NAROPA *the puppet, and tries to hand them to him, along with a knife.*
NAROPA *the puppet shakes his head, no, and backs off. The* BUTCHER, *however, grabs him.* NAROPA *the actor remains lying down but gives a little
jump when the puppet is grabbed.*)

BUTCHER: (*Taunting, to* NAROPA *the puppet.*) Hey there, little Mr. Ac-ac-
ac-ac-ac-ac-ademic Unipro Versity Fessor, 'fraid of a knife?

(*The white screen is placed over the* BUTCHER, *the animal, and* NAROPA *the
puppet.*)

BUTCHER: (*From behind the screen.*) How're you going to cut anything out
of yourself if you're 'fraid of a knife?

(NAROPA *the actor gets up slowly, stunned. The sunset light is more pronounced.* NAROPA *travels on, but more slowly. He is tired. The music is
softer, more tired.*)

MUSICIANS: Om hri, ha ha hum hum phat ... the bear went over the
mountain....

MONK: (*Speaking.*) Naropa was tired but he traveled on, though more
slowly now. Then, at sunset, by the side of the river, he came upon a
man kneeling over someone.

(*The white screen is moved aside to show a man hunched over another man. The first man is a* SURGEON. *He has his hands in a bowl of (warm) water. We hear the sound of the water as several times he puts his hands in the water and takes them out. Only when the* SURGEON *moves slightly do we see that he is bathing the exposed stomach sac of his patient, dipping his hands in the warm water, letting the water run over the patient's stomach sac, and dipping his hands in the water again. The patient is* NAROPA *the puppet.* NAROPA *the actor stands by helplessly, like a child, kneading his own stomach unconsciously.* NAROPA *the puppet seems to be grasping at the air with his hands straight up — thus we know the patient is alive.*)

NAROPA: I — I-I-I-I-I-I-I am . . . . . loo-loo-loo-loo-loo-loo — I . . . .

SURGEON: (*Soothingly, speaking to the puppet* NAROPA.) Nice warm water. Very nice. Very soothing. Very nice. Nice warm water. Very soothing. Very nice.

(NAROPA *the actor begins to cry quietly, still kneading his own stomach. Now the* SURGEON *begins to lecture as to an audience of medical students watching him operate.*)

SURGEON: (*Chanting a little, not stopping what he is doing.*) The body is by nature pure. The body is by nature pure but it gets clogged, you see, with dirt. The body is by nature pure but it gets clogged with the dirt of habit-forming thoughts. (*Now he talks to his patient again.*) Nice warm water. Very soothing. Very nice. (*Now in his lecturing tone again.*) The body is by nature pure but it gets clogged, you see, with the dirt of habit-forming thoughts. (*Now, again, to his patient.*) Nice warm water. Very soothing. Very nice.

(*The screen is placed in front of the* SURGEON *and* NAROPA *the puppet.* NAROPA *sits by the side of the river sobbing.*)

NAROPA: My stomach hurts. I want some water. I want my mother.

(*As* NAROPA *sits crying the* MUSICIANS *sing a reprise of part of the Song of Samsara.*)

MUSICIANS: I'm a fragile water plant.
   In the mist the moon sits on the rippling pond:
   Bubble of enchantment, I cannot touch it.

(*The music turns soft, almost crooning. The light turns rosy-apricot. As he lies sleeping* NAROPA *is surrounded by the Great Gate and wall of a puppet city — it advances slowly on him. Then the Gate opens, and he is inside the city, as if his own dream were overtaking him.*)

MONK: (*Chanting.*) It was then that Naropa came to a city, the capital of a kingdom. He stood a while in front of the Great Gate, admiring its workmanship. When he entered he found the city fair: its houses were rosy-colored and clean, its people were healthy. He stood a while watching in

the Great Square, a wooden roof painted gold shading his head. The people were having a festival.

(*The Gate and high mountain city are beautiful (in architecture and feeling like Kathmandu in Nepal). It is a sunny day; the light on the houses
with their gold trim and wooden roofs is soft and rosy.* NAROPA *stands up
with his staff and bowl. His head is almost touching the ornate sloping
highest roof in the city, that of the palace. There is as much movement as
can be contrived: dancing, flowers, etc., music* ... *This whole visit of*
NAROPA *to the city is light and seductive: a 'bubble of enchantment.' The
people at the festival may be very small puppets, or the illusion of their
presence may be created by dancing and moving pastel-colored silhou-
ettes.*)

FIRST GUARD: (*A taller than average puppet.*) Look at that! (*He means*
   NAROPA.)
SECOND GUARD: Look how tall he is!
MONK: In this city the taller you are, the more important.
FIRST QUARD: He must be very important. I'll go tell the king.

(*The* FIRST GUARD *goes into the palace through a small door near*
NAROPA's *leg. The festival continues.* NAROPA *stands still, holding his bowl
and staff. Suddenly there is a loud Tibetan horn and a cymbal crash. The
(relatively) large main doors of the palace open and an (also relatively)
large and elegant sedan chair is pushed forward onto the main square.
Another horn fanfare and the* KING, *a puppet, smaller of course by far
than* NAROPA *but still larger than his guards or any of his people, steps out
of the door of the chair. The people cheer and bow. The* KING *bows to*
NAROPA. NAROPA *bows to the king. The people cheer again.*)

KING: (*To* NAROPA) Isn't it a beautiful day? Such a day! The gods bless us.
   We know who you are, Great Abbot. Your presence here is a real treat.
   We're honored.
NAROPA: Noble Sir, I am looking for my teacher, Tilopa.
KING: Of course you are. Everybody knows that. (*He motions to the sedan
   chair.*) I want you to meet my daughter Maya.

(*The* KING *hands his (large puppet) daughter, the* PRINCESS MAYA, *out of
the sedan chair and walks her to* NAROPA. *She is beautiful and sexy but
every inch a princess. She moves deliciously, has long dark hair, wears a
few costly jewels and a soft melon-colored silk sari trimmed with gold. She
bows her head modestly to* NAROPA. *He bows to her. The* KING *motions the
(actual)* MUSICIANS *to play as he leads* NAROPA *and his daughter in a formal promenade around the square. The people cheer, the* MUSICIANS *play
festival music, the people dance—all more or less in the style of high
Himalayan civilization.*)

KING: (*As they promenade.*) We've heard of you, Naropa, of course. Everyone has. You're so famous. And now that we see how tall you are ...

well! We give you our daughter's hand, and half our city, mountains
and gold as a dowry!

NAROPA: But —

KING: Do you find our city fair?

NAROPA: Oh, yes, but —

KING: Do you find our daughter fair?

NAROPA: Oh, very fair, but —

KING: Then that's settled. The Princess Maya finds you famous and tall,
don't you dear? (*The* PRINCESS *nods in agreement. The* KING *shouts to
the people.*) She finds him famous and tall! He finds her fair! (*The people cheer.*) Start the wedding march!!

(*The people cheer loudly. The Tibetan horns, cymbals, etc., play loudly
and long. The* KING *joins* NAROPA's *and his daughter's hands. More cheers,
music, etc. The lights dim almost out. The* KING *steps back. Lavender and
rose curtains are pulled across and around the stage. The music plays a
joyous rhythmic noise climaxing in a large horn and cymbal sound. Then
to a single dreamy mountain flute the curtains in front are drawn back to
reveal* NAROPA *in bed with the* PRINCESS *of his dreams. The bed and room
are merely suggested by curtains all around.* NAROPA *and the puppet* PRIN-
CESS *are naked or nearly so under the sheets: the* PRINCESS's *sari and
NAROPA's robe, staff, and bowl are lying by. The puppet* PRINCESS's *fleshly
appearance is as attractive as her dressed appearance.*)

PRINCESS: Are you happy?

NAROPA: (*Dreamily.*) Oh, I'm happy, yes, but —

PRINCESS: Shhhhh. (*She turns to him as he lies on his back, kissing his
lips.*) We'll go riding today. We'll look at the mountains my father gave
you.

NAROPA: (*Beginning to wake up a little.*) What's happening? Something is
too easy.

PRINCESS: (*Kissing him again.*) Shhhh. When my father dies you and I will
be king. You'll be the tallest king this kingdom has ever had.

NAROPA: My father was a king. I could have been a king in my own country, 'though it's not as rich as yours. I've had a wife, 'though she wasn't
as beautiful as you. I left to become a monk. I taught at the University
. . . then — I'm looking for my teacher. (*He sits up in bed.*) I'm looking
for my teacher, Tilopa.

PRINCESS: My father will help you find anyone you want.

NAROPA: (*Getting out of bed.*) Nuts!

PRINCESS: (*Sitting up, pulling the sheet up over her breasts.*) What are you
doing?

(*He is putting on his robe. She pulls the bell-rope behind her. Almost immediately the door opens and the* KING *enters with his guards behind him.
The* PRINCESS, *holding the sheet to cover her, moves to him.*)

KING: (*Angry.*) You only appear to be a civilized man, Naropa. Until you

become sensible you will stay locked in this bedroom — forever, if need
be.

(*The* KING *leaves with his guards, pulling the* PRINCESS *with him. There is
the sound of a heavy bolt being shut.* NAROPA *breathes heavy and quick,
preparing to break down the walls.*)

NAROPA: I'll huff and I'll puff, and I'll blow these walls down! My right arm
will be a hammer!

(*He stands, puffs out his chest, and does karate chops with his arms, going
toward a wall. An exasperated man's voice, which we will later recognize as*
TILOPA's, *is heard from behind the curtains. The music stops.*)

TILOPA'S VOICE: Oh, Naro, Naro, what are you doing now? Are you going
to cut a dream in half with a sword? Has Baby been tricked again by his
own magic show? Did you imagine you would find Tilopa in bed with
the princess? Naro . . .

(*The curtains lift. The light is green.* NAROPA *is in a forest, but he is so
feisty, giving little karate chops here and there, jumping around like a box-
er, that he hardly knows where he is. A young* HUNTER *sits quietly sharpen-
ing his arrows with a sharp knife. His spear, also sharp, and his bow, are
beside him. Hunters were considered disreputable. This one is dressed
scantily and roughly—the local equivalent of a semi-outlaw; his presence is
seductively physical and strong.*)

HUNTER: Need a weapon?

(NAROPA *is so feisty he doesn't hear him. After a long while, maybe ten seconds,* NAROPA *suddenly hears the question and spins on the* HUNTER,
aware of his presence.)

NAROPA: What?
HUNTER: (*Calmly.*) Need a weapon?
NAROPA: (*Suspiciously.*) What for?
HUNTER: (*Shrugging his shoulders.*) I don't know.
NAROPA: My teacher's name is Tilopa. I'm looking for him. He's tricky.

(NAROPA *is at this moment furious with* TILOPA. *He continues karate chops
and feistiness.*)

HUNTER: A knife maybe? Sharp. Or a spear?
NAROPA: (*Suspicious, spinning on him again.*) What for?
HUNTER: You could kill yourself a deer. (*He pulls back the bow, demon-
strating its strength.*)
NAROPA: (*Fascinated, then remembering who he is.*) I don't kill. Monks
don't kill. "All living beings are our brothers and sisters."
HUNTER: (*Smiling.*) You're not hungry?
NAROPA: (*Who is.*) No.
HUNTER: (*Smiling more.*) You wouldn't like some nice venison?

NAROPA: (*Walking off angrily and with as much dignity as he can muster.*) No. I would not.

TILOPA'S VOICE: (*Coming from somewhere behind the hunter.*) Too bad, Naropa. If you won't shoot the arrow of your beautiful mind from the bow of your beautiful body, if you won't kill all those prefabricated notions, you ain't gonna find nobody.

(NAROPA *spins around but the* HUNTER *leaps behind the white screen and is gone.*)

TILOPA'S VOICE: And tomorrow I'm goin' fishin'.

(NAROPA *leans for a moment against a tree, recovering his composure. Then he takes a few deep breaths and begins to travel again, only this time a little faster—he walks fast.*)

MUSICIANS: (*At a faster pace.*) Om hri, ha ha hum hum phat. Om hri, ha ha hum hum phat. Om hri, ha ha hum hum phat ... etc....

MONK: (*Speaking.*) And then Naropa came to a mountain lake in which he could see fish jumping. 'Surely here,' he thought by this large and quiet lake, 'I will find my teacher.'

(NAROPA *sits by the lake, carefully composing himself into a lotus meditating position, closing his eyes. His meditation, which may be accompanied by a quiet flute, is soon interrupted by the voices of peasants approaching from one side of the lake, a* MAN *and a* WOMAN.)

OLD MAN'S VOICE: Aay-up. Guh. (*Pause.*) Guh. Aay. Oop. (*Sound of teeth clicking, sound of slurping, loud.*) Aaayuh. Gimmie that 'un.

OLD WOMAN'S VOICE: (*After she clicks her teeth.*) Et it.

OLD MAN: Shit. Aayup. Got it! Big un.

(NAROPA *remains in his meditating posture, doing his best to ignore these uncivilized sounds. The flute tries to go on. A slovenly* OLD MAN *and a slovenly* OLD WOMAN *enter ploughing. As they plow they are grabbing at worms and insects in the furrow and eating them. The* OLD MAN *and the* OLD WOMAN *are played by puppets. They look as gross as can be.*)

OLD MAN: Gimmie that 'un.

OLD WOMAN: (*Clapping the worm into her mouth.*) Et it.

OLD MAN: Greedy bitch. Next un's mine. And the next un too. Aayup.

(OLD MAN *grabs an insect and eats it.* NAROPA *has not been able to stop himself from opening his eyes to these activities. He is disgusted but trying not to be. With some effort he turns from the lake to address the peasants.*)

NAROPA: Hello? Excuse me.

OLD MAN: (*Grabs another worm.*) Mine.

OLD WOMAN: (*Grabbing another.*) Mine.

NAROPA: Hello!

(They look at him.)

NAROPA: I'm waiting for my—for Tilopa. Ti-lo-pa! He's fishing. Have you seen him?

OLD WOMAN: *(Shouting in the* OLD MAN'*s ear.)* It wants its Ti-lo-pa.

OLD MAN: Well, tell it.

OLD WOMAN: Ti-lo-pa said 'wait.'

OLD MAN: Give it some food.

(The OLD MAN *goes off continuing to plough. As* NAROPA *watches in horrified fascination the* OLD (PUPPET) WOMAN *lights some wood under a pot (which is in a size appropriate to her). Then from a rusty barrel she takes some live worms and a frog and puts them into the cooking pot.)*

NAROPA: *(Getting up.)* I ... thanks ... but I ... I'm a vegetarian. Thanks. I'm fasting. I don't eat. Thanks.

(He turns away from the OLD WOMAN *and stands facing the lake. He is retching, trying to hide it.)*

MONK: *(Speaking.)* Naropa wondered what he had done in this lifetime, or any other, to be invited by an old grandmother to eat worms and frogs boiled alive.

(The OLD MAN *now returns. He looks as he did before, only now he is played by an actor rather than a puppet. He is carrying a dead ox on his shoulders, grunting under its weight.)*

OLD MAN: *(To* OLD WOMAN*)* Did you make it food?

*(*OLD WOMAN *wiggles her finger at her head, then at* NAROPA, *indicating that* NAROPA *must be crazy.)*

OLD WOMAN: I made it food but—it won't.

OLD MAN: Shit! Shit on it.

(He drops the ox carcass right onto the boiling pot, etc., crushing and annihilating fire, pot, etc.)

OLD MAN (To NAROPA): Shit on you! Shit! How're you going to learn anything if you won't eat? You won't even eat your own thoughts. You stand there like a dried-out turd mulling things over! Shit.

(The lights go out.)

NAROPA: Shit.

TILOPA'S VOICE: *And* I'm goin' to kill them whether you like it or not.

(The lights come up again on the MAN *we saw earlier torturing his* PARENTS. *Now he's stabbing them each with a knife again and again, formally, pausing between stabs. The puppets who play the* PARENTS *are the same puppets who played the* OLD PEASANT MAN *and the* OLD PEASANT WOMAN—*but they look younger as the* PARENTS.*)*

TILOPA'S VOICE: (*Gently.*) Don't split everything into this and that, little Naro. You'll never find me if you won't look inside yourself.

(*The white screen is placed in front of the* MAN *with his* PARENTS.)

TILOPA'S VOICE: Tomorrow I'm going begging.

(NAROPA *can barely get himself to walk, but he does, and from a walk into a fast walk, and from that into a run. He is jogging.*)

MUSICIANS: (*At the appropriate faster and faster rhythm.*) Om hri, ha ha hum hum phat. Om hri, ha ha hum hum phat. Om hri, ha ha hum hum phat.

(*Then the* MUSICIANS *are silent as* NAROPA *continues to jog.*)

NAROPA: (*To himself.*) Om hri, ha ha hum hum phat.
FIRST YOUNG MONK: (*One of the* MUSICIANS.) Who is *that*?
SECOND YOUNG MONK: (*Also a* MUSICIAN/NARRATOR.) It's the old abbot of Nalanda. The one who's gone crazy.

(*The two* MONKS *go out onto the stage.* NAROPA *stops running. They both prostrate themselves to him.*)

SECOND MONK: You do this hermitage honor, Sir.
FIRST MONK: We're honored, Sir, by your visit to our monastery.
NAROPA: Get up. I'm not an abbot.
SECOND MONK: (*To first.*) Go get the superior.
NAROPA: I'm looking for my teacher, Tilopa.
SECOND MONK: Yes, Sir.
NAROPA: Have you heard of Tilopa?

(*The* FIRST MONK *returns with the* SUPERIOR *from the* MUSICIANS' *platform. He also prostrates to* NAROPA, *as does the* FIRST YOUNG MONK *again.*)

SUPERIOR: Glorious abbot. Saint.
NAROPA: No, no, stop that. I'm looking for Tilopa.

(*They stand.*)

SUPERIOR: Well, as it happens, Sir, there's a beggar in our courtyard who says his name is Tilopa.

(*They turn toward the white screen which is lifted to reveal a* BEGGAR *squatting by a fire. He has gray hair tied back in a knot, a wiry dark body, and he wears only white cotton around his middle. He takes two live (puppet) fish from a pail of water and tosses them into a frying pan. The* MONKS *react angrily, pulling at him, beating him with their hands.*)

MONK: What are you doing? Evil! This is a monastery. Frying live fish! Live! Desecration!
BEGGAR: Sirs, sirs, what's the matter? Don't you like fish?

SUPERIOR: Cooking live fish is a desecration!
BEGGAR: (*Snapping his fingers in a casual way.*) Fish, go home.

(*The fish seem to fly straight up into the sky.* NAROPA *prostrates himself to the* BEGGAR.)

NAROPA: Tilopa, venerable Tilopa, please give me instruction.

(*The* BEGGAR *reaches into a rusty container.*)

BEGGAR: Here.

(*He thrusts his hand out aggressively to* NAROPA.)

FIRST MONK: (*Looking into the* BEGGAR's *hand with disgust.*) Lice.
BEGGAR: (*To* NAROPA.) Kill these.

(*All the* MONKS *are horrified.* NAROPA, *on his knees, backs away from the lice. The* BEGGAR *pushes them a little closer to this face.*)

BEGGAR: Here. If you want to kill your ignorance, kill these.

(NAROPA *is unable to agree.*)

MONK: (*Chanting.*) And how will you learn anything, Naropa, the beggar said, if you won't kill the lice of habit-forming thoughts which are inside you?
ANOTHER MUSICIAN: (*Chanting from elsewhere on the stage.*) And how will you learn anything, Naropa, the beggar said, if you won't kill the lice of habit-forming thoughts which are inside you?

(*The* BEGGAR *has gone.* NAROPA *gets up slowly and lurches out of the hermitage as the lights dim. He continues to lurch from stylized figure to stylized figure spread out on the plain, as all the characters present chant, in turn and overlapping and in unison (but so that the words are heard clearly) as in Tibetan chanting, the whole producing a droning noise like many bees gathering nectar on a bush. This low Tibetan-style chanting is accompanied by the Tibetan musical instruments, climaxing later in the scene into a joyous 'calling forth of the god' but never losing a continuity that is like the extension of a single moment, hallucinatory in that way.*

The whole stage is used for this scene, including the musicians' platform—as great an impression of width as possible should be given. The DEAF MUSICIANS *referred to are the actual* MUSICIANS. *The* LEGLESS MAN *moves in a constant tiny circle on a small wheeled platform. The* TONGUELESS MAN *says what the others are saying but in sign language only. The* CORPSE's *face is painted white and it is lying, fanning itself slowly with a large feather.*

During this whole scene NAROPA *is 'lurching' in slow motion from character to character, looking for* TILOPA.)

CHANTER: To find your teacher, Naropa, you must learn to see with your teacher's eyes, then you will learn to see your teacher....

CHANTER: And Naropa found himself on a wide plain where the light was as on the desert just before the sun rises, where the light was white on the horizon but dark blue above with a few stars still shining...and the plain seemed to extend all around him without interruption by house or tree...and the people on the plain appeared to be ordinary and the people on the plain appeared not to be ordinary.

CHANTER: There was a one-eyed soldier cleaning his gun ...

CHANTER: And a one-eyed priest conferring blessings ...

CHANTER: And a blind painter painting a buddha ...

CHANTER: And a one-eyed merchant weighing goods ...

CHANTER: And deaf musicians playing ...

CHANTER: And a tongueless man speaking ...

CHANTER: And a legless man moving ...

CHANTER: And a corpse in white silk gently fanning itself with a feather ...

(Here there is a moment of horn-blowing or a single unexpected strong instrument.)

CHANTER: If you learn to see with your teacher's eyes, you will learn to see your teacher....

(Another musical underlining.)

CHANTER: Assume the courage of your convictions.

CHANTER: Be worthy.

CHANTER: Be devout.

CHANTER: Be confident.

(Another musical underlining.)

CHANTER: If you learn to see with your teacher's eyes, you will learn to see your teacher ...

CHANTER: Wield the razor of intuitive understanding ... you'll come to the viewpoint.

CHANTER: Pay attention to all things. That is the method.

CHANTER: Free yourself from the voices of this and that.

CHANTER: Ride the horse of bliss and radiance....

CHANTER: By your own light will you know ... By your own light ... by your own light

(This is a joyous climactic place emphasized by the instruments. Then the chanting starts low again.)

CHANTER: *(being the* BLIND/PAINTER *on the plain.)* Most people see only with one eye ...

ANOTHER ONE-EYED CHANTER FROM THE PLAIN: Most people see without seeing a thing.

MUTE: *(Singing only, accompanied by a droning instrument but not by other voices.)* Most people speak, saying nothing.

THE LEGLESS MAN: (*Chanting.*) Don't you know, Naropa, that we're all lame?
CHANTER: Don't you know, Naropa, that this world is a world of the lame . . . .
CHANTER: That lameness is just a way of moving slowly.
CORPSE: (*Chanting; all sound having become very soft by now.*) And the still-
ness of death is only a breeze from the place of no beginning.

(*Very little music, fading. A cymbal crash. Lights out.*)

(*The lights come up again almost immediately. This time the light is perfectly
ordinary, not colored at all, and there are no* MUSICIANS *or* CHANTERS *or
anyone on the stage but* NAROPA. *He has a small box with him, and he is
carefully but systematically taking a razor out of it, etc., preparing to kill
himself.*)

NAROPA: (*Simply.*) Although I've met various manifestations of my teacher, I
haven't met Tilopa. I've failed. I'm ashamed to go back. Since this body
and mind have held me back, I'm going to discard them. I resolve to meet
my teacher in a later life.

(*Very calmly he is about to slit his wrist when* TILOPA's *voice is heard loud,
from nearby, calling.*)

TILOPA'S VOICE: Naropa! How will you find your teacher if you kill the
Buddha?

(*He appears, the* BEGGAR *we saw in the hermitage, but not fierce now, and
cleaner-looking.*)

TILOPA: Is it not me your evil thoughts desire?

(NAROPA *is very moved.* TILOPA *holds him.* NAROPA *drops his head.*)

NAROPA: How could I have thought the truth was in what is uncertain and
passing like a cloud? Now, please . . . accept me as your student.
TILOPA: Ever since you first met me in the form of a leper we haven't been
apart. We've been like a body and its shadow, you and I. The visions
you had of the world arose from the poisons of your own past. (*He
chants the last two lines unpretentiously, just a little different from
speaking.*) Now you are immaculate and radiant, you are worthy to be
taught.

(*From backstage a long single horn sound. Lights dim out.*)

Starluster

John Wellman

for Yolanda

©1980 Copyright by John Wellman.
CAUTION: No performances or readings of this work may be given without the ex-
press authorization of the author's agent. For production rights contact: Helen
Merrill, 337 West 22nd Street, New York, N.Y. 10011.

Starluster was first performed on February 8, 1979, in The Basement Space of The American Place Theatre, New York. It was directed by Carl Weber, and the cast included:

MARIE. . . . .*Robin Groves*
NICHOLS . . . .*Kevin O'Connor*
ANNA . . . .*Ellen Barber*
CLERK . . . .*Dominc Chianese/Ted Hoffman*
HOUGH . . . .*David Rasche*

Sets: Sally Locke
Music: Michael S. Roth
Costumes: Mary Brecht

NICHOLS.
ANNA.
MARIE.
HOUGH.
THE CLERK.

The first four are young Americans, aged from twenty-five to thirty. The CLERK is older, perhaps fifty. They are all rather elegantly dressed and should resemble a collection of thirties' gangsters and molls. HOUGH's appearance is a touch more sombre than the rest. All, except the CLERK, are hatted at one time or another.

The setting is an hotel in the Fado district of Lisbon, Portugal. The action takes place during the winter of 1975-76, but should be imagined as an approximate present.

The Ballad of Bad Weather. Music composed by Michael Roth. In The American Place production this was sung as a prologue to the play. The *Ballad* is always to be sung by MARIE.

A note on the chess. In scene four HOUGH is perusing a copy of Kotov's *Alexander Alekhine.* R.H.M. Press, 1975, which contains the specified game between Alekhine and Reti: a sprightly *Ruy Lopez* finishing in a draw after thirty-seven moves. The game was played in Vienna, not Lisbon; and was played in 1922, not in 1925. But it is a masterpiece. In scene twelve HOUGH departs from the game on his sixteenth move, and within five or six moves crushes NICHOLS. It is perhaps superfluous to note that neither NICHOLS nor HOUGH is in any way remarkable as a chess player. In scene eight and thereafter HOUGH and NICHOLS each possess a copy of Kotov.

THE BALLAD:

>   Rode we two the beacon's glare down to sea,
>   Under a white sky and a jet-black sun;
>   They faded slate, my truelove's blue-eyes,
>   Without no rhyme or reason.
>
>   But bad weather had swallowed up the light,
>   Without no rhyme or reason;
>   Till by Lisbon town they had faded quite,
>   Under a white sky and a jet-black sun.
>
>   I stood on the pebble beach, much alone,
>   Under a white sky and a jet-black sun;
>   Some thin witch had claimed his eyes for her own,
>   Without no rhyme or reason.
>
>   What matter of man he was, to betray,
>   Without no rhyme or reason,
>   Wicked seabirds knew, but would not say,
>   Under a white sky and a jet-black sun.
>
>   But I hung bat-blind in my love, *so much!*
>   Under a white sky and a jet-black sun
>   That I clung to what I could not touch,
>   Without no rhyme or reason.
>
>   But I found my bitter life none too free
>   Without no rhyme or reason;
>   That gray weather cleared. Oh, I could see,
>   Under a white sky and a jet-black sun.

So gathered berries-blue to scotch his sight,
Under a white sky and a jet-black sun;
How the weather's bitch had nursed her spite,
Without no rhyme or reason!

For I recalled some witching *I had known*,
Without no rhyme or reason;
That witch I brained with an old cow-bone,
Under a white sky and a jet-black sun.

Now bad weathers comes too frequently
Under a white sky and a jet-black sun;
Rode we two the beacon's glare down to sea,
Without no rhyme or reason.

So I hide my heart in silver. My love's my love despite;
Without no rhyme or reason;
But bad weather had swallowed up the light,
Under a white sky and a jet-black sun.

For he that's blind, must be mine alone,
Under a white sky and a jet-black sun;
I stand on the pebble beach, very much alone,
Without no rhyme or reason.

Scene one. The lobby of an old hotel in the Fado district of Lisbon.
NICHOLS *sits on a chair at a table. He is hunched over a collection of objects that includes a hash pipe, bottles, incense sticks, a small idol, burning candles, and a radio. He is wearing a headset. The* CLERK *remains motionless in the shadows behind his desk.* ANNA *enters as indicated, carrying two suitcases. She approaches* NICHOLS *from the rear, and so does not see his face.*

NICHOLS:

Break this
Spell of rain,
Starluster,
And the fogs . . .
Spell of rain,
Starluster,
The numbers!
Still no three
From two. He's really
Tough nut to crack.
"The Eastern Star
Calls with its
Hundred knives,"

                    Starluster,
                    Burn the cities!
                    Burn the cities!
                    Double one oh
                    Seven forty
                    Seven three,
                    Do you read me?
                    It's *The Prize*!
                    The Prize! Fog,
                    Nothing but
                    Fog, drizzle,
                    "The war of clouds."
                    Starluster,
                    Send me four
                    Seven two and it's
                    "Little girls
                    Jumping rope."
                    Break this
                    Spell of rain,
                    Starluster, it's
                    Burn the cities!
                    Burn the cities! Read me? Double
                Or nothing. *Cryptic, man, cryptic*!
                And just once more, Starluster,
                Conchita's sweet nookie . . . *oops*!

(ANNA *enters*.)

                    No way. The weather does not allow.
                    Three thirty-three. She's too stupid, read me?
                    I can't see you, Starluster, I can't see you!
ANNA: Hey, I've been looking for you, buster. *No, it's not you.*
NICHOLS: Who are you?
ANNA: Is there
                Anybody here?
NICHOLS: "That depends on
                Who you're looking for . . ."
ANNA: Idiot.
CLERK: May I help you, madame?
ANNA: Is this place . . .
                Hotel *Mirafunda*?
NICHOLS: Oh this?
                Just a little sympathetic magic.
                It's a kind of short-wave, deep-brain
                Sign language.

ANNA: I'd like a single-bath American room . . . I mean,

A single room. *Per favore. Por favor.*

CLERK: Of course, madame.
       With private bath?

ANNA: Yes, please.

CLERK: Your first visit to Lisbon, madame?

ANNA: Yes, it's my first.
      I mean *no*. I've been here before, once,
      A long time ago. Say, you wouldn't, by any chance,
      Happen to know a man by the name of . . .

(She stares suddenly at NICHOLS, *who has been inspecting her suitcases.)*

NICHOLS: It's just my way
         Of loosening up, metaphysically,
         So to speak. All the poets speak of that.

ANNA: *(To the* CLERK.)
      I'm looking for a man named Hough.

CLERK: I am sorry, madame.
       The rules of the hotel do not permit.

NICHOLS: Do you know Blake, William Blake?

ANNA: *(To the* CLERK.)
      Oh, I see, well, thank you.

CLERK: I am sorry, madame, but those are our rules.
       That man over there, he is your compatriot.

ANNA: Indeed.

CLERK: He may be able to enlighten you.

ANNA: Indeed he may.

NICHOLS: I was a prodigy.

ANNA: *(To the* CLERK.)
      Thank you. It's not important.
      May I see the room?

CLERK: But of course. Follow me.

ANNA: *(To* NICHOLS.)
      Pardon me.

NICHOLS: Yes?

ANNA: I want to speak with a man named Hough.
      He is purported to be ensconced in this hotel.

NICHOLS: Perhaps you mean *reported* . . .

ANNA: I mean *purported*. It is a theoretical question.
      I see his hat on the hat-rack, *but*,
      On the other hand, many hats look alike.
      Tell him Anna's here, which he knows
      Anyway, but just tell him Anna's here.

(She begins to leave.)

NICHOLS: The Woman's Movement opened me up
         To my own passionate sublimity.

ANNA:	Well, blind me!
NICHOLS:	I know my own death. They can't take that from me.
	A true poet must epitomize the insignificant.
	Clouds are my best friends. And the numbers 3,5,8.
	My role is poet; I marshall all the lies and constraints
	Of America.
ANNA:	You certainly do.
NICHOLS:	For my own uses. From New York?
ANNA:	Don't waste time, do you?
NICHOLS:	New York! That's where I belong. One of the places ...
ANNA:	One of the places ...
NICHOLS:	There are many. The Revolution will begin there.
	All the health food restaurants. People there really care
	About the food they eat.
ANNA:	(*To the* CLERK.)
	Sir, show me to my room. I feel weary.
	The train ride was long ...

(*To* NICHOLS.)

	And tedious.
NICHOLS:	You must mean Hough. He's staying here too.
	He writes poems and plays. Quite promising.
	I keep an eye on things. My name is Nichols.
	He's upstairs talking to my old lady Marie.

Scene two. ANNA's *hotel room. The furniture in the room is simple and nondescript.* MARIE *follows* ANNA *into the room, inadvertently taking her by surprise.*

ANNA:	*Starluster* ...
	Hype. That's what that is. *Jesus Christ!* Who are you?
MARIE:	Marie. I'm in the next room.
ANNA:	Place is crammed with Americans.
MARIE:	I have renounced America. All I do is keep
	The passport. It's useful.
ANNA:	I'll say.
MARIE:	I'm Marie.
ANNA:	Have you been here long?
MARIE:	A week or two.
ANNA:	You must like it here
	In Lisbon.
MARIE:	Hate it.
ANNA:	Then why do you stay?
MARIE:	Business. Not really something
	To talk about. That's a pretty dress.

	Where'd you get it?
ANNA:	In the States, but it's Italian. It is nice, isn't it?
MARIE:	Tell me, what's it like out today?
ANNA:	How do you mean?
MARIE:	The weather.
ANNA:	Oh, it's quite foggy and damp. Cold. Haven't You been out yet?
MARIE:	No. Not today. I don't like to.
ANNA:	What? Go out?
MARIE:	That's right. What lovely boots!
ANNA:	You like them?
MARIE:	Very much.
ANNA:	Well I don't. They pinch my feet. Say, Who's that guy downstairs in the lobby?
MARIE:	Only Louis. Nichols. We're traveling together. He's a genius. *I'm not feeling well* . . .
ANNA:	Oh, have you been sick?
MARIE:	Off and on. I always am. I don't like to travel Particularly.
ANNA:	That's why you don't go out?
MARIE:	That's right.
ANNA:	Well, *I am* going out. Can I get you something?
MARIE:	No. Thanks anyway.
ANNA:	Where's Hough?
MARIE:	He went downstairs. Do you know him?
ANNA:	Vaguely.
MARIE:	He's nice. He got some things for me. That's why I don't need to.
ANNA:	Yes. He's nice.
MARIE:	What's your name?
ANNA:	Oh, I'm sorry. It's Anna. Anna Farrar. I want To clean up a bit. Let's go for a coffee later on, All right?
ANNA:	Yes, I'd like that. Good-bye, Anna.
ANNA:	Good-bye, Marie.
MARIE:	Don't fuck him.
ANNA:	*What?!*
MARIE:	Please don't fuck him. He's got the crabs anyway.
ANNA:	What on earth do you mean? Fuck *who?*
MARIE:	Nichols. Don't. Please.
ANNA:	I have no intention Of fucking him.
MARIE::	Please.

ANNA: Go away. I need some rest.

MARIE: Good-bye, Anna.

Scene three. A small cafe in the hotel, adjacent to the lobby. NICHOLS *is sitting at a table reading a newspaper. On the table are a chess board and pieces.* ANNA *enters, in a huff.*

ANNA: Did you ask?

NICHOLS: What? What do you mean?

ANNA: Did you ask *Starluster* whether it is
           All right to have a cup of coffee with me?

NICHOLS: Bitch. You must really get off on
           Being unfriendly. The life of the imagination
           Knows no division.

ANNA: Is that so? Well,
           You can fuck me, if you want,
           But only from behind, like an animal.

NICHOLS: What the hell!

ANNA: Be grateful.

NICHOLS: You're incredible!

ANNA: What's the Portuguese word for *thank you*?

NICHOLS: What the hell are you up to?

ANNA: Tell me, shithead, the word for *thank you*!

NICHOLS: *Obrigado.* It's obrigado.

ANNA: What?

NICHOLS: O-bri-gado.

ANNA: Obrigado? Obrigado. Now say it, go ahead, say it!

NICHOLS: I don't believe you.

ANNA: Say it, shithead, say it!

NICHOLS: Obrigado!

ANNA: I won't fuck you. You're too much of a shithead.

(*She leaves.*)

NICHOLS: Obrigado.

Scene four. The lobby. HOUGH *and* NICHOLS *are playing an impromptu game of chess. The latter seems somewhat anxious, and spends much of the scene, especially the first half, on his feet.*

HOUGH: Why do you say that Nichols?

NICHOLS: Because half the house must come down.

HOUGH: Which half?

NICHOLS: The bottom.

HOUGH: Tell that woman, when she asks, that I'm
            Not here.
NICHOLS: I win; I always win
            Because I've accepted my own insignificance,
            And lived my own death. You could beat me
            And I'd still win. It's my *karma*. Your move.
HOUGH: They pursue you to the far ends of the earth.
NICHOLS: It's freaky.
HOUGH: (*Showing him a book*.).
            Do you know this game? Reti and Alekhine
            Played it here, right here in this hotel.
NICHOLS: Incredible.
HOUGH: Incredible if you think about it;
            Everyone in flight . . .
NICHOLS: What did you say?
HOUGH: Nothing.
NICHOLS: You look cross-eyed.
HOUGH: Cause I'm thinking.
NICHOLS: Want some dope?
HOUGH: Not now . . . Hey, I've got an idea.
NICHOLS: Good for you.
HOUGH: Have a seat, I insist.
NICHOLS: Hemorrhoids . . .
HOUGH: Kneel then.
NICHOLS: What is it?

HOUGH: We'll play chess . . .
NICHOLS: I thought that was what we were doing.
HOUGH: Look, we'll play out this game. The one
            I showed you: *Reti-Alekhine, Lisbon 1925*.
NICHOLS: It was a draw.
HOUGH: (*He begins to set up the chess pieces*.)
            So?
NICHOLS: So, what's the good of that?
            I mean I can get into deception,
            But this stinks.
HOUGH: No, idiot.
NICHOLS: *What's idiot?* It was a good game,
            But it's been played, so to speak.
HOUGH: You can depart from the game
            At some point.
NICHOLS: Then it's not the same.
HOUGH: Either player can depart from the game
            At any point. It becomes ours then.
            Since this game was a draw the safest
            Bet will always be to stick to the text.
            Move.

(HOUGH *makes his first move: P-K4.*)

	... Move.
NICHOLS:	You're a fiend.
HOUGH:	I'm serious.
NICHOLS:	You mean, like, if we follow along up to, say,
	The twenty-fifth move which is, say, pawn to knight
	Four, and I decide to move a totally different piece
	I just do it?
HOUGH:	Right, and we play it out from there.
	Loser pays for dinner.
NICHOLS:	Give me the book.

(*Pause.*)

HOUGH:	Sure, I spent some time in the Movement,
	But it's dead.
NICHOLS:	It's like a re-enactment.
HOUGH:	Everyone I know is a Buddhist, or a minimalist ...
NICHOLS:	It's like an exorcism.
HOUGH:	The fags have everything tied up tighter
	Than ...

(NICHOLS *makes his first move:* ... *P-K4.*)

NICHOLS:	Your move.
HOUGH:	Than ...
NICHOLS:	There's something
	In your coffee.

(HOUGH *moves: N-KB3.*)

HOUGH:	Fly shit.
NICHOLS:	My move? I like this.
	It's very existential, replaying a famous game
	Of chess. In the same hotel. Fifty years later.
	It's like voyeurism
	Because it's like looking into someone
	Else's soul. I'm really into voyeurism
	Because it's how you get to know the Big Lie.
	And we are all part of the Big Lie.

(NICHOLS *moves: N-QB3.*)

HOUGH:	Yeah, the same poses,
	The same bullshit.

(HOUGH *moves: B-QN5.*)

NICHOLS:	Poetry is voyeurism too.
HOUGH:	You know.

I'm beginnning to feel oppressed by my own
Generation. I'm trying to learn how to write,
But now I see that's very difficult, and well,
None of us ever bothered to master anything that was
Difficult.
    Oppressed by my generation! I can't even
Talk about it without invoking a half-dozen
Thunderous cliches, and sounding like a
Kind of scrambled headline from the *Voice*.

(NICHOLS *moves*: . . . *P-QR3*.)

NICHOLS: Did I ever tell you about this film
            That Marie and I made in Denmark?
            We lie on the beach and she sucks me off,
            But the best part is, in the backround,
            We played the music from the *Flying Nun*, or
            That nun song, whatever it was. Do you
            Remember?
HOUGH: Everyone is a conceptualist.
            Everyone on a grant, or handing them out.
            Everyone *into this*, or *into that*. Well, I'm the same,
            I guess. I want all the same things.

(HOUGH *moves*: *B-QR4*.)

NICHOLS: She didn't want to do it at first.
            But I told her, look Marie, we all have to
            Get into our own lies.
HOUGH: I came here to visit a city I used to love,
            And find *the same kind* of people. Don't take it
            Personally; I mean, I'm glad to see you.

(NICHOLS *moves*: . . . *N-KB3*.)

NICHOLS: Then we got stoned,
            And she did it. That was a revolutionary act.
HOUGH: If you hadn't noticed, I am quite fond
            Of contrivances.

(HOUGH *moves*: *N-B3*.)

NICHOLS: You know, you and I are different . . .
HOUGH: (NICHOLS *moves while* HOUGH *is speaking*: . . . *P-QN4*.)
            You know
            I was in love with this crazy woman once.
            She was so beautiful! I can still recall at least
            Six of her scents. I don't mean to be too obscure.
            One was her basic smell, a bit like coffee, resonant.
            One was a kind of mint, only a touch more

Aromatic in the upper registers. One was like salt.
Sweat, but sweet. The other three were indescribable.

NICHOLS: We are different, I think.
We are going to have to work this out.

HOUGH: (*He moves while speaking*: B-N3.)
She slept with everyone, including
My friends. That was the end of it, finally,
After a whole lot of grief. But I remember now,
How I got angry one time and demanded an
Explanation of one thing. An apology is what I wanted.
And she said: "Hough, you know me better than anyone."
And that struck me. Later on it occurred to me that
I didn't know her at all. It was that simple. But at
The time, I didn't know what to say.

NICHOLS: My move, the sixth. That's right.

(NICHOLS *moves*: . . . B-QB4.)

HOUGH: In case you're interested it was not her.
It was not her!

(CLERK *enters*.)

CLERK: Message for you, Senhor Hough.

(CLERK *leaves*.)

HOUGH: Be back in a minute.

(HOUGH *moves*: NxP, *then leaves*.)

NICHOLS: What did black do? Oh, ok . . .

(NICHOLS *moves*: . . . NxN.)

———————

Scene five. The lobby. HOUGH *and* NICHOLS *are back at the chess game.*

NICHOLS: I remember lying on my back, at my farm,
Watching the bombers fly overhead. To Viet-Nam.

HOUGH: To Jersey City.

(HOUGH *moves*: P-Q4.)

NICHOLS: You and me, we're survivors.

HOUGH: Speak for yourself.

NICHOLS: My sexual needs are flowers.

HOUGH: Mine are vegetables. Move.

NICHOLS: I walk in the woods
And sleep there.
Sometimes it rains.

(NICHOLS *moves*: . . . *B-Q3*.)

HOUGH: *What am I doing here?*
NICHOLS: I believe absolutely
             In the godlike nature
             Of most poets.

(HOUGH *moves*: *PxN*.)

HOUGH: *Most.*
NICHOLS: I'm not interested
             In another person's
             Weaknesses.

(NICHOLS *moves*: . . . *BxP*.)

             . . . Move.
HOUGH: You know I dreamed last night
             I murdered someone, but I couldn't
             Make out who it was.
NICHOLS: I believe they will crucify
             Us all, the poets first.
HOUGH: Nail us up on the fucking telephone poles.

(HOUGH *moves*: *P-B4*.)

NICHOLS: Marie has these hangups;
             I need a lot of women
             To satisfy me.
HOUGH: *The more the merrier!* Move.
NICHOLS: What do you mean?
HOUGH: Move.
NICHOLS: My poems are for me alone.
             I need others who are like me.
HOUGH: Anybody I know? Move.
NICHOLS: You know, you and I are different.
HOUGH: Move, slowpoke.

Scene six. The lobby at night. It is quite dark. ANNA *and* HOUGH *are walking about slowly. They sit down and get up from time to time. The interrupted chess remains as it was at the end of the preceding scene.*

ANNA: You know my father hated Jews so much
             He fell off a ladder yelling at one. Then
             He found out he was Jewish. Around that time
             He began to beat us kids. Then he left.
             Is that the kind of man you are?
HOUGH: I have my own needs.

ANNA:	Thoughts run through my mind;
	Some connect and some don't.
	Shut the window please; it's drafty! I
	Listen to myself; and
	I wonder how long it can go on like this,
	In fact . . .
HOUGH:	It all seems so obvious. *So damn obvious!*

(*Long pause as the* CLERK *emerges from his office behind the desk, pauses to light a cigarette, and strides out.*)

ANNA:	You're so full of contempt.
	How can I reach you?
	How can you be reached?
HOUGH:	I don't for the life of me
	See what your game is.
ANNA:	That has nothing to do with this;
	I am not sorry. I will not apologize.
HOUGH:	What do you mean?
ANNA:	I can imagine myself accomplishing something
	Quite grand, but only with someone's help.
HOUGH:	Don't tease, Anna.
ANNA:	Hough's always the same.
	Everyone else changes, they change
	All the time. But Hough stays the same.
HOUGH:	Who was it?
ANNA:	My feelings are my own. I can do
	Just as I please with my life.
HOUGH:	What the hell are you talking about? I am
	Asking you who put you up to this.
ANNA:	How can you threaten everything
	Over this arcane little fantasy of yours?
HOUGH:	I don't know
	A damn thing that's of any use. You think
	You can make a revolution with phone numbers,
	Names on a list.
ANNA:	You can make a revolution out of anything
	If you want to.
HOUGH:	You wouldn't know a revolution from a
	Garbage strike.
ANNA:	Now listen to me carefully. The whole
	Thing could blow up sky-wide any time . . .
HOUGH:	*Wide? sky-wide?*
ANNA:	High . . . sky-high.
HOUGH:	What do you believe in, anyway?
ANNA:	I've never killed anyone. Yet. Who's that

	Creep you play chess with?
HOUGH:	A creep.
ANNA:	I am not a criminal.
	A crime is something you do, by yourself,
	For yourself. Now you, what do you believe in?
HOUGH:	I never said I did.
ANNA:	Nothing, nothing, nothing, nothing, nothing . . .
HOUGH:	No, dearie, it's not the same as nothing.
ANNA:	Here we stand. The self-indicted. It seems
	I'm the philosopher today. You don't believe in anything . . .
HOUGH:	Correct.
ANNA:	But that's not the same as believing in nothing?
HOUGH:	Correct.
ANNA:	So what is this *it* that you do believe in, anyway?
HOUGH:	It's not the same as nothing. But I won't tell you.
	You're a mocker. I wouldn't give you the satisfaction.
ANNA:	*I'm the mocker?*
HOUGH:	Why'd you ask that about Nichols?
ANNA:	Only you know all the Operators.
	The ones that Joe, Caspar, and Bones know.
	Don't know Bones, Caspar, and Joe.
HOUGH:	Tsk! Tsk!
ANNA:	We need your help.
HOUGH:	You smell like shit.
ANNA:	It'll happen anyway.
HOUGH:	Keep out of what doesn't concern you. Don't
	Bother me anymore. Pack your bags. Leave.
	Go back.
ANNA:	We are not going to harm anyone. Not in
	Lisbon. You're so *bourgeois*.
HOUGH:	Bourgeois my ass!
	You and your nasty little German friends
	Can go stuff your nasty little narrow minds
	Up your collective ideological asshole.
	If you can't see through that crowd of . . .
	Of . . .
ANNA:	You're giving me a headache.
HOUGH:	It always eludes me. It always eludes me . . .
	I just can't find the words. I get so fucking mad
	I could walk through a brick wall without feeling
	It, but I lose the words. I can't find a way of
	Saying it. Sick of punk. Of the *Stones*. Of potheads.
	Poltergeists. Blank consciousness. Auras. Health
	Food. Fist-fucking. The *new this*, the *new that* . . .
ANNA:	You sound like a reactionary.
HOUGH:	A mossback . . .

Fuck the Sixties! Stuff it. But I still want to bring down
The banks, bureaucracies, unions, cartels, all of it. The
Whole fucking chess game.

ANNA: I feel terrible.

HOUGH: Take a pill. Over there. In my left coat-pocket,
I think.

ANNA: What is it, an upper, a downer?

HOUGH: A leveller.

ANNA: What's that?

HOUGH: Aspirin.

ANNA: Why? Why not? Why not in Lisbon?

HOUGH: So you like Portugal, do you? Well, tell me,
Who is Alvaro Cunhal? Or Vasco-Goncalves?
Do you know how Spinola was forced from
Power? Or who the CIA resident is? Or what
Plans they have in store for us? Well?

ANNA: Ok ... Have it your way. I'm going. But
I'm not going anywhere. We're not through
With this.

Scene seven. The lobby of the hotel. HOUGH *is talking on the* CLERK's *desk-telephone while the latter stands motionless behind his desk.* NICHOLS *saunters in, and realizing what is happening, stops in his tracks to eavesdrop. He departs as indicated, in a hurry.*

HOUGH: So you
want me
to wait ...
Should I
tell her
the names?

(NICHOLS *enters.*)

Yes, he is
here, and
we are
getting ac-
quainted.
He talks a
mean chess game,
as for being
a poet I'm
not so sure.
Of course.

Of course.
Then it's
going to
start right
here in
sleepy old
Lisbon?
Bank of this,
Bank of that.
Which one first?
Banco di
Spirito Santo,
a major dis-
ruption of
cash flow
and re-dis-
tribution of
assets to the
four winds,
operations
in the States
only of a
diversionary
nature . . .
Quel surprise!
In four days
eh? That soon!
Well, I'll be
damned! Who?
No, he does
not have a
clue. No idea.
Impossible.
Yes, yes, yes,
I read you.
Of course.
Of course.

(*Pause as* NICHOLS *scurries out.*)

I shall
keep you in-
formed. So
far it's de-
ceptively
even. I'll
sign off

for now.
Viva, etc.

(NICHOLS *leaves*.)

HOUGH: I'm afraid he's heard it all, Joao!
CLERK: As you say, *hook line and sinker*.

Scene eight. The lobby as before. NICHOLS *and* HOUGH *continue their chess game. Each sits at a separate table over separate, but identical, chess sets. When one moves a piece at his table the other responds as though the move had taken place at his board.* NICHOLS'*s table is upstage on the right,* HOUGH'*s is downstage on the left. They do not look at each other.*

NICHOLS: (*He moves while speaking: BxN.*)
There's something about that in Merwin's book
The Tennis Court Oath. I like his stuff.
It is mysterious. Like mine. It's that quality
Of mystery that's important. You know I could write . . .
HOUGH: (HOUGH *moves: PxB.*)
Move.
NICHOLS: I could write academic verse — sonnets and the like —
If I tried.

(NICHOLS *moves*: . . . *OO*. HOUGH *moves: P-K5*.)

HOUGH: Thought that was Ashbery's book. Move.
NICHOLS: No. He wrote *The Mice*. That's a good book too.
HOUGH: He must be an interesting man, Merwin.

(NICHOLS *moves*: . . . *P-B4*. HOUGH *moves: B-R3*.)

NICHOLS: You want to meet him? I'll introduce you
Some time.
HOUGH: Move.
NICHOLS: He doesn't say much.
HOUGH: Move.
NICHOLS: He's very quiet.
HOUGH: Move.
NICHOLS: That's his *karma*.
HOUGH: Move.
NICHOLS: My move?

Scene nine. The lobby, as before. HOUGH *gets up from his table, goes over to* NICHOLS. *Both wear masks. He carries a chapbook of poems and a ball-point pen, which he offers to* NICHOLS *as indicated. The second pen should be a very fine one.* NICHOLS *moves:* ... *Q-R4.*

HOUGH:	Say, would you mind autographing this.
NICHOLS:	What is it?
HOUGH:	You wrote it.
NICHOLS:	So it is ...

(NICHOLS *autographs the book.*)

HOUGH:	But that's just a scrawl!
NICHOLS:	What do you mean?
HOUGH:	That's not good enough. Sign it again, Over here.
NICHOLS:	What on earth do you mean? That's the way I sign my name.
HOUGH:	Sure is unaesthetic.
NICHOLS:	If I had a better pen maybe I could Do something about it. How do you expect A self-respecting poet to sign his work With a pen like that?

(HOUGH *produces the second pen.*)

HOUGH:	Well, try again.
NICHOLS:	I will not.
HOUGH:	Please.
NICHOLS:	No.
HOUGH:	Come on.
NICHOLS:	This is ridiculous. You can take it The way it is, or forget about the whole Thing. What do you think I am?
HOUGH:	Take your damn poetry. I don't Give a crap about it.

(HOUGH *throws down the chapbook and then, quickly retrieving it, leaves.*)

Scene ten. The cafe of the hotel. It is empty. The CLERK *busies himself about an espresso coffee machine as* ANNA *enters and sits at one of the larger tables. Fado music is playing. After a short time the* CLERK *sees her and walks over to take her order.*

ANNA:	Yes, I'd like An espresso, make that A double espresso, please.
CLERK:	I am sorry, but could you move To a smaller table? These tables are Reserved for groups of three or four.
ANNA:	I *am* a group of three or four.

CLERK:	I am sorry, that's our rule.
ANNA:	I would like four espressos. One here. And here.
	One there. And there. I will be a party of four.
CLERK:	Please, Madame.
ANNA:	Don't you *please madame* me!
	That's my order. Four espressos.
	S'il-vous plait!

(NICHOLS *enters and joins* ANNA *at her table. For a moment both are silent.*)

	I don't believe a word of it.
NICHOLS:	Don't blame me if he vanishes.
ANNA:	I need time.
NICHOLS:	Don't blame me.
ANNA:	Why is he so important?
NICHOLS:	Who said he was?
ANNA:	Not until you show me some credentials.
NICHOLS:	I burn down forests, blow up dams,
	Change the weather, blight crops.
	I can kill, as well,

(*Pause.*)

	But I am a gentle person.
ANNA:	You have no authority.
NICHOLS:	If you don't give me the names
	I'll do whatever needs to be done.
ANNA:	I don't like threats, shithead.
NICHOLS:	Look, it's his *karma*.
	People get used up. He's through.
	Finished. It's like you think he's
	Some kind of demigod. Look, lady,
	I've been around for a long, long
	Time. I need those names.
ANNA:	He won't tell me.
NICHOLS:	After all, I am a poet. Of sorts.
	I see through the veils of eternity.
ANNA:	People do get used up . . .

(*The* CLERK *brings on the four espressos, and sets them down.*)

NICHOLS:	Expecting someone?
ANNA:	I am being all four of us.

Scene eleven. MARIE's *room. She is sitting on a high stool downstage holding a guitar. Music is playing on a record-player.* HOUGH *enters and sits in a chair at some distance from her.*

HOUGH: Listening to the music?
MARIE: And making my own.
HOUGH: Theodorakis, isn't it?
MARIE: It's Greek.
HOUGH: *Mauthausen Songs*. Great stuff.
MARIE: Right on . . .

(*She turns off the music.*)

HOUGH: You like it here?
MARIE: Not really.
HOUGH: Why not?
MARIE: It's not that I don't like it, it's just
            That I don't belong here. I don't really
            Understand how I got to be here.
HOUGH: That makes two of us.
MARIE: You, you're supposed to be the
            Big wheel. We're all here because
            Of you, I think.
HOUGH: I'm afraid you're right.
MARIE: What about you? What's your story?
HOUGH: I came here to write. Like Nichols.
            A lot of wasted time. Now I go where
            It's comfortable. Read some. Write not much.
MARIE: Sounds all right to me. I like you.
HOUGH: *You're crazy!*
            Can you speak to him? Does he
            Make any sense to you?
MARIE: He's warm and generous and . . .
HOUGH: I've heard all that before.
            Have you known him a long time?
MARIE: Six months.
HOUGH: Not long.
MARIE: That's long.
HOUGH: What will you do when you go
            Back to the States?
MARIE: Not me.
HOUGH: What do you mean? Why not?
MARIE: Too much of a hassle. Don't
            Let's talk about it.
HOUGH: Sorry. Just curious. You mean
            To stay here then?
MARIE: Can't stay here. No bread. Don't much
            Like it here.
HOUGH: Then where?
MARIE: Where we go. Wherever.
HOUGH: Come on!

MARIE:	You're pretty hard Sometimes.
HOUGH:	Where're you from?
MARIE:	Milwaukee. Out of town. And you?
HOUGH:	Chicago. The same.
MARIE:	I don't go back much.
HOUGH:	Neither do I.
MARIE:	That's a pretty ring. Did you Get it here?
HOUGH:	Family. My mother was a singer. She traveled a lot. She must've got it In Europe. I like it.
MARIE:	Do you want . . . something?
HOUGH:	What do you mean?
MARIE:	Nothing. Let me tell you A story. When I was fourteen I ran away from home. Folks didn't care. Old Uncle tied me up. Raped me. Then he Took me back. Folks took me to a Home When I told 'em what happened. He'd caught Up to me in Chicago . . .
HOUGH:	Who had?
MARIE:	My Uncle. But later, in the Home, they Beat me. I got out after my father died. My mother killed him, I know that because She threatened to pin it on me. He had Another woman. I knew her, it was me. I got into trouble a lot. Got into real trouble. That Uncle . . .
HOUGH:	Go on.
MARIE:	Fed up. Don't want to talk.
HOUGH:	Did you make up all that stuff?
MARIE:	You know me.
HOUGH:	No.
MARIE:	You really know me.
HOUGH:	Marie, I want to leave here, but I don't know where to go, or how To get there . . . That's all bullshit. Sorry. What I mean to say was I am Going to have to leave here Soon. It may be quite sudden.
MARIE:	I thought we had to wait.
HOUGH:	Change of plans. Sorry about that.
MARIE:	I don't mind waiting. I don't mind waiting, at all.

HOUGH:	You see, I know where I'm Going, I just don't know how I am going to get there.
MARIE:	Airplane, I'd say.
HOUGH:	Forget it.
MARIE:	Maybe we could elope.
HOUGH:	Elope?
MARIE:	With bells on our toes and heels.
HOUGH:	Leaving a big scandal and a big Hotel bill.
MARIE:	It's about Anna, isn't it?
HOUGH:	It's about Anna. And other things.
MARIE:	You sure don't give a person much To hold on to.
HOUGH:	What do you mean?
MARIE:	I mean, don't you ever ... I mean, Just let it all out ... let go ... say What you are ... let yourself be Known?
HOUGH:	All people want, mostly, is a list. A, *your name*. B, *where you're from*. C, *what you do for a living*. My name I don't tell people Because I don't much care for it. Where I come from doesn't interest me. And what I do for a living, well, that's Not exactly the sort of thing that makes For openers at a cocktail party.
MARIE:	Missed my point.
HOUGH:	Guess I'd rather know, than be known.
MARIE:	Sounds lonely.
HOUGH:	It is.
MARIE:	It's safer not to know too much.
HOUGH:	I'll say. Are you going to sing?
MARIE:	Ok. Here's an old song I found. It's about Lisbon. Or takes place here. Something like that. Anyway. Here goes. It's hard. But I'll try ...
HOUGH:	Sing the damn song.
MARIE:	Ok. Here goes. It's called *The Ballad of Bad Weather*.

Scene twelve. The lobby again. HOUGH *and* NICHOLS *playing as before, that is, seated facing each other over one board. In rapid succession they*

make the following moves: HOUGH, *00.* NICHOLS, *QxB.* HOUGH, *PxN. Both
are intensely involved in the game.*

NICHOLS: The economic system of America
Is predicated on death. Do you know
How many cats it takes to make one
Tennis racket?

(NICHOLS *moves:* . . . *P-B5.*)

HOUGH: It's turning into a draw. So what,
I'll just take the fucking pawn!

(HOUGH *moves: PxP.*)

NICHOLS: So it's for real now?
HOUGH: Move.
NICHOLS: The only people I want to talk to
Are artists.

(NICHOLS *moves:* . . . *PxB.*)

. . . Gotcha!
HOUGH: I didn't see that. Hmm.

(HOUGH *moves: BPxP.*)

NICHOLS: I sometimes think that the only hope
Lies in extinction.
HOUGH: What?
NICHOLS: I mean, just look at what we've done
To this fucking planet.

(NICHOLS *moves:* . . . *KxP.*)

HOUGH: You're crazy . . .

(HOUGH *moves: R-B3.*)

NICHOLS: I am talking about
The extinction of the entire human race.
After all, without love what is there?

(NICHOLS *moves:* . . . *B-N2.* HOUGH *moves: Q-Q4ch.*)

HOUGH: Check.

(NICHOLS *moves:* . . . *P-B3.*)

If you do that
You lose a piece.
NICHOLS: "If I leap into the flame
I become Empedocles" . . .
That's from one of my poems.

(HOUGH *moves: QxPch.*)

HOUGH: Check.
NICHOLS: Took it, eh?

(NICHOLS *moves: . . . R-B2.* HOUGH *moves: R-N3ch.*)

HOUGH: Check.
NICHOLS: Looks bad. I'll try this.

(NICHOLS *moves: . . . K-R1.* HOUGH *moves: QxR.*)

HOUGH: Had enough?

(NICHOLS *moves: . . . Q-B4ch.*)

NICHOLS: Check.

(HOUGH *moves: K-R1. He pauses, then gets up to leave.*)

              Let me think about this.
HOUGH: Take your time.

(HOUGH *leaves.*)

Scene thirteen. In the darkened lobby, very late at night. ANNA *enters walking swiftly, and only sees* HOUGH *seated at a table when he lights a cigarette.*

HOUGH: I don't want you to talk
              To Nichols anymore.
ANNA: Why not?
HOUGH: You've already jabbered
              Too much.
ANNA: I think he's an asshole. A nobody
              Who's got it into his head
              That he's a somebody.
HOUGH: He's a definite somebody
              All right. You're in danger.
ANNA: Horse-shit.
HOUGH: I'm not kidding.
ANNA: Tell me who to talk to.
              At the Endowment, at least.
HOUGH: You'll blow it.
ANNA: Why are you being so difficult?
              They told me . . .
HOUGH: Who told you?
ANNA: None of your business. Anyhow
              They told me there'd be no problem.

A list. Then the transmission. And then
The first operations. Simple as that . . .
          And that Nichols would be here
To relay some messages.

HOUGH: I'm not sure of him.

ANNA: Why? Why not?

HOUGH: I don't know. He cheats at chess.

ANNA: He's an asshole.

HOUGH: He's dangerous.

ANNA: For you, maybe.

HOUGH: What do you mean?

ANNA: I'm giving you two days.
Then it's all over. You'll be out.
You know, I think he's kind of cute.

HOUGH: *Cute?*

ANNA: Nichols. I like his mustache.

HOUGH: Who put you
Up to this?

ANNA: Bye-bye . . .

HOUGH: Wait, Anna.
Wait a minute. There's
Something I want to say.

ANNA: Go ahead. I'm listening.

HOUGH: Don't push so hard. It doesn't
Make things any clearer between
Us. I mean maybe there won't
Be any revolution. Maybe we've
Lost touch. Maybe we have to
Stop and think.

ANNA: What we want
For ourselves?

HOUGH: A bit that. And something else.
Look, I don't know how to say this . . .

ANNA: Well, I do . . .
I wish you wouldn't be so damned
Suspicious. Look, Hough, you know
You mean a lot to me. One reason
I got mixed up in this is because
I thought we'd have a chance to . . .
Well, speak . . .
          I know you think I'm just a
Dizzy spoiled American brat. But
I'm not. *I can help.* And I don't
Want that much out of it, *for me.*
Maybe I'm not as clear-headed

As you think I ought to be, but
Jesus Christ, give me a chance,
Will you? I'm new at this.
I really do want to change things
So that . . .
So that everything we used to
Talk about can happen.

HOUGH: And what if I can't tell you?
ANNA: *Two days.*
That's all.

(*She starts to leave.*)

HOUGH: Trust me.
ANNA: Hey,
I'm not a terrorist!
HOUGH: What's the weather
Like outside?
ANNA: Did you ever trust me?
HOUGH: Yes, and look what happened.
ANNA: I need those names, believe me.

(*Pause.*)

Look, it just happened that way.

(*Pause.*)

I need them *in two days.*
HOUGH: I believe you.
ANNA: Then you'll help?
HOUGH: I'll do what I can.
ANNA: You're an infuriating man.
HOUGH: *What is lasting the poets provide . . .*
ANNA: Some poet said that, I suppose.
HOUGH: A madman as well.

Scene fourteen. The lobby of the hotel. It is just after dawn. The CLERK *is preparing for the day. The light is quite brilliant and should seem to emanate from an altogether different source than that of the other scenes.* HOUGH *is checking items off a list on a small notebook. Later he burns a piece of paper in an ashtray. As usual, the chess game is visible on its table.*

HOUGH: Joao, can you arrange
Everything for this afternoon?
CLERK: Certainly, Senhor Hough.
HOUGH: I'd still like to get
A couple of silk shirts.

CLERK:	The shops open at ten.
HOUGH:	He may have tipped them off Already. He's on to me for sure.
CLERK:	It is a beginning, Senhor Hough. Even in such a large country as yours It is necessary to make a small beginning.
HOUGH:	I'm worried about her.
CLERK:	She has told him nothing.
HOUGH:	That's not what worries me.
CLERK:	Only her pride will be injured.
HOUGH:	Joao, do you play chess?
CLERK:	His position is, I think, very difficult.
HOUGH:	The Germans call it *zugzwang*. Any way he moves he loses.
CLERK:	One thing troubles me about her.
HOUGH:	I don't want to hear it.
CLERK:	She is very, very rude.

Scene fifteen. The lobby. NICHOLS *is hunched over the chess, apparently in deep concentration.* HOUGH *enters, carrying a box of silk shirts.*

NICHOLS:	I didn't play well.
HOUGH:	(*He holds up a bright red shirt.* NICHOLS *nods approvingly.*) Who do you work for?
NICHOLS:	Are you crazy?
HOUGH:	Caspar, Little Joe, or someone else?
NICHOLS:	They've changed. Caspar is very committed.
HOUGH:	They have not changed. He is the same kind of Moral fanatic that his Uncle In the SS was.
NICHOLS:	If you hate all Germans You're worse off than they Are.
HOUGH:	I don't hate all Germans. Look, your cover's blown. Tell me who you really Work for, *Nichols*.
NICHOLS:	I am a committed person.
HOUGH:	To what?
NICHOLS:	Pawn to king four.
HOUGH:	You'd better get out of sight.
NICHOLS:	Are you going to move?
HOUGH:	Thought by sucking up To Anna you'd find things

	Out.
NICHOLS:	You're nuts.
HOUGH:	You know Dr. Johnson's definition
	Of a patriot?
NICHOLS:	What do you mean?
HOUGH:	*The last refuge of a scoundrel.*
NICHOLS:	You can't beat me remember that. *I always win.*
HOUGH:	You name isn't Nichols. Nichols is dead.
NICHOLS:	You couldn't find a rat
	In a cup of coffee.
HOUGH:	Sell Starluster that.

(*Shows* NICHOLS *a newspaper clipping.* NICHOLS *arises and begins to pack his belongings. He continues to do so through the following speech.*)

NICHOLS: No sirree, I did not play well . . .
            I was always fascinated with emblems
            And insignias of things, you know.
            I loved to draw them, all kinds. When
            I was a kid, you know.
                You make a Star of David out of
            Two triangles, it's real easy, but I didn't
            Know what is stood for. So I made it my own
            Symbol. Marked everything I had with that
            Crazy six-pointed star. I was just a kid. Now
                My dad liked hunting. He was into Indian
            Lore when he was a kid. That was back in
            The Twenties. Well, he carved these funny
            Twisted crosses on some of his things. It was
            The swastika, but that was before the Nazis;
            Only his swastika bent the other direction.
            I mean, like, I'm no Jew. And, hey, I ain't no Nazi.
            But Jesus how I loved those emblems! Even if
            I didn't know what they stood for. Just a kid!
                But you now. Hey Hough! Weren't you
            Ever a kid? You were never a kid, were you?

HOUGH: What were your instructions?
NICHOLS: To keep an eye on you.
HOUGH: You've blown it. It's begun. But in the States.
NICHOLS: Hey, man! Today is Saturday, all day long.

(NICHOLS *begins to leave.*)

HOUGH: Still, I am curious
            Who you really are,

(*Pause.* NICHOLS *stops for a moment, and looks back at* HOUGH.)

            Though it doesn't matter.

(NICHOLS *leaves.*)

Scene sixteen. The lobby, brightly lit. The CLERK *is reading a newspaper while standing behind his desk.* ANNA *enters, in a furious state.*

ANNA: Hough! Hough! Where's Hough? It's begun!
Hough, for Christsakes, where are you?
I don't need you anymore! It's begun. Oh hell,
Where is he? Pardon, Sirrah, have you seen,
By any chance, Mr. Hough?

CLERK: He has checked out, madame.

ANNA: Checked out?

CLERK: And he left this note for you.
But there is trouble. The lady, the other
American lady, she has tried to suicide
By jumping off a bridge. Unfortunately
A garbage boat had come under the bridge,
She did not see it. She landed on the, ah,
Garbages. It is all right. She is not injured.
But she sent this note for you. It says
You must come immediately. The police have
Arrested her.

ANNA: Marie? A suicide?

CLERK: It was not a successful suicide, madame.

ANNA: "Anna, had to return quickly. Things have
Begun. Nichols works for you know who.
I could not tell you. Please come quickly.
Now. I can be reached at the following
Address. Forgive me."
The son of a bitch! Nichols! Where's Nichols?

CLERK: He has departed also. In his case without
Paying his bill, which is substantial.

ANNA: Shithead!

CLERK: The police will arrest him.

ANNA: "I can be reached ..." I would like to pay
My bill. And I would like to speak with a
Travel agent. Immediately.

CLERK: Of course, madame.

ANNA: Alone. Well, bust my ass! Alone.

CLERK: Here's the check, madame.

ANNA: Will this do?

(*She hands the* CLERK *a credit card.*)

CLERK: Yes, madame.

ANNA:	And the travel agent?
CLERK:	I am telephoning now, madame.
	But there is still the problem of the lady
	Who is being held by the police. She desired
	That I convey to you her urgent wish that ...
ANNA:	Fuck her.
CLERK:	I beg your pardon, madame.
ANNA:	I said *fuck her*. Have you got the travel agent
	Yet?
CLERK:	The line is engaged.
ANNA:	Damn it! Alone. That son of a bitch.
	I've got to get out of here.
CLERK:	I'll keep trying, madame.
ANNA:	*Alone*. Fuck. Shit. Cunt. Hell. Fuck shit ...
CLERK:	Madame ...
ANNA:	What is it?
CLERK:	You appear to have *fallen off the stool*,
	As we say.
ANNA:	What do you mean? What's that?
CLERK:	It is said that our late dictator Salazar's decline began with a fall from a high stool. He injured his head in the fall, and began to lose his mind. In particular he developed an obsession, you would have to call it, for telling dirty jokes. He would go on telling dirty jokes, one after the other. In fact he could no longer administer the government. But, out of love for him, his assistants would stage cabinet meetings and he would go on solemnly reciting dirty jokes. Everyone would politely listen as though they were discussing important things. And so we say that someone has *fallen off the stool*.
ANNA:	I see what you mean, I guess.
	I sure am a flop as a revolutionary.
CLERK:	Madame, we are all failures
	At something. You Americans
	Are so concerned about success.
ANNA:	But, look, a revolution that is not a success
	Just doesn't make it as a revolution.
CLERK:	I was not talking about
	That.
ANNA:	I know. I'm trying not to hear you.
CLERK:	I did not wish to scold you.
ANNA:	I'm going upstairs to pack.
CLERK:	If you like
	I shall make a reservation in your name
	For a flight at the earliest possible
	Time. But what destination shall I give?
ANNA:	You read the note.

CLERK: No, madame, I did not. You see,
          I too am a failure as a revolutionist.
ANNA: It's
          New York. New York.

(*She leaves. There is a short pause, and she enters again.*)

          You never liked me, did you?
CLERK: No, madame, I do not.
ANNA: I don't like you either.

(*She leaves a second time, this time for good.*)

———

I would like to express my sense of profound gratitude as follows: without Bonnie Marranca and Gautam Dasgupta I would not have known where to start; without Leslie Farber I would not have had the courage to begin; without Carl Weber the work would not have been well-done; without Yolanda it would not have been worth doing.

Authors' Biographies

Maria Irene Fornes has been a prominent figure in the off-Broadway theatre scene since the mid-sixties. A three-time Obie award winner for *Promenade, Fefu and Her Friends,* and *Eyes on the Harem,* she has also served as President of New York Theatre Strategy since 1973. Her early plays are collected in a volume entitled *Promenade and Other Plays.*

William Hauptman's plays have been performed at the American Place, the Public Theatre, and at numerous regional theatres in the United States and Canada. *Domino Courts* won a 1976 Village Voice Obie for Distinguished Playwriting. He has held several fellowships, including a Guggenheim, and also wrote the pilot episode of *A House Divided,* a series for Public Television.

Richard Nelson received a 1979 Obie Award for *The Vienna Notes* which has been presented at Playwrights' Horizons, the Mark Taper Forum, the Guthrie II, and the Sheffield Crucible Theatre in England. His play, BAL, was produced this season by The Goodman Theatre in Chicago. His other plays, which include *Jungle Coup, Conjuring an Event, The Killing of Yablonski* and *Scooping,* have been seen at the American Place, PAF Playhouse, the Mark Taper Forum/Lab; and Arena Stage. His translation of Moliere's *Don Juan* was directed last season by Liviu Ciulei at Arena Stage, and his translation of Brecht's *The Wedding* was presented by the BAM Theatre Company.

Ronald Tavel, who founded and named the Theatre of the Ridiculous movement in 1965, has written over twenty-five plays, among them *Shower, Kitchenette, The Life of Juanita Castro, Gorilla Queen, How Jacqueline Kennedy Became Queen of Greece, The Last Days of British Honduras* and *Big-*

foot. He received two Obie Awards in playwriting, and has published a novel, *Street of Stairs,* and many poems and essays. As Andy Warhol's scenarist and sometime director-actor, he wrote fourteen films. He was appointed Artist-in-Residence at The Yale University Divinity School in 1975 (believed to be the first such position at a Protestant divinity school) and Playwright-in-Residence at Cornell University in 1980.

Jean-Claude van Itallie, who was born in Belgium, served as Playwright-in-Residence for the Open Theater, 1963-68. He has taught at Princeton University and the Naropa Institute. Among him many plays are *America Hurrah,* for which he won an Obie, *The Serpent, A Fable, The Sea Gull* (adapted from Chekhov), and *The Bag Lady.* He scripted the recent documentary *Picasso: A Painter's Diary* on PBS television.

John Wellman is a poet and playwright who lives in New York. He has written several plays and texts for Dutch radio. These include *Nobody* (1972) and *Fama Combinatoria* (1973); a stage version of the latter premiered in Amsterdam in 1975. His published works include *In Praise of Secrecy* (1977), a book, of poems, and *Opera Brevis* (1977), a play; *Satires,* a new collection of poems, is forthcoming from New Rivers Press. Wellman's other plays are *Memory Theater of Giordano Bruno, Harm's Way, Land of Cockaigne* and *Energumen.*

PERFORMING ARTS JOURNAL PUBLICATIONS

PLAYSCRIPTS

Theatre of the Ridiculous (2nd. printing)
Plays by Kenneth Bernard, Charles Ludlam, and Ronald Tavel.
$11.95 (hbk); $5.95 (pbk).

Animations: A Trilogy for Mabou Mines
Plays by Lee Breuer, with 70 illus.
$35.00 (limited signed); $15.95 (hbk); $8.95 (pbk).

The Red Robins
Play by Kenneth Koch.
$7.95 (hbk); $3.95 (pbk).

The Women's Project
Plays by Joyce Aaron/Luna Tarlo, Kathleen Collins, Penelope Gilliatt, Rose Leiman
  Goldemberg, Lavonne Mueller, Phyllis Purscell, Joan Schenkar.
$14.95 (hbk); $6.95 (pbk).

Beelzebub Sonata
Plays and essays by Stanislaw I. Witkiewicz.
$14.95 (hbk); $6.95 (pbk).

BOOKS

American Dreams: Sam Shepard and His Plays (Criticism)
$15.95 (hbk); $7.95 (pbk).

Hawk Moon (Fiction)
Sam Shepard
$35.00 (limited signed); $12.95 (hbk); $4.95 (pbk).

Collective Consciousness
Art Performances/Art Shows in the Seventies
$20.00 (hbk); $12.00 (pbk).

PERIODICALS

Performing Arts Journal
LIVE

Write to:

Performing Arts Journal Publications
P.O. Box 858
Peter Stuyvesant Station
New York, N.Y. 10009

844047